IMAGES
of America

HOPKINTON AND CONTOOCOOK

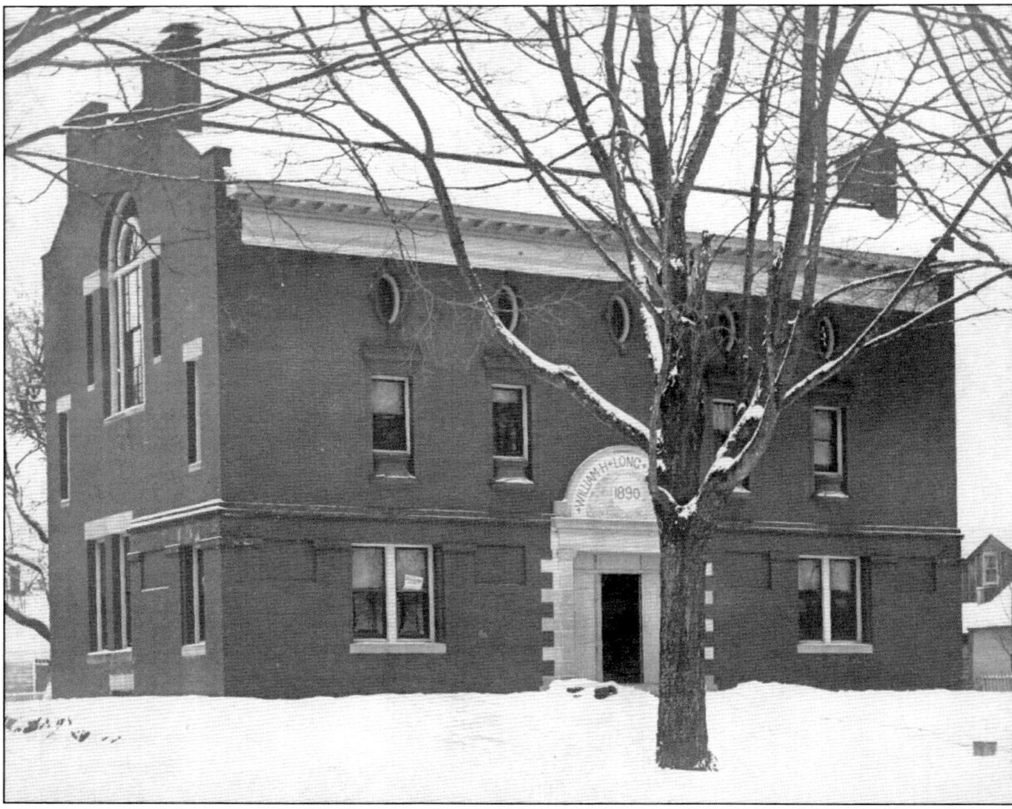

The Hopkinton Historical Society was founded as the Philomathic Club by George H. Crowell, Darwin C. Blanchard, and Silas Ketchum. Over the years the club transformed, and in 1875, the former literary group incorporated as the New Hampshire Antiquarian Society. The group's collection of antiquities was housed above Ketchum's store in Contoocook Village, but in 1890, Mrs. Lucia A.D. Rollins Long had built and dedicated the William H. Long Memorial Building in memory of her husband for the purpose of providing a permanent home for the New Hampshire Antiquarian Society. The striking brick building in Hopkinton Village, seen here in 1905, is the oldest purpose-built museum for a historical society in the United States and is listed in the National Register of Historic Places. Known now as the Hopkinton Historical Society, it continues to collect important artifacts from the town's history and welcomes visitors to enjoy its many exhibits. (Photograph by Leon Kelley, courtesy Hopkinton Historical Society.)

On the Cover: Established on March 5, 1831, the post office at Contoocook was located at the northern end of the Curtice Block from about 1869 until it was relocated to the railroad depot next door. In 1892, after removing old horse sheds at the southern end of the Curtice Block, the post office was moved again and remained there until December 29, 1958, when a new post office was built at the current location of the bank just east of the Curtice Block on Main Street. The post office is now located on Park Avenue. The cover photograph shows Contoocook postmaster John A. Fuller and mail carrier Mr. Hazelton in front of the post office in the Curtice Block. (Courtesy Hopkinton Historical Society.)

IMAGES
of America

HOPKINTON AND CONTOOCOOK

Mala Duclos Tyler in cooperation with
the Hopkinton Historical Society

ARCADIA
PUBLISHING

ISBN 978-0-7385-9137-7

Published by Arcadia Publishing
Charleston, South Carolina

Printed in the United States of America

Library of Congress Control Number: 2011945638

For all general information, please contact Arcadia Publishing:
Telephone 843-853-2070
Fax 843-853-0044
E-mail sales@arcadiapublishing.com
For customer service and orders:
Toll-Free 1-888-313-2665

Visit us on the Internet at www.arcadiapublishing.com

To Mom, Dad, Tim, Joe, Morgan, and Beck for their love and encouragement. And to the generations that came before for the roots and guidance.

Contents

ACKNOWLEDGMENTS

The desire to write this book was born of a true love and appreciation of this town, its people, and its history. Generations of my family have called Contoocook their hometown and I truly can't think of a better place to say that about. Creating this book has been an enlightening and enjoyable labor of love.

First and foremost I would like to thank the Hopkinton Historical Society, especially executive director Heather Mitchell, for allowing me access to the society's invaluable collection and for offering answers and guidance. Of course I would also like to thank the Hopkinton Historical Society as a whole, past and present, for its efforts in preserving our history.

Many of the photographs presented in this book were donated to the Hopkinton Historical Society by residents wishing to preserve them for future generations, an act I'd like to express great gratitude for and encourage others to consider for the preservation of their own collections. Amongst the treasures at the Hopkinton Historical Society are the images of Hopkinton photographer Leown Kelley, who beautifully captured glimpses of life around the turn of the 20th century, many of which are featured in this book.

A debt of gratitude goes to those who have captured and preserved history in writing, including Charles Chase Lord, Mildred M. Raymond, and Rosalind Putney Hanson.

Special thanks go to those who shared their personal collections with me, including Tim Goodwin, William Stevens, Faith Duclos, Marion Duclos, the Contoocook Riverway Association, Barbara Brown Carpenter, and Edith Carr.

The list of those who have offered information, answered questions, and given guidance is too long to name, but includes Robert Duclos, Tim Goodwin, Mike Kirk, Blanche Conant Roberts, Deb Young, Dorothy Young Carruthers, Dane Malcolm, Judy George, Patty Cass Smith, Steve Lux, and Doug Clemons.

I would like to thank my editor at Arcadia Publishing, Lissie Cain, for her encouragement and ever-present support.

Thank you to writer and dear friend Beverly Jenkins for encouraging reassurance and words of wisdom.

And lastly, my deepest gratitude goes to my parents Robert and Faith Duclos for their enthusiasm for this project, and to my husband Joe and children Beck and Morgan for making this dream possible.

Introduction

Whether strolling down the picturesque, maple-lined Main Street in Hopkinton or standing at Fountain Square in Contoocook, it is not difficult to imagine what these villages looked like 100 or more years ago. Historic buildings and homes of prominent figures in the town's history still stand, indifferent to time and beautifully preserved. Hopkinton has managed to grow and at the same time be true to its roots and steadfast in its beauty and charm. A quintessential New England town, its history is celebrated and very much alive around every corner.

Originally granted in 1735 by the Massachusetts Bay Province to the citizens of Hopkinton, Massachusetts, "Number Five" was among a string of land grants from the Connecticut River to the Merrimack River. The following spring Richard Potter, believed to be the first settler, was granted £5 to settle the land with his family. By October 1738, Number Five, which was renamed New Hopkinton by its inhabitants, had become sufficiently settled to host a legal meeting in the township.

In 1740, the fledgling settlement was dealt a setback when King George II decreed that the land was no longer part of Massachusetts Bay, but part of land which had been granted to Sir Ferdinando Gorges and Capt. John Mason, the latter naming his portion of the grant New Hampshire. The current owners of the grant agreed to give preference to the original grantees; however, many of the township's settlers were living in a section known as the Bow Claim, and for years a bitter battle was fought over land rights. In 1763, these settlers were obligated to repurchase land they believed they already owned, but in doing so established that they were indisputably residents of Hopkinton.

Meanwhile, threats of another nature plagued the township. Three garrisons were erected for the settlers' protection due to conflicts with the native inhabitants: the Putney Garrison upon Putney Hill, Kimball Garrison near the spot where Routes 202 and 9 divert from Route 89, and Woodwell's Garrison, which was situated closer to Contoocook near Penacook Road. Despite the efforts, eight people were captured from Woodwell's Garrison in 1746. The captives were marched to Canada and it took great time and effort to secure the return of six of them while two others died as prisoners. In 1753, Abraham Kimball—the first white child to be born to the township—and Samuel Putney suffered a similar attack but were saved by the Flanders men of Boscawen and returned to their families just one day after their capture.

At long last, conflicts over boundaries and hostility with the Indians seemed to have passed, and in 1765 Hopkinton was incorporated and held its first town meeting. The town began to flourish and a meeting house was constructed at the site of the present Soldiers Monument in Hopkinton Village. Over the next few decades, mills, roads, and bridges were erected, and as the northern territory was settled, Hopkinton became a prominent spot along the route from Boston to Montreal. In December 1792, the State of New Hampshire decided Hopkinton was an ideal location to hold the following May's Supreme Court sessions as well as the September and December terms of the Court of Common Pleas and General Court (state legislature) sessions, hence making the town a half-shire of Hillsborough County, of which it was a part at that time. Without a permanent capital, the state legislature alternated its meetings in the state's four half-shire towns, which also included Amherst, Exeter, and Portsmouth. Hopkinton's power and influence soared as it became a hub for commerce and legal business. The New Hampshire state legislature met in Hopkinton four times between 1798 and 1807. These meetings were held in the court house built in 1796 on land given by Benjamin Wiggin—the location of the current town hall. Delegates, lawyers, and others filled the town and its businesses, taverns, and inns prospered. The beauty of the town and its position as a half-shire led many prominent political and business leaders to build stately homes in Hopkinton.

But the tide of prosperity began to turn in 1814 when Concord was selected to become the permanent home of the state legislature, and suffered further decline when Hopkinton was incorporated into the newly-established Merrimack County in 1823, thereby losing its status as a half-shire town. An era of prominence had ended, but Hopkinton persevered and adapted as business and industry developed in Contoocook while Hopkinton Village became a peaceful destination for generations of summer residents and seasonal guests.

The water power of the Contoocook River in Contoocook made it an ideal location for mills. As early as 1791, Eliphalet Poor owned the first mill in the village. Fulling mills, sawmills, a clapboard mill, a copper shop, and a grist mill were built on the river's banks in the early years. In 1826, Joab Patterson, father of Civil War hero Col. Joab N. Patterson, manufactured woolen cloth in a mill on Cedar Street that stood where the Grange building stands now, and which was later the site of Frank I. Morrill's sawmills. Inventor Walter S. Davis built an impressive mill building on the south side of the river in 1893 that housed three manufacturers. The prosperous village was created by the power of the Contoocook River, but at times, also suffered from its wrath.

From its humble beginnings, Hopkinton has grown, thrived, and persevered. Throughout challenges and successes it has remained a beautiful town filled with character and charm. Descendants of early settlers still call Hopkinton their home, speaking well of the town's long and true roots. Homes of its distinguished residents, such as Dr. Ebenezer Lerned, Walter S. Davis, Comm. George H. Perkins, Col. Edwin C. Bailey, and Chicago businessman Horace Gair Chase can still be seen today. Customers can still walk through the doors of the Curtice Block, the Bailey Block, and the building that once housed Ward Rand's store and Reddy's Market. Many of the town's churches, built in the 18th and 19th centuries, still welcome parishioners. Hopkinton has successfully preserved its past while thriving in the present.

One

Hopkinton Village

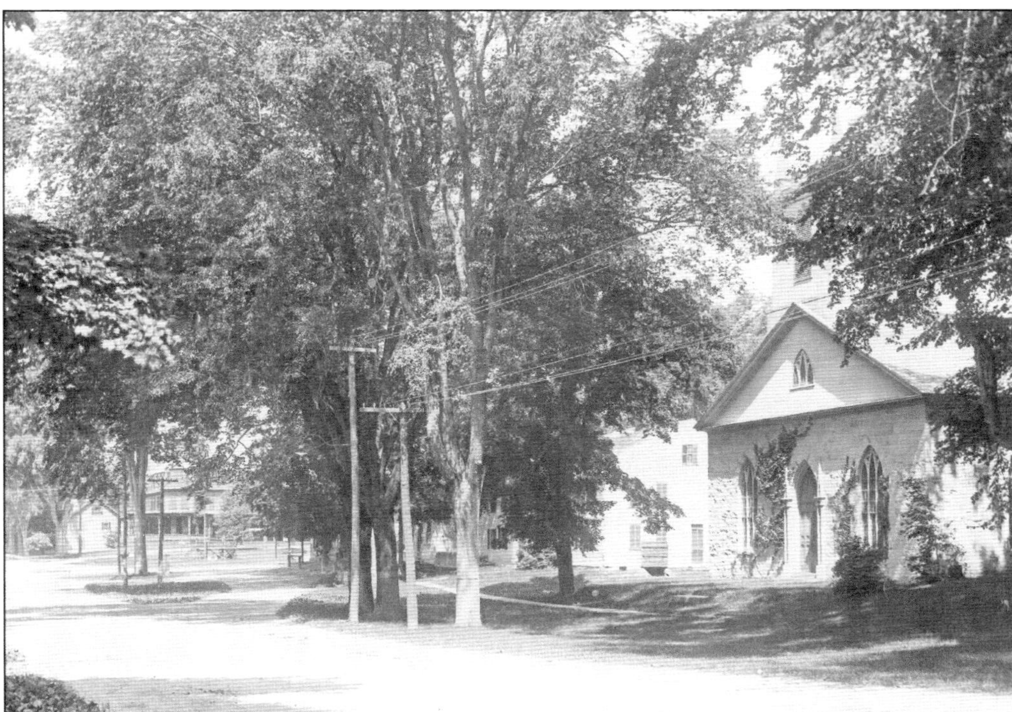

This photograph shows a view of Main Street in Hopkinton Village looking northwest around the late 1800s. Visible in the distance is the Perkins Inn (left), and in the foreground is St. Andrew's Episcopal Church (right). To the left of the church is the former home of Benjamin Wiggin and Wiggins Tavern. (Photograph by Leown Kelley; courtesy of Hopkinton Historical Society.)

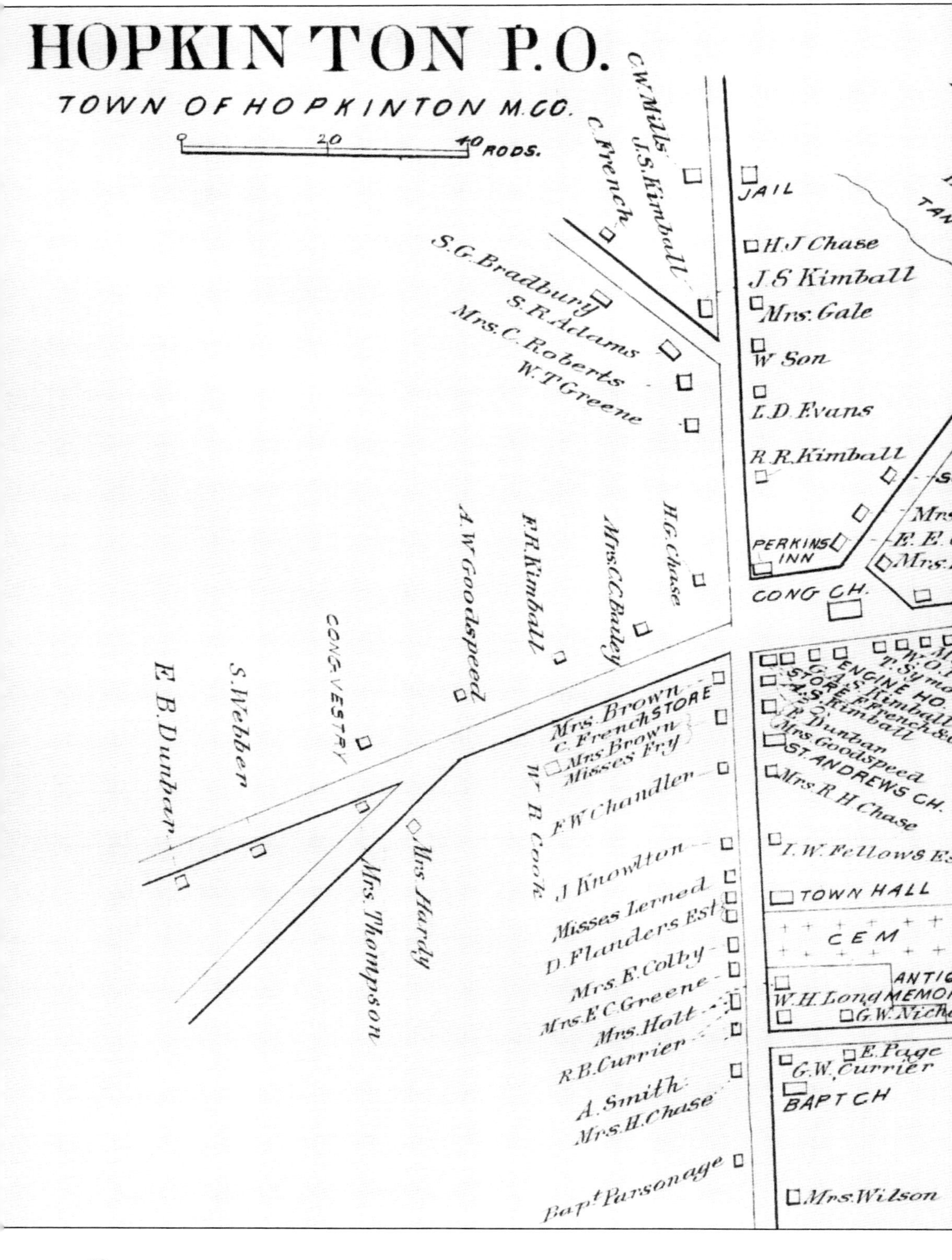
HOPKINTON P.O.
TOWN OF HOPKINTON M.CO.
0 20 40 RODS.
C.W. Mills
J.S. Kimball
C. French
JAIL
H.J. Chase
J.S. Kimball
Mrs. Gale
W. Son
E.D. Evans
R.R. Kimball
S.G. Bradbury
S.R. Adams
Mrs. C. Roberts
W.T. Greene
PERKINS INN
CONG CH.
H.G. Chase
Mrs. C.C. Bailey
F.R. Kimball
A.W. Goodspeed
CONG. VESTRY
S. Webber
E.B. Dunbar
Mrs. Brown
C. French STORE
Mrs. Brown
Misses Fry
W.R. Cook
F.W. Chandler
J. Knowlton
Misses Lerned
D. Flanders Est
Mrs. E. Colby
Mrs. E.C. Greene
Mrs. Holt
R.B. Currier
A. Smith
Mrs. H. Chase
Bapt Parsonage
Mrs. Hardy
Mrs. Thompson
ENGINE HO.
G.A.S. Kimball
STORE F. French & Co
A.S. Kimball
P. Dunbar
Mrs. Goodspeed
ST. ANDREWS CH.
Mrs. R.H. Chase
I.W. Fellows Es
TOWN HALL
CEM
W.H. Long
G.W. Nich
E. Page
G.W. Currier
BAPT CH
Mrs. Wilson

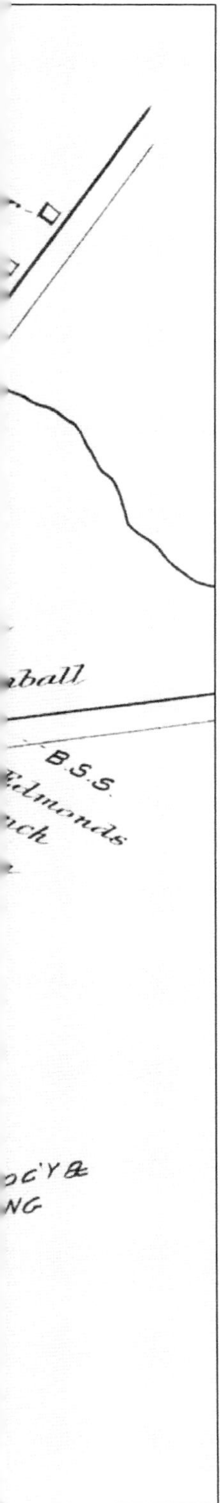

This map was created in 1892 by D.H. Hurd and Company and shows the different buildings and dwellings in the village of Hopkinton, complete with the property owners' names. These maps were created from government surveys, investigations, and county records. Of special interest is the road configuration at the village's square. In 1927, four buildings on the southeast corner of the square burned in a single night and later the road was readjusted to meet highway requirements. Main Street is lined with the homes of many recognizable names from Hopkinton's history. Many of those stately homes still stand today, beautifully preserved. (Courtesy of Mala Duclos Tyler.)

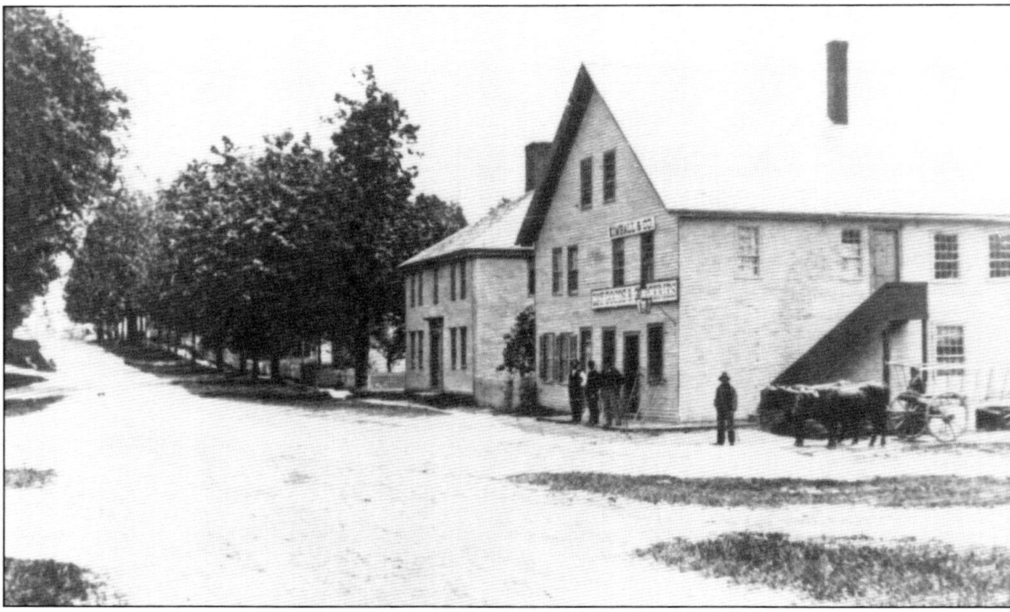

A view from the Hopkinton Village square looking southeast down Main Street shows Kimball and Company's Dry Good and Groceries, currently the home of the Cracker Barrel Old Country Store. The home next to the store once served as a tavern owned by Theophilus Stanley, one of the town's earliest taverners. Stanley also owned a tannery at Mill's Brook, where Kimball Lake is now. (Courtesy of Hopkinton Historical Society.)

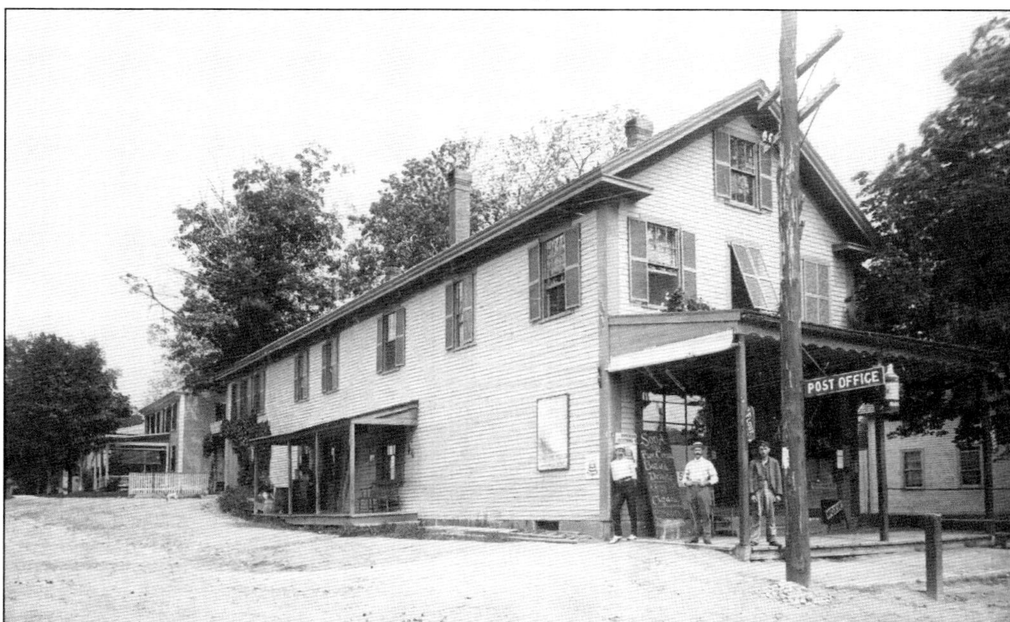

On the northeast corner of the village square stood this store at the intersection of Main Street and Briar Hill Road. The store, owned by Kimball and Company, contained a telephone station that was opened in 1884. Later that year, a telephone station opened in the depot in Contoocook. (Courtesy of Hopkinton Historical Society.)

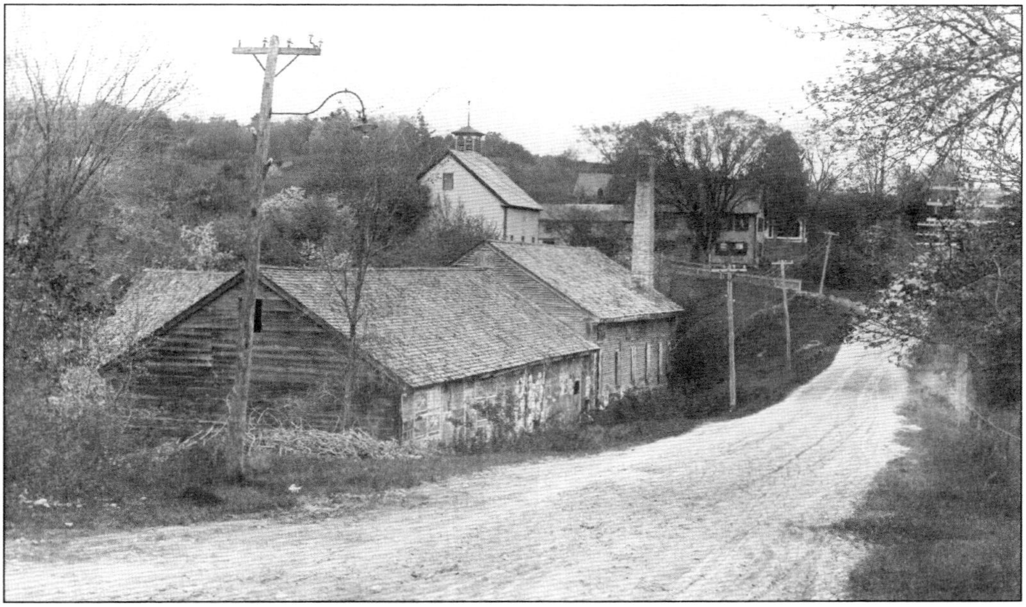

Around 1815, Thomas Kast began producing leather at this tannery located about one quarter of a mile northwest of Hopkinton Village on Hopkinton Road (Route 103). In 1828, it was sold to Jonathan Osgood. In 1853 the tannery was owned by Horace J. Chase, who produced leather for Concord Coaches for 45 years. The remnants of the mill's dam are still visible today. (Courtesy of Hopkinton Historical Society.)

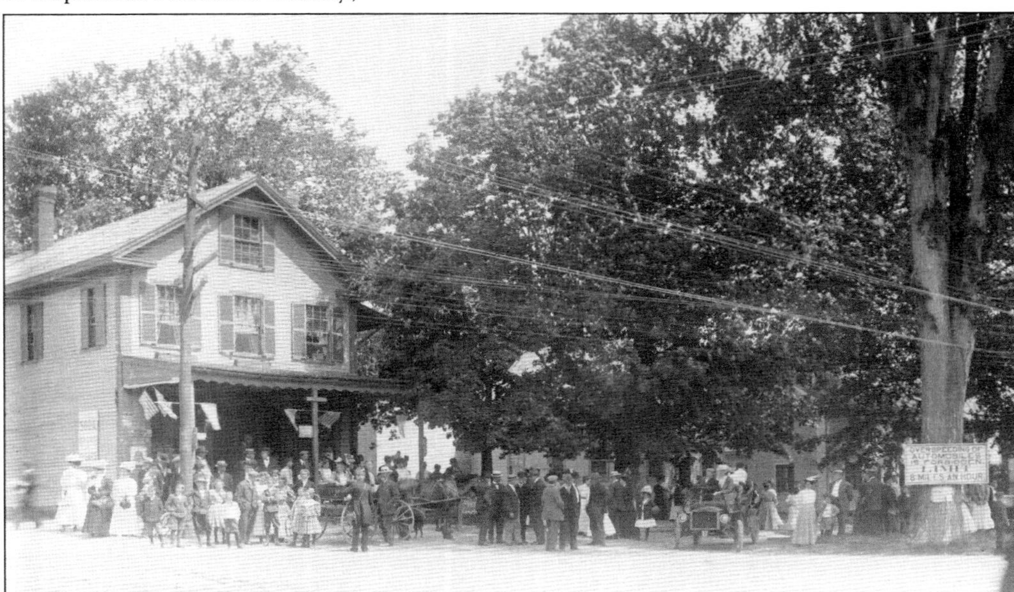

Townspeople gather outside the store in Hopkinton Village during the early years of the automobile in this undated photograph. Note the sign posted on the tree to the right warning, "Overspeeding of automobiles is forbidden. Limit 8 miles an hour." With no train depot in Hopkinton, the village was relatively quiet until the advent of the car, which many complained was loud and dangerous. (Courtesy of Hopkinton Historical Society.)

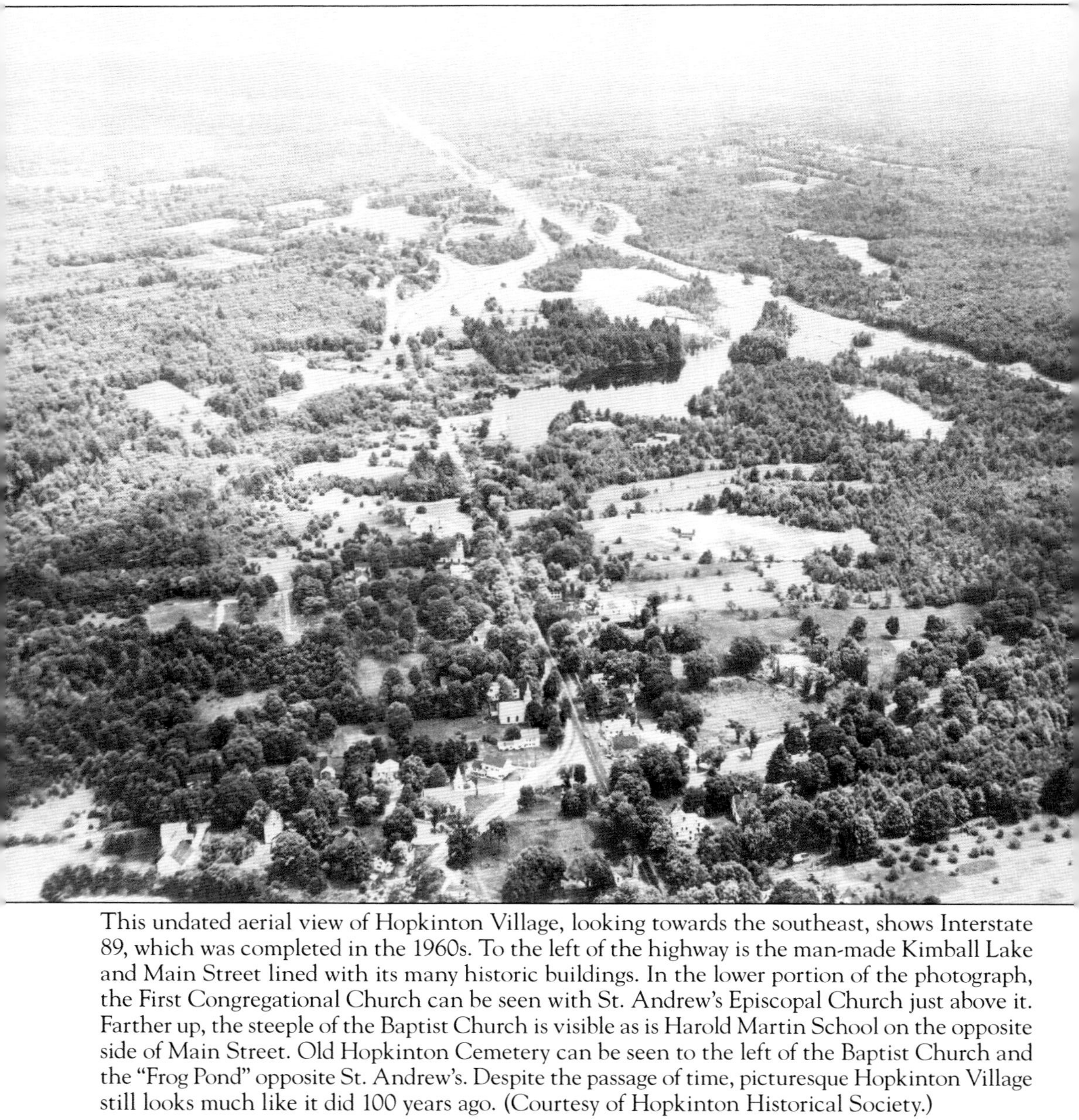

This undated aerial view of Hopkinton Village, looking towards the southeast, shows Interstate 89, which was completed in the 1960s. To the left of the highway is the man-made Kimball Lake and Main Street lined with its many historic buildings. In the lower portion of the photograph, the First Congregational Church can be seen with St. Andrew's Episcopal Church just above it. Farther up, the steeple of the Baptist Church is visible as is Harold Martin School on the opposite side of Main Street. Old Hopkinton Cemetery can be seen to the left of the Baptist Church and the "Frog Pond" opposite St. Andrew's. Despite the passage of time, picturesque Hopkinton Village still looks much like it did 100 years ago. (Courtesy of Hopkinton Historical Society.)

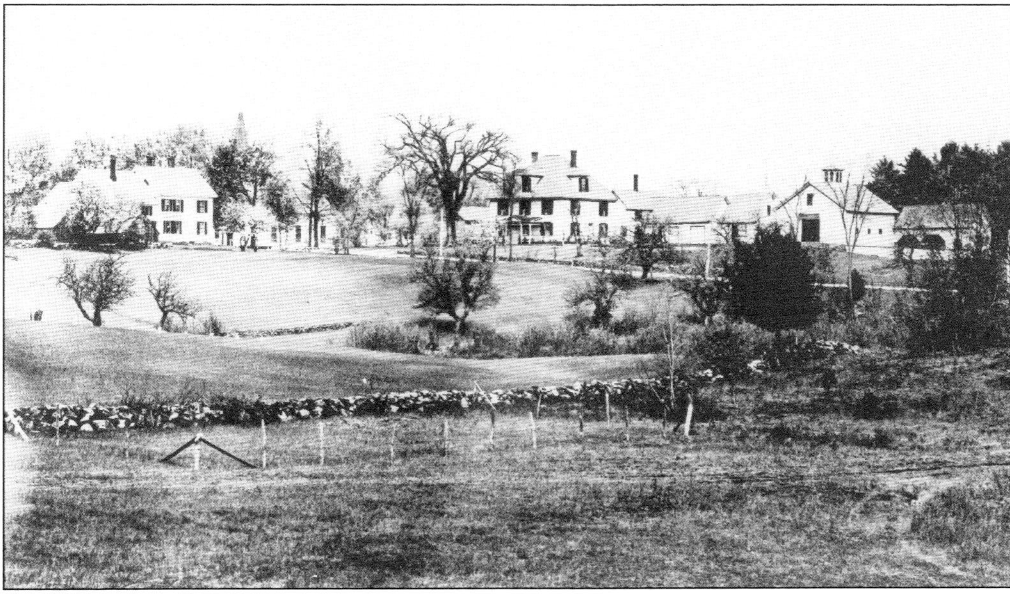

Looking north across Main Street at the east end of the village, the steeple of the old Baptist Church is visible in the distance and the church's parsonage is on the left. The Darrahs owned the house on the right and were well known in Hopkinton's social circles. The large, unique building was later known as the "beehive," and now contains apartments. (Courtesy of Hopkinton Historical Society.)

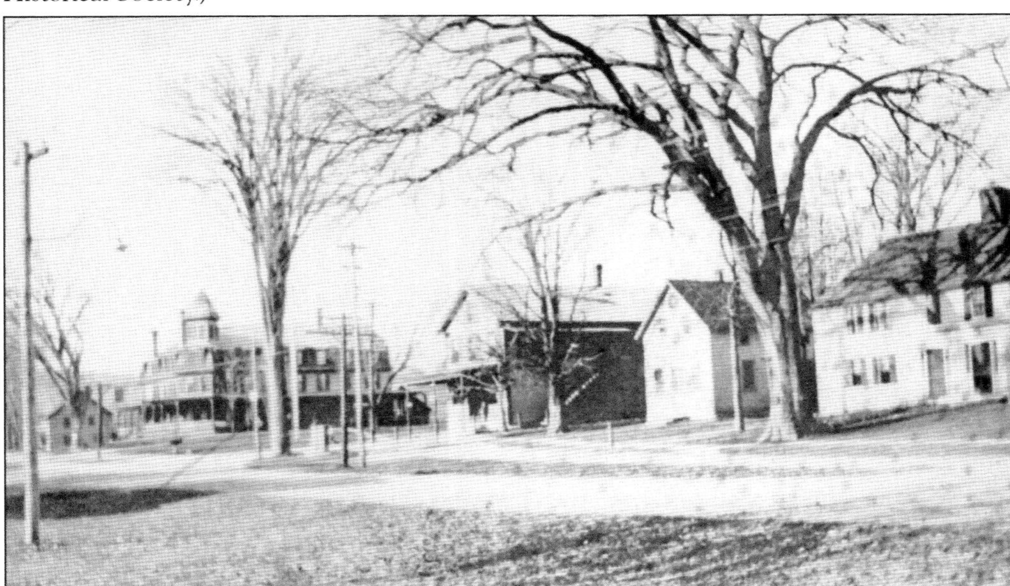

This undated photograph shows the intersection of Main Street and Briar Hill Road in Hopkinton Village. On the far left is a home that would later become the Hopkinton Inn. The large edifice beside it is the Perkins Inn, and to the right of the inn is the village store, the post office building, and Wiggins Tavern. Of these, only the Hopkinton Inn survives today. The first post office was established in Hopkinton on April 1, 1811, with John Harris as the first postmaster. (Courtesy of Hopkinton Historical Society.)

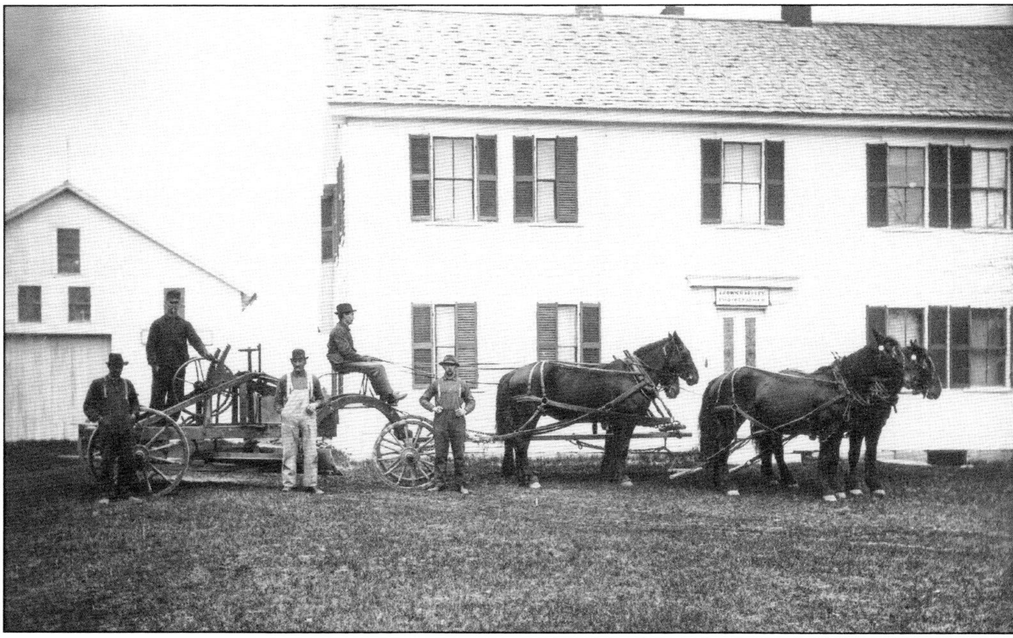

Keeping roads passable was an arduous task in the days of unpaved roads. Seen in this undated photograph is the horse-drawn road grader used to maintain roads. The equipment and its crew stand in front of a home located east of Hopkinton Village on Hopkinton Road. It was the studio of photographer Leown Kelley. (Photograph by Leown Kelley; courtesy of Hopkinton Historical Society.)

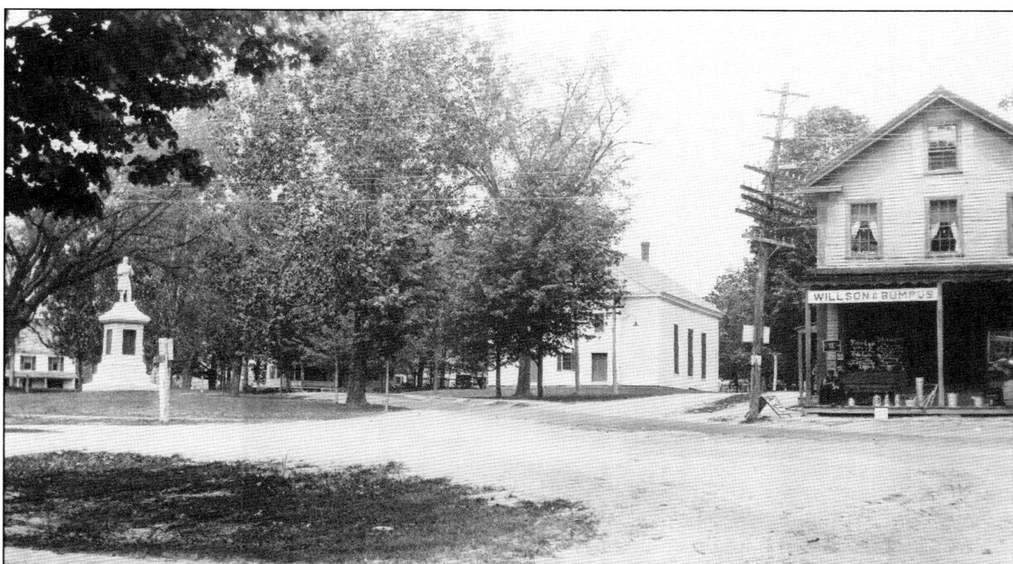

Hopkinton Village is seen in this undated photograph showing the Willson and Bumpus Store on the right, which burned down in the fire of 1927. To the left is the Soldiers Monument with the First Congregational Church in the middle. Briar Hill Road runs between the church and store and Hopkinton Road (Route 103), between the monument and the church. Later this intersection would be altered to meet highway requirements. (Courtesy of Hopkinton Historical Society.)

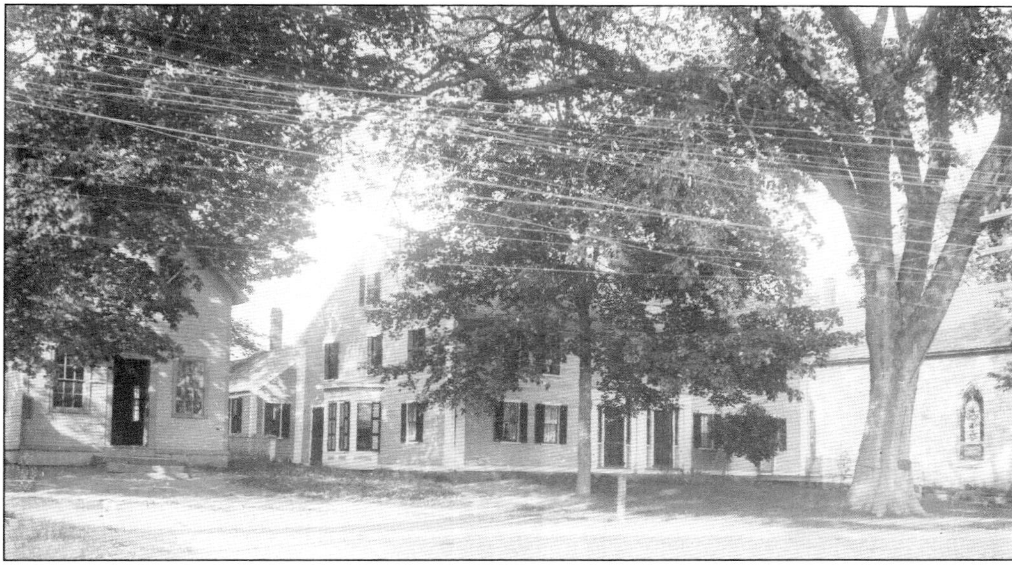

Benjamin Wiggin came to Hopkinton in 1774, and in his time was a landlord, postmaster, merchant, and justice. He served as a selectman from 1776 to 1790, and donated the site for the Hopkinton courthouse where the town hall now stands. Wiggin was one of the earliest tavern owners. His home and tavern, seen in this undated photograph, stood between the post office and St. Andrew's Church. (Courtesy of Hopkinton Historical Society.)

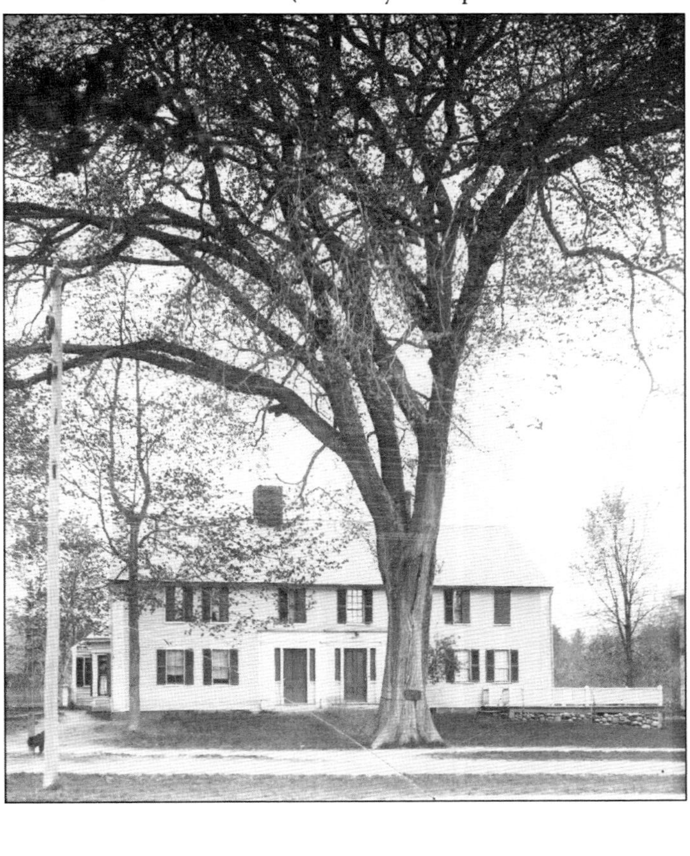

In the summer of 1825, under the elm in front of the Wiggins House, a public reception was held for General Marquis de Lafayette, who aided the American cause during the Revolution. Ironically, it is believed that Benjamin Wiggin himself favored the British side in the war. The house and the tree were both destroyed in a fire in 1927. (Courtesy of Hopkinton Historical Society.)

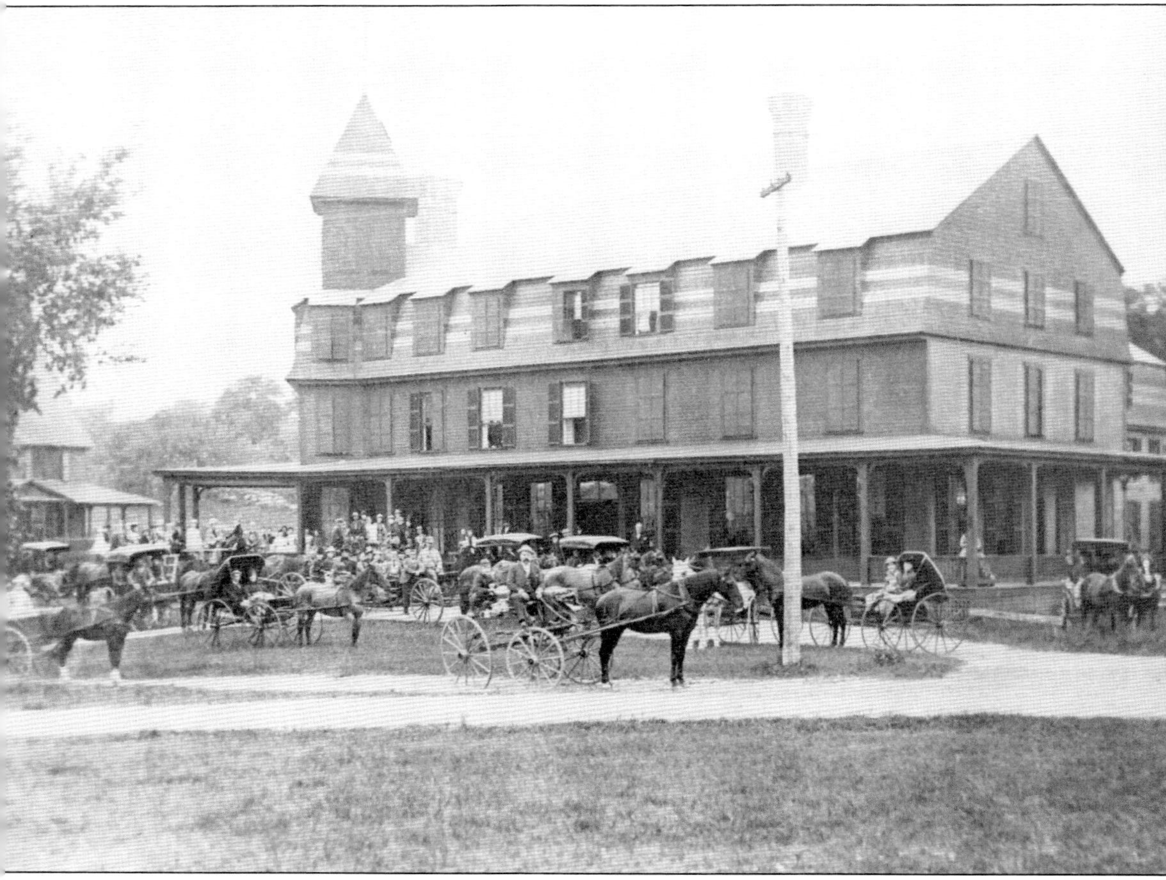

At the northwest corner of the junction of Hopkinton Road (Route 103), Old Henniker Road (Route 202), and Main Street in Hopkinton Village stood the grand Perkins Inn. Possibly as early as 1786, Maj. Isaac Babson kept a tavern on this site. Here, his wife Eleanor Babson, daughter of John and Molly Stark, welcomed guests with great hospitality. After 1800, it was purchased by Roger E. Perkins; it was sold to Brimsley Perkins in 1826. Under his care, the tavern became the most noted public house between Montreal and Boston. In 1847 the inn closed to the public with the death of Perkins's wife and the decline of Hopkinton's population and influence. David B. Story, sheriff of Belknap County and proprietor of the Weirs Hotel, reopened the grand edifice in 1864 for summer boarders; however, on October 5, 1872, the inn burned. Feeling the need for guest accommodations in the village, Kate P. Kimball spearheaded the effort for a new hotel. The Perkins Inn, pictured in this 1888 photograph, opened on July 4 of that year. Sadly, it too was destroyed by fire, set by an arsonist, on March 22, 1907. (Courtesy of Hopkinton Historical Society.)

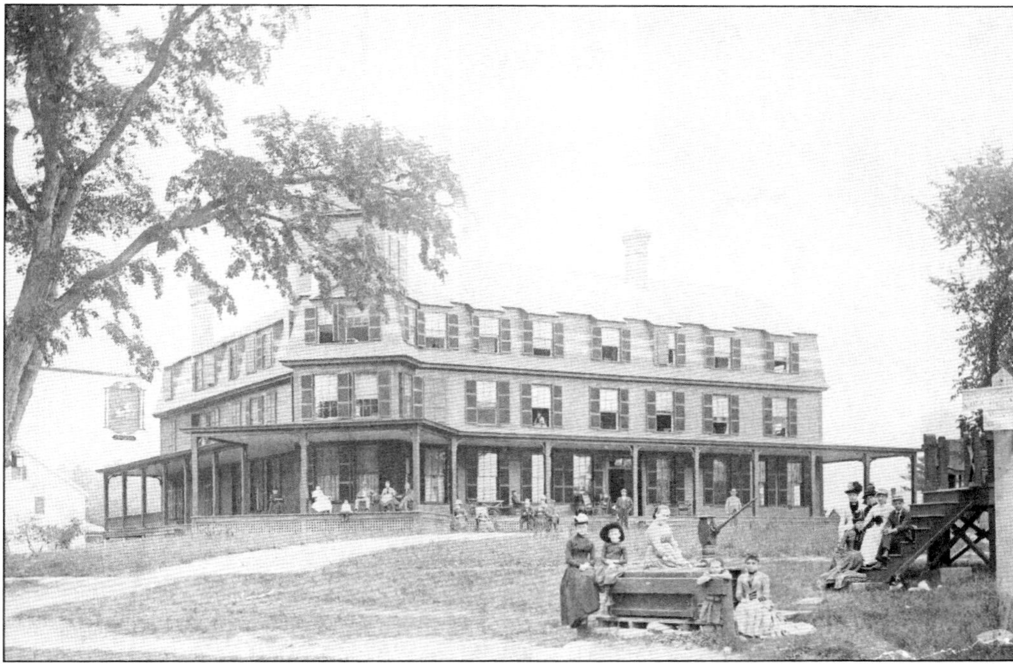

This undated photograph of the Perkins Inn shows Mrs. George Shepard, Frances Greene, Cornelia Dearborn, Robert Warren Kimball, and his mother Mary Theresa (Greene) Kimball gathered around the pump. (Courtesy of Hopkinton Historical Society.)

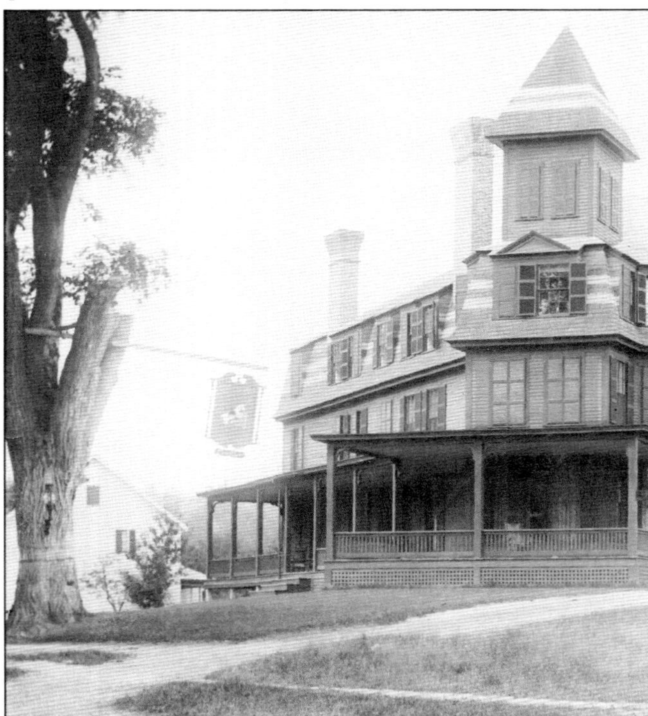

The old swing-sign inviting guests to the Perkins Inn, shown here on the elm tree to the left, originally hung outside the Wiggins Tavern in Hopkinton Village. Benjamin Wiggin was a tavern keeper as early as 1786, a date that is inscribed on the sign. The old sign, bearing an oddly disproportionate man on horseback, finds its current home in Northampton, Massachusetts, at Wiggins Tavern, founded by a descendant of Benjamin Wiggin. (Courtesy of Hopkinton Historical Society.)

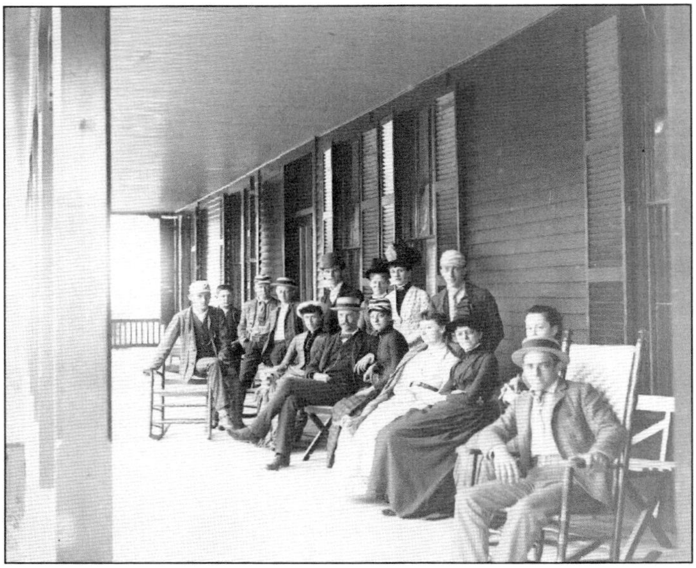

Perkins Inn's guests enjoy the porch facing South Road. The inn offered 52 guest quarters, steam heat, and "modern plumbing and lighting." Every room had a window that opened to Hopkinton's scenic beauty and guests enjoyed fine dining and afternoon teas. Two hundred yards northeast of the inn, guests could enjoy the Beech Hill Golf Club, which offered Saturday teas and weekly golf contests with prizes. (Courtesy of Hopkinton Historical Society.)

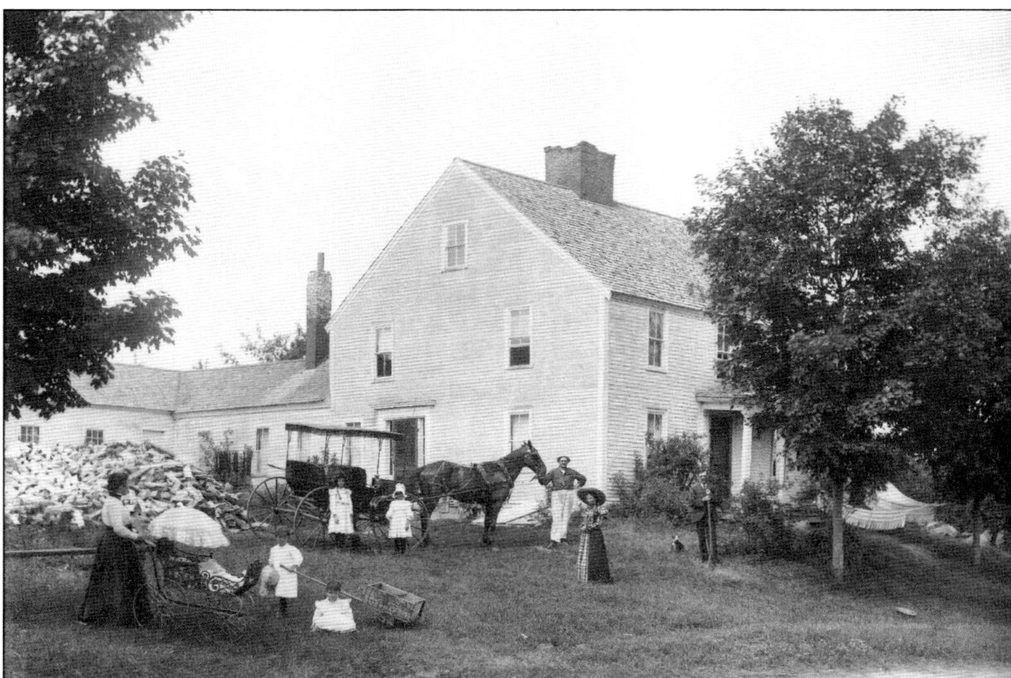

Gould Hill, located on the northern brow of Putney Hill, northwest of Hopkinton Village, was named after the Gould family. Joseph Gould was one of Hopkinton's original proprietors. His sons Christopher and Moses settled on what would become known as Gould Hill. Christopher Gould built the homestead pictured here around 1760. Robert Truman Gould, great-great grandson of Moses Gould, turned the family farm into a successful apple orchard. This original home was dismantled around 1899. (Courtesy of Hopkinton Historical Society.)

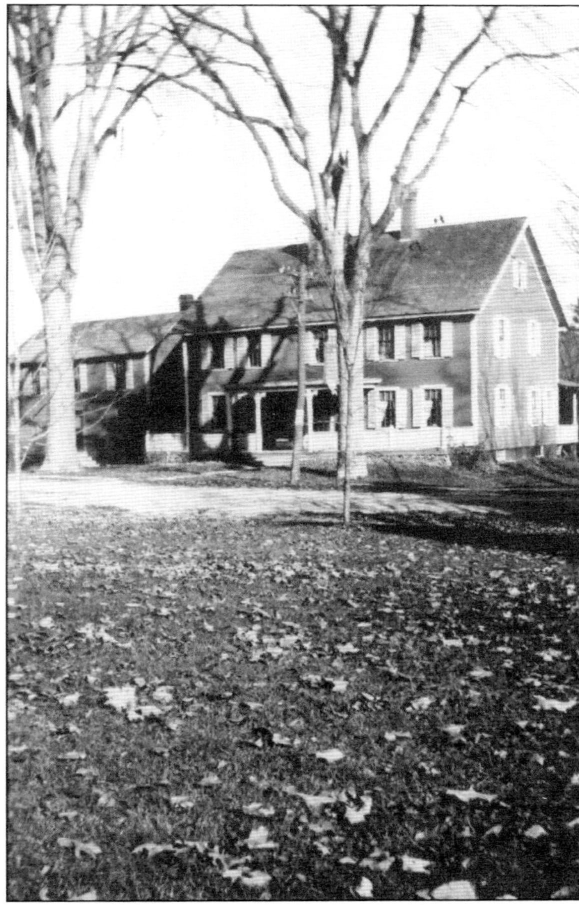

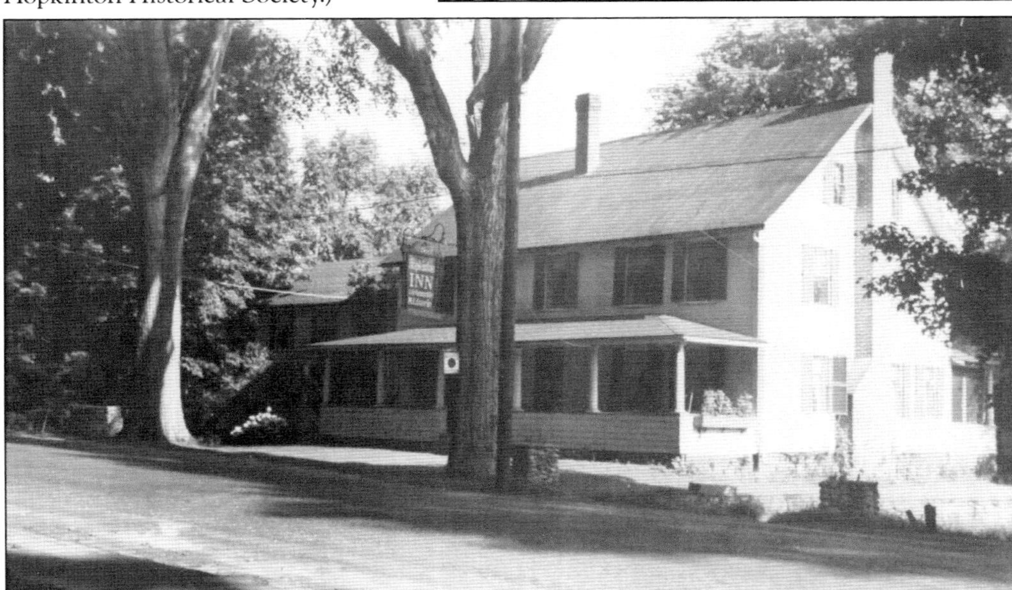

The Hopkinton Inn was located just west of the Hopkinton Village square on Old Henniker Road (Route 202). The sign reads "1786 Entertainment by M.E. Guerin." Guerin owned the inn, which was open year round to guests and served tea in the afternoon to private parties. Hopkinton resident Tim Goodwin recalls fond memories of the inn in the 1960s when his mother, Clara Goodwin, would run it on occasion for owner Mabel Fish. At that time, only the main part of the house was used and it offered four guest rooms, while the annex on the left side of the building held up to six additional guest rooms. Out-of-town visitors would enjoy the beautiful country setting and home-cooked breakfast and dinners. The Hopkinton Inn ceased operations by the early 1970s and the beautiful building is now a private home. (Courtesy of Hopkinton Historical Society.)

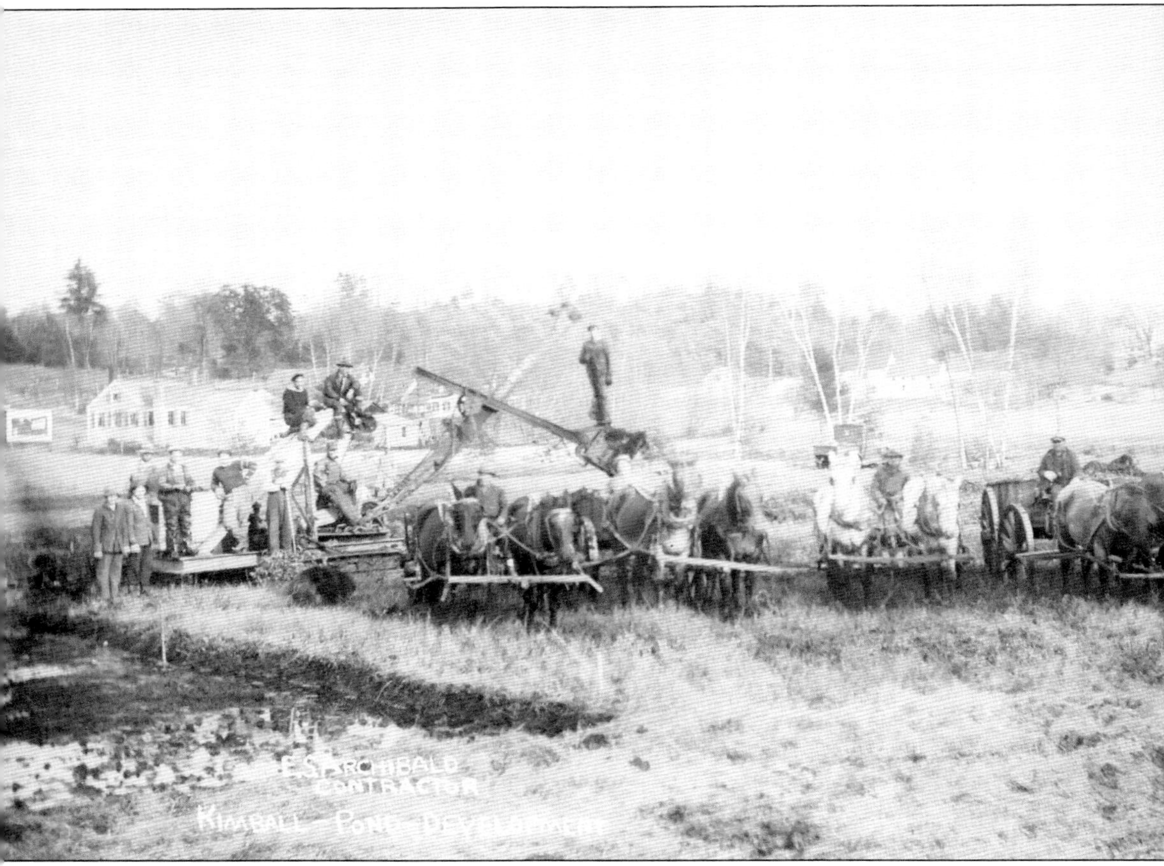

In the midst of the Great Depression, Hopkinton natives John P. Kimball and Harold C. Kimball decided to excavate Ardow—or Mill's Brook—and its accompanying pond to create a lake and resort area just east of Hopkinton Village. Harold C. Kimball was the founder of Indian-Walk Footwear Company in New York, and it was the profit from this endeavor that funded his vision of creating jobs for struggling townsmen by building a sportsmen's resort. The Kimball brothers contracted local builder Ernest Archibald to hire the town's unemployed laborers at 40¢ an hour to build a dam across Mill's Brook and dig out 20 acres of swampland to create a pond. Additionally they built log cabins and nature trails and stocked the pond with trout. Kimball also purchased John Derry's blacksmith shop, where 17 tons of horseshoes (as calculated by Ripley's Believe It or Not) were stacked outside. The building later served as a restaurant for many years. (Courtesy of Hopkinton Historical Society.)

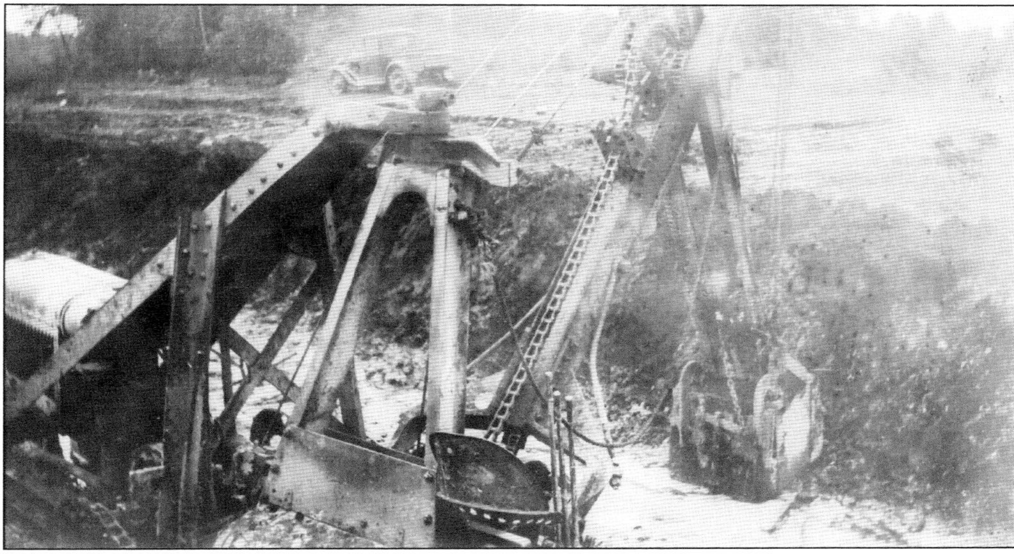

Much of the laborious excavation of Kimball Lake was done by men equipped only with hand shovels. The sole piece of machinery for the immense task was a steam shovel, shown here in photographs dated June 7, 1932. Digging out muck and old vegetation at times five or six feet deep, the steam shovel then loaded the debris onto horse-drawn wagons for removal. Ernest Archibald, the project's contractor, recalled, "One time I dang near lost the shovel for good. She sunk almost out of sight and the men were a week and a half getting her out." (Courtesy of Hopkinton Historical Society.)

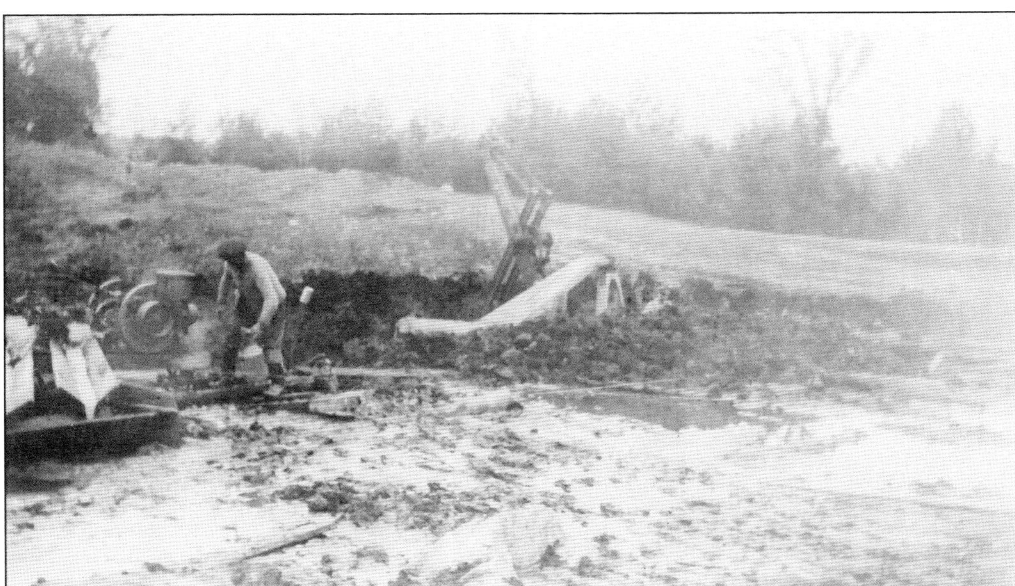

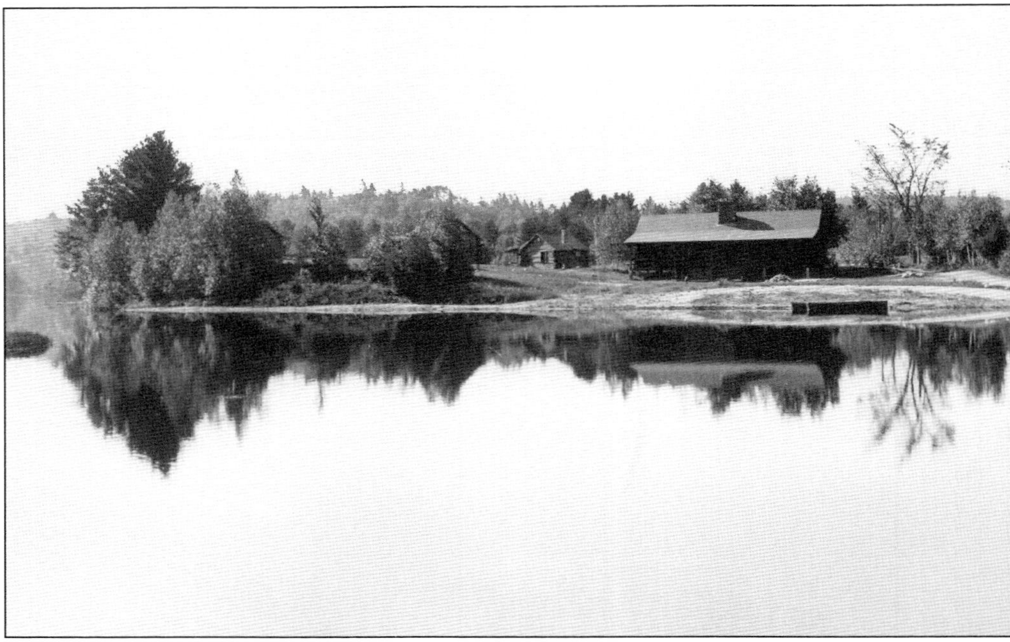

In 1936, the Kimball brothers' 31-acre pond was filled and stocked with trout. A brochure for the resort advertised the rates as $1.50 per day per guest, or $8.75 for the week. For an additional $5.50, a guest could rent a boat and catch his daily limit of a dozen trout. (Courtesy of Hopkinton Historical Society.)

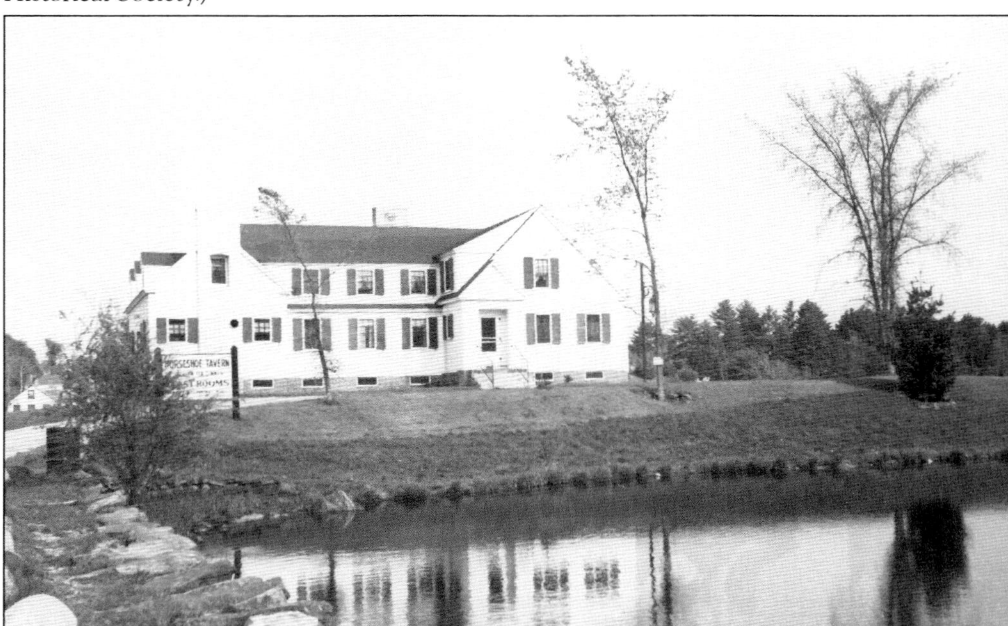

Located next to Kimball Lake, the main section of this house was built by Joseph and Lucinda Mills in 1858. Harold C. Kimball purchased it in the early 1930s and included it as part of his Kimball Lake retreat. He later sold it as a restaurant and although it has changed owners several times since, it remains a dining establishment today. (Courtesy of Hopkinton Historical Society.)

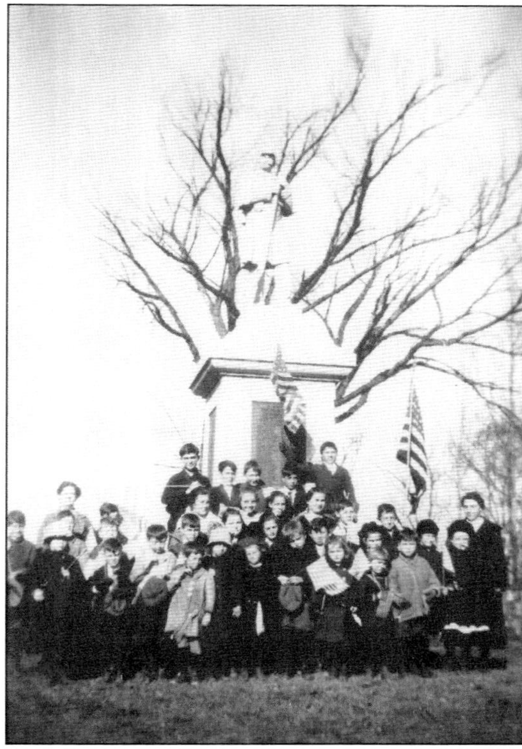

School children gather around the Soldiers Monument in the undated photograph at right. Just northwest of the Hopkinton Village square, a small park honors Hopkinton's heroes. The statue, dedicated in 1916, lists the names of those who fought in the Revolutionary War, the War of 1812, the Spanish American War, and the Civil War. Other monuments in the park honor those who have served in World War I, World War II, and wars since. A fountain near the Soldiers Monument commemorates the formation of Hopkinton's Aqueduct Association in 1840, which was spearheaded by Horace Chase. The waters were drawn from springs about a half mile away on the eastern slope of Putney Hill on land owned by Abraham Burnham. (Courtesy of Hopkinton Historical Society.)

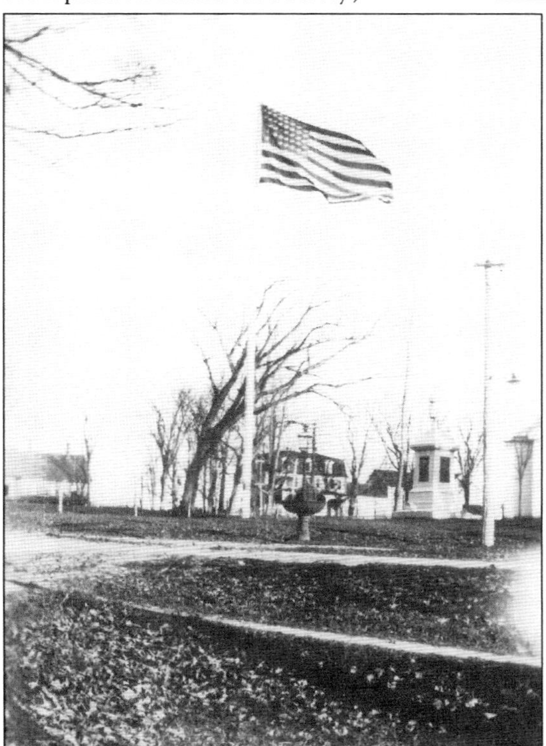

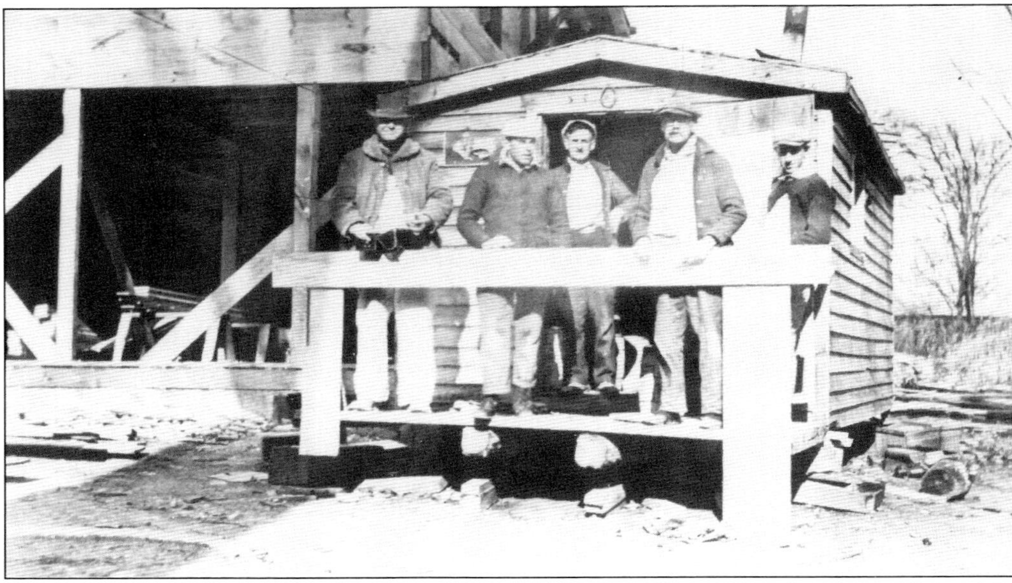

Men pause for a photograph while working to rebuild the village store after the 1927 fire. The blaze destroyed the Willson and Bumpus Store along with three other buildings. Pictured from left to right are Jack Farley, Guy Goodwin, Frank Hoyt, Walter Hoyt, and an unidentified man. (Courtesy of Hopkinton Historical Society.)

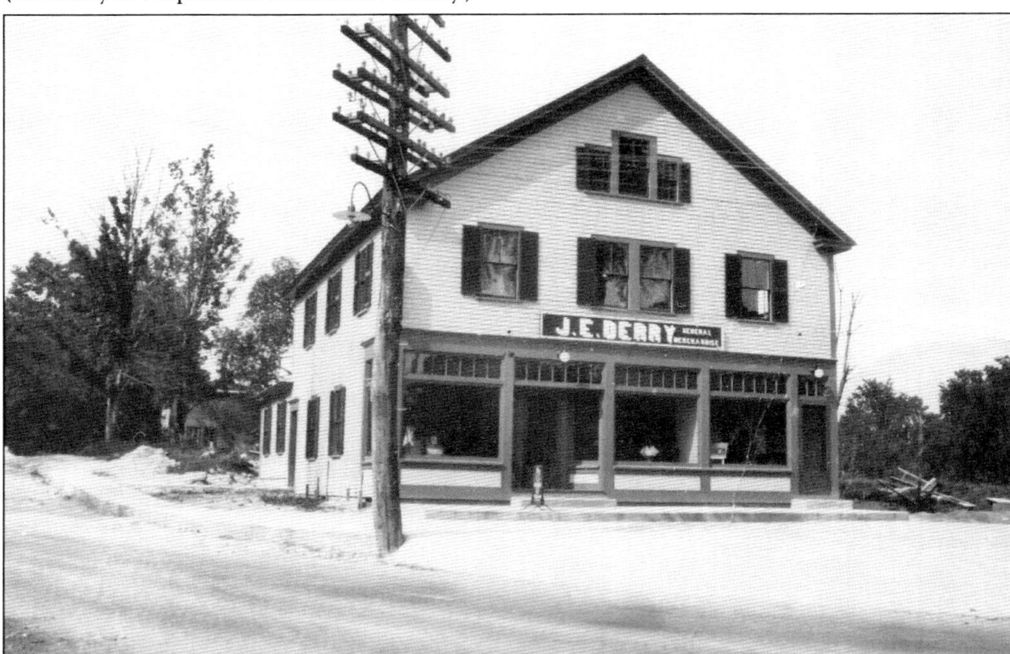

This undated photograph shows the newly-constructed village store after the fire of 1927 that destroyed the previous store and three other buildings. Joseph E. Derry constructed the new building and opened a general merchandise store. Derry also owned a blacksmith shop less than a half mile southeast on Main Street that attracted much interest for its massive pile of horseshoes, measuring at one time nearly eight feet high. (Courtesy of Hopkinton Historical Society.)

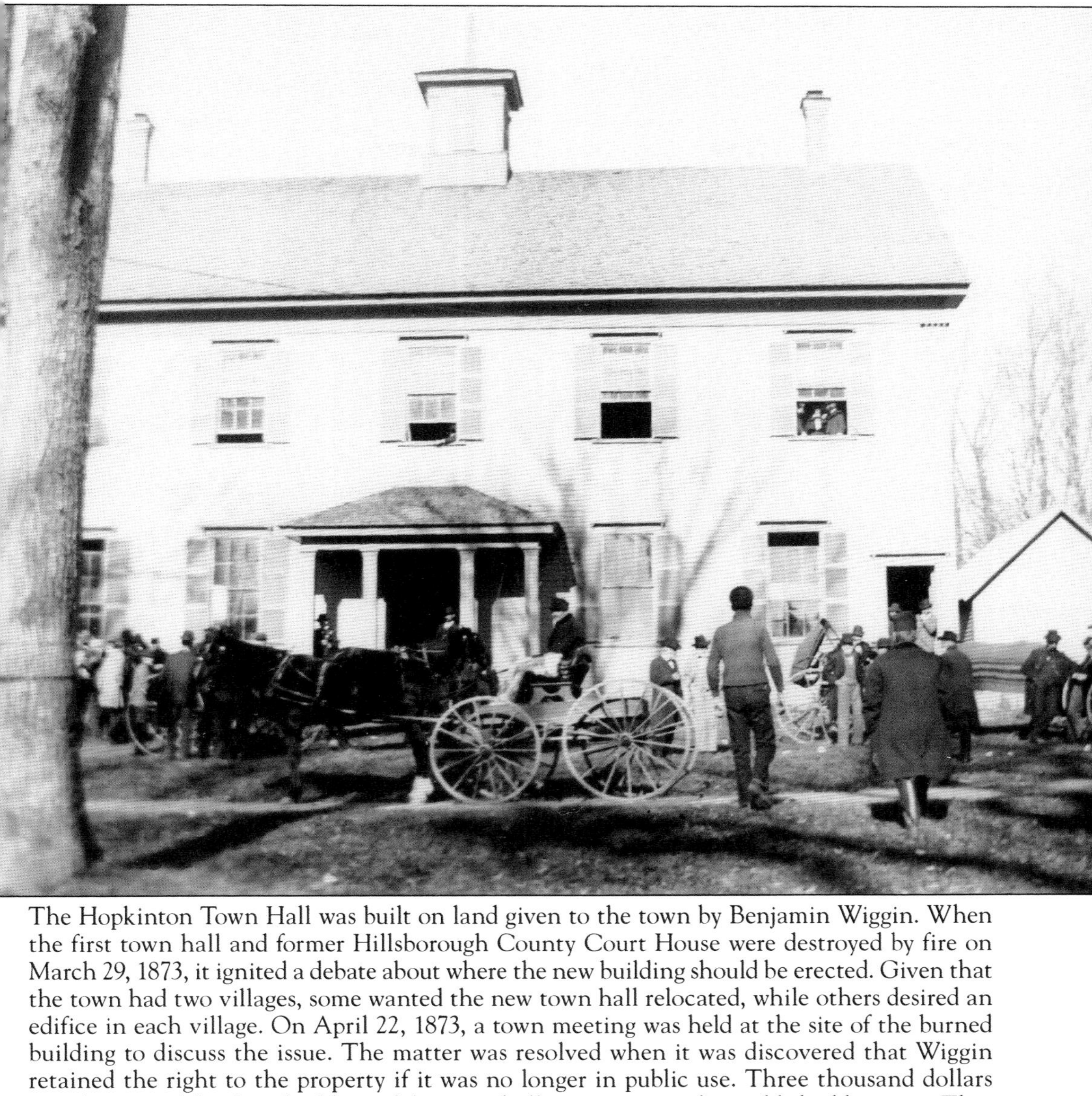

The Hopkinton Town Hall was built on land given to the town by Benjamin Wiggin. When the first town hall and former Hillsborough County Court House were destroyed by fire on March 29, 1873, it ignited a debate about where the new building should be erected. Given that the town had two villages, some wanted the new town hall relocated, while others desired an edifice in each village. On April 22, 1873, a town meeting was held at the site of the burned building to discuss the issue. The matter was resolved when it was discovered that Wiggin retained the right to the property if it was no longer in public use. Three thousand dollars was then voted for the rebuilding of the town hall on its previously-established location. That decision, however, did not squelch opposition and the construction was plagued by resistance, funding issues, resignations of committee members, and court injunctions. Fortunately, the building seen here was completed in 1874 and a dedication celebration was held that March 3. (Courtesy of Hopkinton Historical Society.)

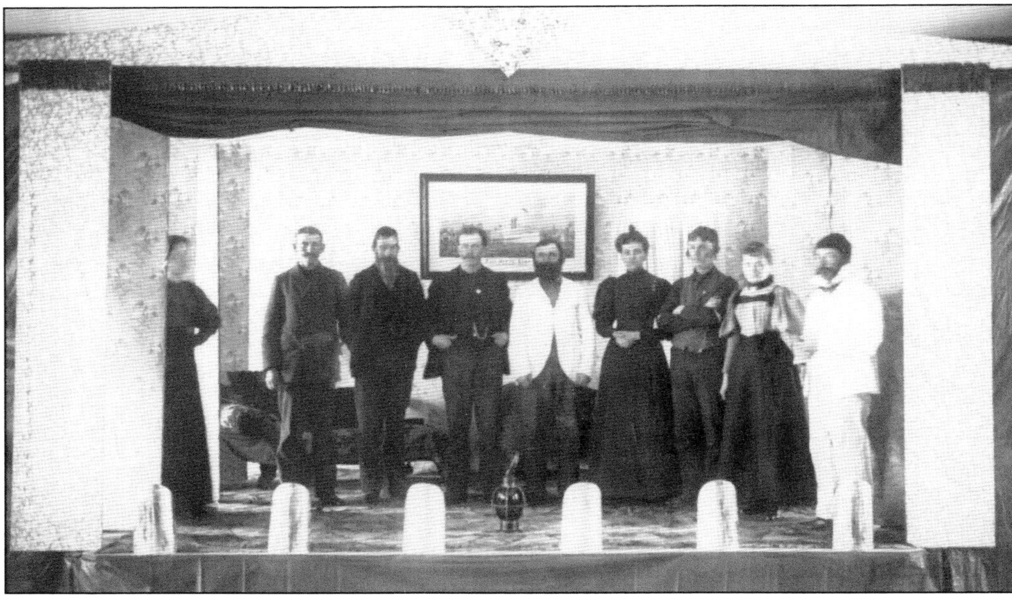

When the new town hall was being planned, the residents of Hopkinton wanted a second floor added to accommodate a hall for public use, such as plays, as depicted in this undated photograph. Private funding was pledged to pay for the additional expenses and it was named Lyceum Hall. (Courtesy of Hopkinton Historical Society.)

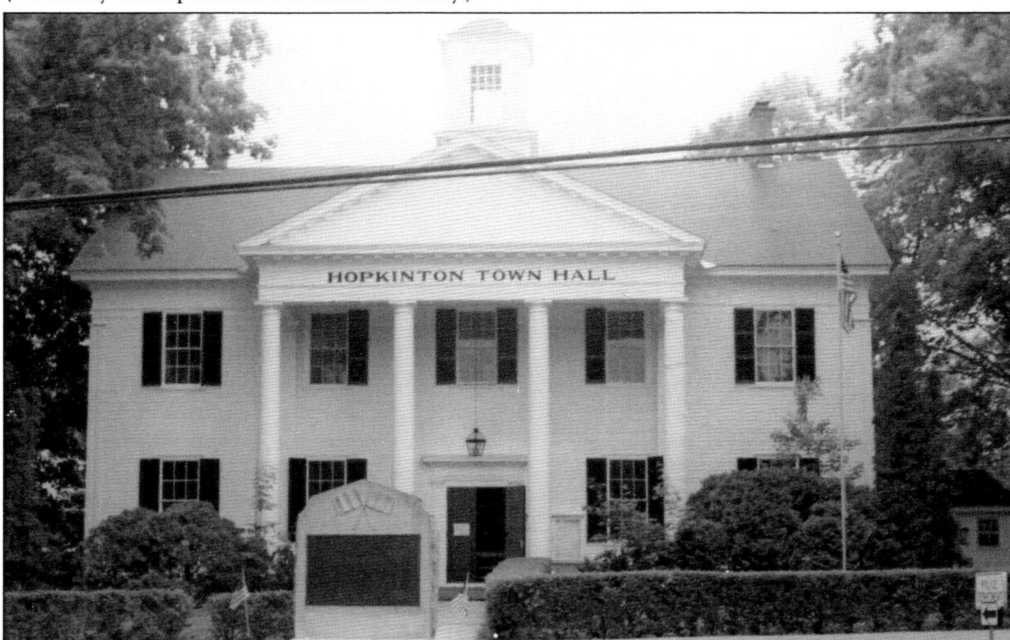

This undated photograph shows what Hopkinton Town Hall looks like today after it was altered in the early 20th century. At that time, the grand portico and cupola were added, the door to the upstairs hall was removed, and the windows were realigned. The grand-looking pillars were also added in the early part of the 20th century, and the building continues to be a hub of town business and affairs. (Courtesy of Hopkinton Historical Society.)

Two

CONTOOCOOK VILLAGE

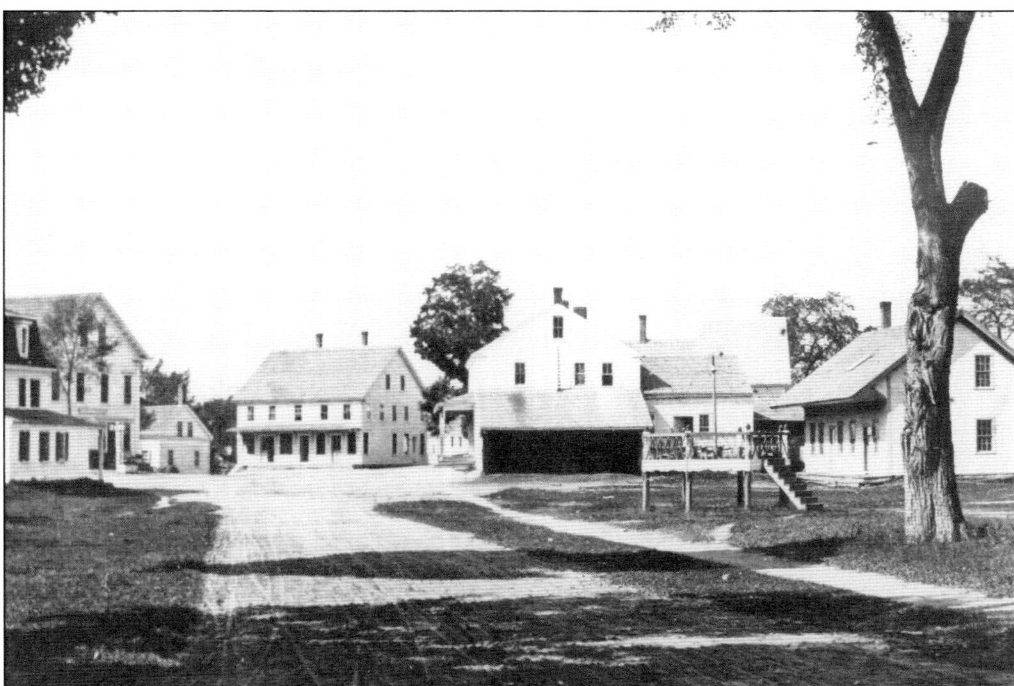

A very early view of Contoocook Village looking west up Main Street shows, from left to right, the corner of the Bailey Tavern, the original Bailey Block, a private home, the Jones Block (original home to the New Hampshire Antiquarian Society, later known as the Hopkinton Historical Society), the Curtice Block with its original horse sheds, and the train depot. (Courtesy of Hopkinton Historical Society.)

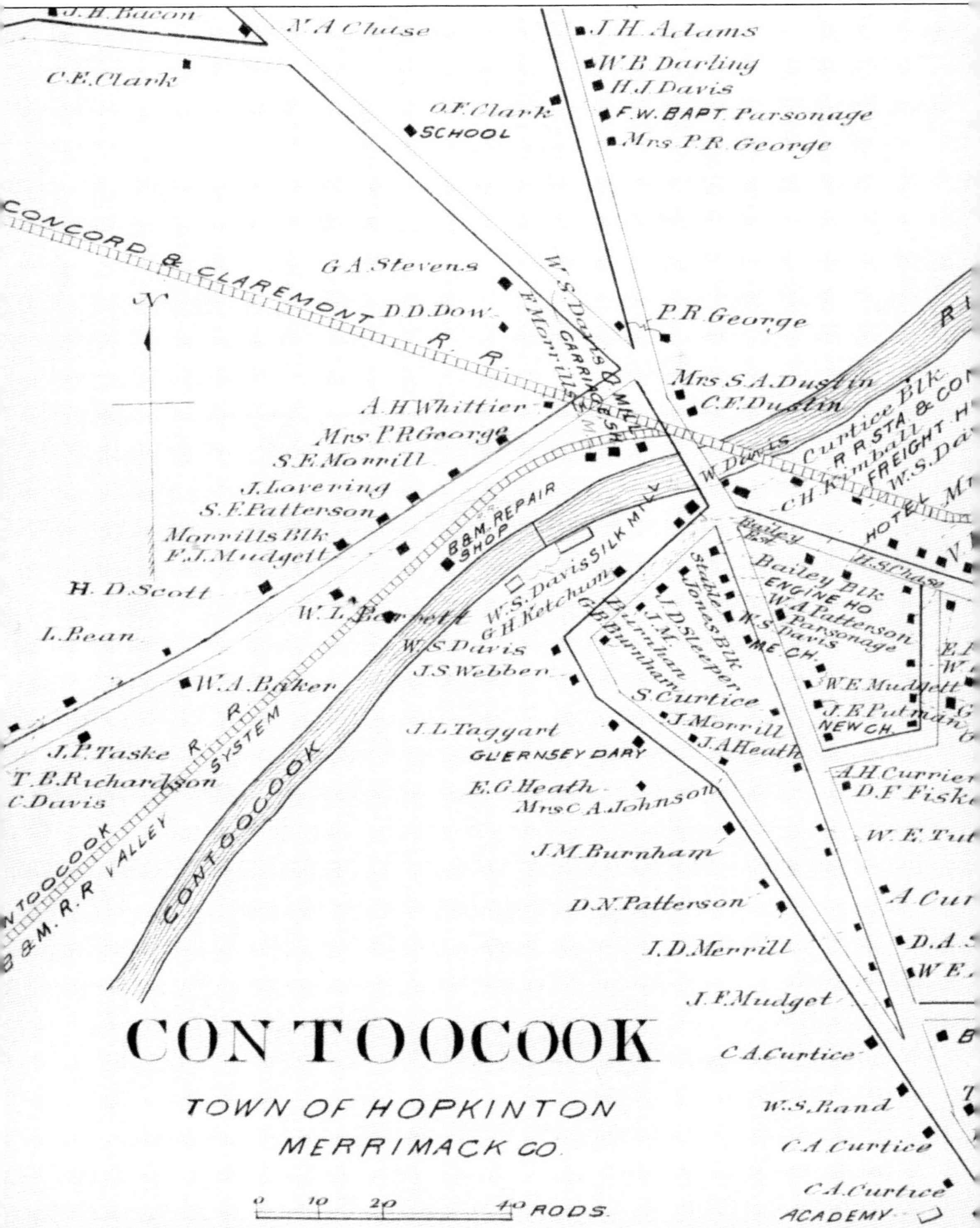
CONTOOCOOK
TOWN OF HOPKINTON
MERRIMACK CO.
0 10 20 40 RODS.
CONCORD & CLAREMONT R. R.
CONTOOCOOK
CONTOOCOOK B & M. R. R VALLEY SYSTEM
B & M. REPAIR SHOP
W. S. Davis Silk Mill
School
F. W. Bapt. Parsonage
Guernsey Dary
Academy
New Ch.
M. E. Ch.
Engine Ho
Bailey Blk
Morrills Blk
Curtice Blk
R R Sta
Freight H
Hotel
J. H. Adams
W. B. Darling
H. J. Davis
Mrs P. R. George
O. F. Clark
N. A. Chase
C. E. Clark
G. A. Stevens
D. D. Dow
P. R. George
Mrs S. A. Dustin
C. E. Dustin
A. H. Whittier
S. F. Morrill
J. Lovering
S. F. Patterson
F. J. Mudgett
H. D. Scott
W. L. Barnett
L. Bean
W. A. Baker
J. P. Taske
T. B. Richardson
C. Davis
J. S. Webber
G. H. Ketchum
J. L. Taggart
E. G. Heath
Mrs C. A. Johnson
J. M. Burnham
D. N. Patterson
I. D. Merrill
J. F. Mudget
C. A. Curtice
W. S. Rand
H. A. Rowell
J. D. Sleeper
S. Curtice
J. Morrill
J. A. Heath
W. A. Patterson
W. E. Mudgett
J. E. Putman
A. H. Currier
D. F. Fiske
H. S. Chase

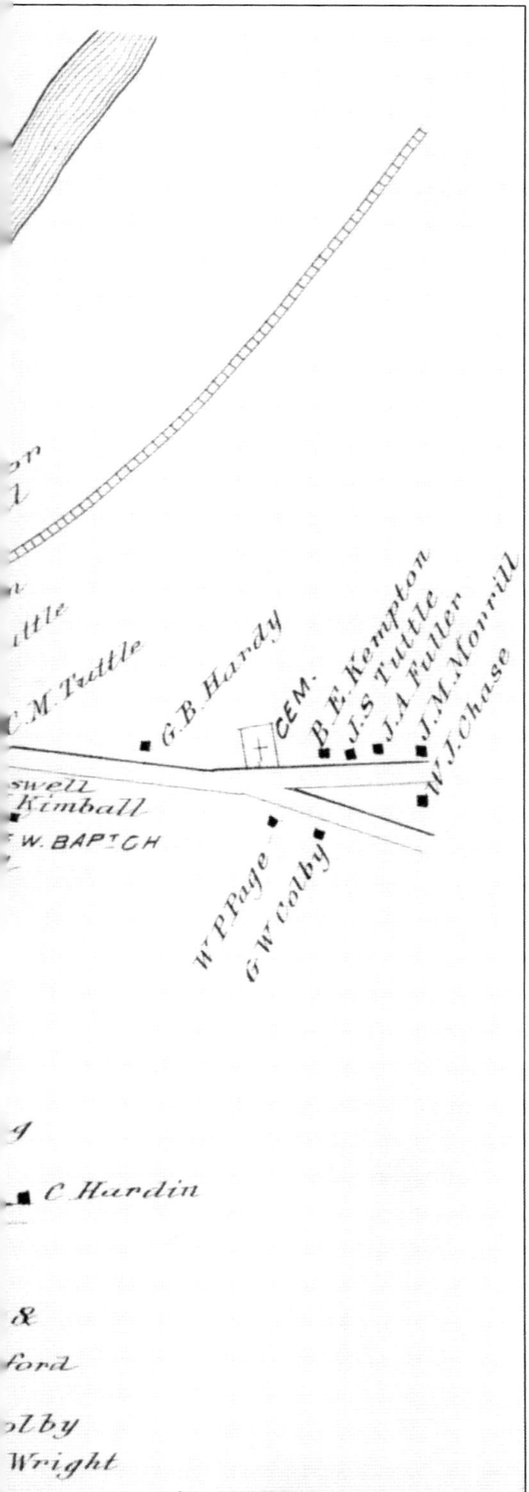

This map of Contoocook Village was produced in 1892 by D.H. Hurd and Company. The map shows Cedar Street running parallel to the southern side of the Contoocook River and then turning sharply to the south. In earlier days Cedar Street, then called River Street, was the main road and went straight across the river over Hill's bridge, near the Grange Hall. This original bridge was built in 1787. (Courtesy of Mala Duclos Tyler.)

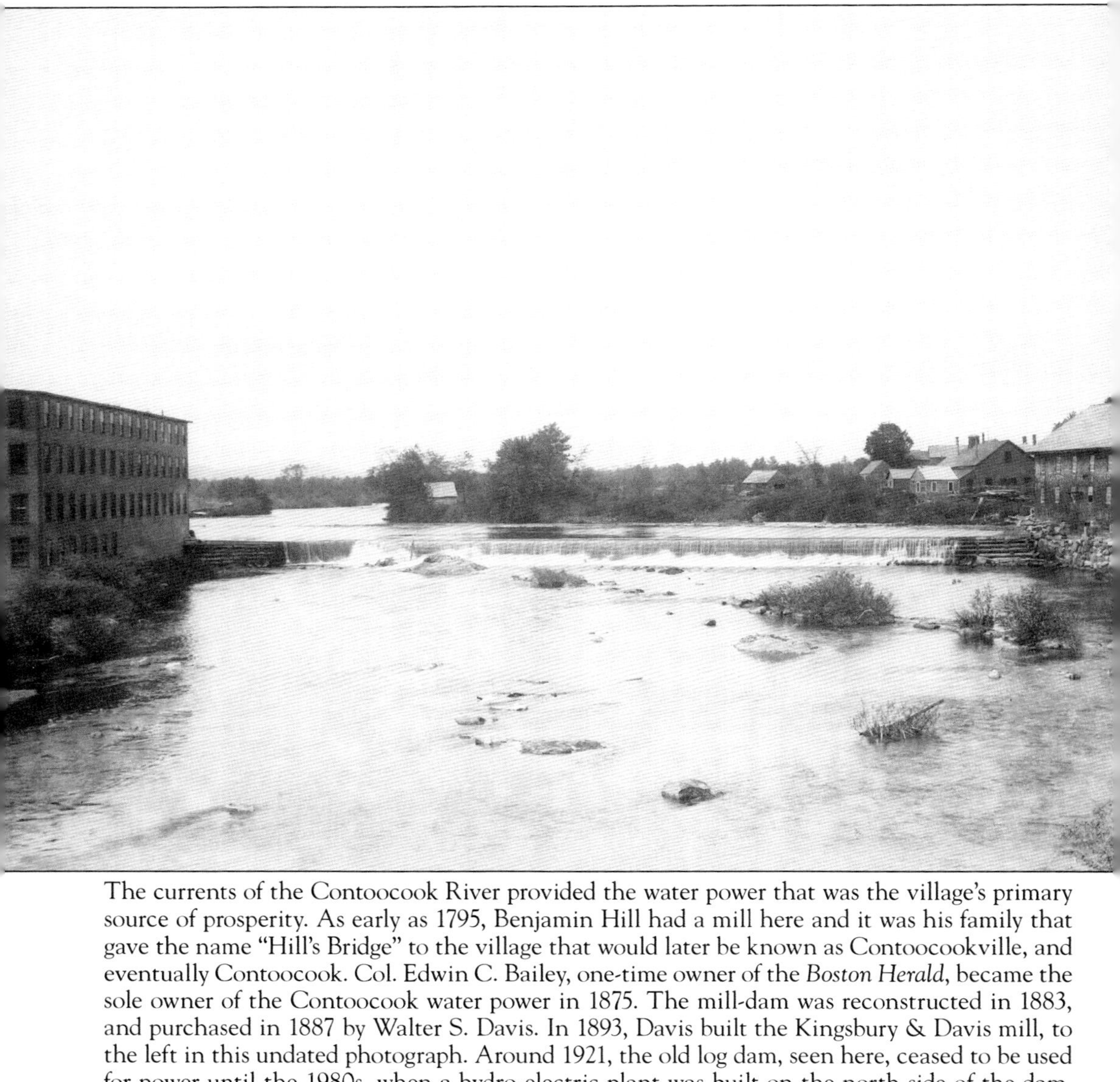

The currents of the Contoocook River provided the water power that was the village's primary source of prosperity. As early as 1795, Benjamin Hill had a mill here and it was his family that gave the name "Hill's Bridge" to the village that would later be known as Contoocookville, and eventually Contoocook. Col. Edwin C. Bailey, one-time owner of the *Boston Herald*, became the sole owner of the Contoocook water power in 1875. The mill-dam was reconstructed in 1883, and purchased in 1887 by Walter S. Davis. In 1893, Davis built the Kingsbury & Davis mill, to the left in this undated photograph. Around 1921, the old log dam, seen here, ceased to be used for power until the 1980s, when a hydro-electric plant was built on the north side of the dam. (Courtesy of Hopkinton Historical Society.)

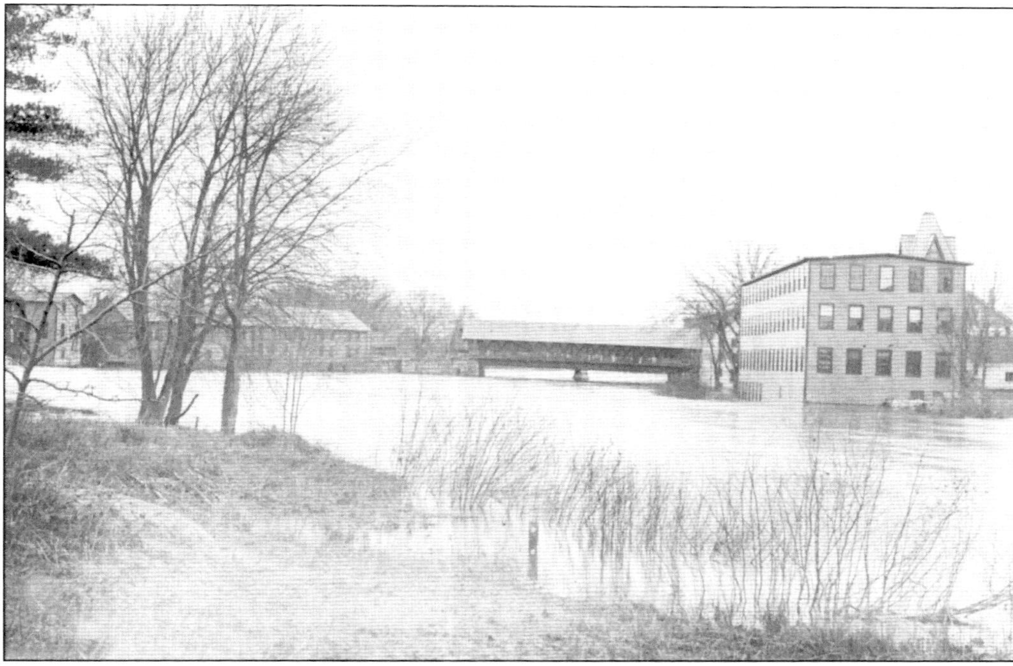

Seen here is a view of Contoocook Village looking northeast down the Contoocook River. The covered highway bridge was built around 1853. To the right of the bridge is the Kingsbury & Davis Machine Company and to the left is the grist mill. The falls of the Contoocook River made Contoocook an ideal location for grist mills, lumber mills, and other industrial endeavours. (Courtesy of Hopkinton Historical Society.)

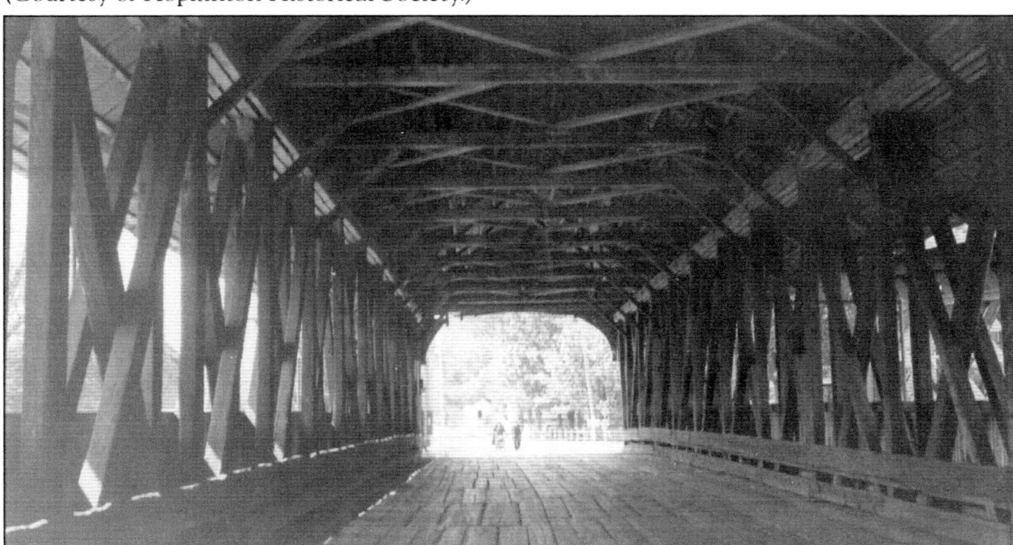

This undated photograph shows a view from inside the covered highway bridge looking northwest on Route 103 towards the Perkins Manor. The bridge, built around 1853, provided a crossing over the Contoocook River for pedestrians, horses and buggies, oxen and wagons, and eventually automobiles during its more than 80 years of service. Prior to this one, a bridge was located further south up the river. (Courtesy of Hopkinton Historical Society.)

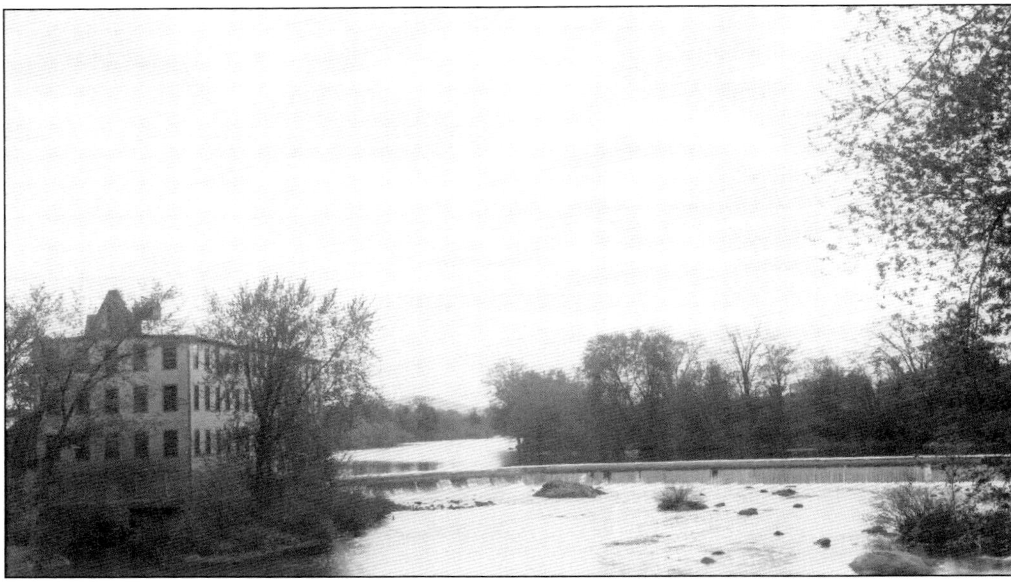

This view of the Contoocook River dam looks southwest from the highway bridge in Contoocook Village after the old log dam had been replaced with concrete. The Contoocook River is one of the few north-flowing rivers in the world. It flows for about 71 miles from Poole Pond in Jaffrey/Rindge to Penacook, where it meets the Merrimack River. (Courtesy of Hopkinton Historical Society.)

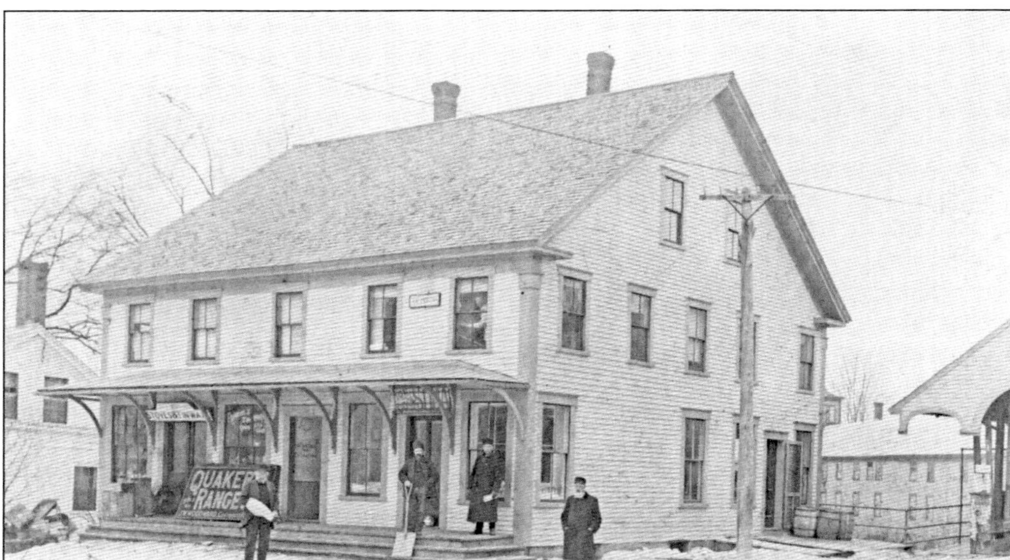

This undated photograph shows a building owned by C.H. Kimball that once stood just south of the covered highway bridge (Route 103). Known as the Jones Building, it was the original home of the New Hampshire Antiquarian Society, later known as the Hopkinton Historical Society. The shops in the building included George Ketchum's stove and tin ware shop, a store selling general merchandise, and a job printing and stationery shop. The building, as well as the house beside it, was later destroyed by fire. (Courtesy of Hopkinton Historical Society.)

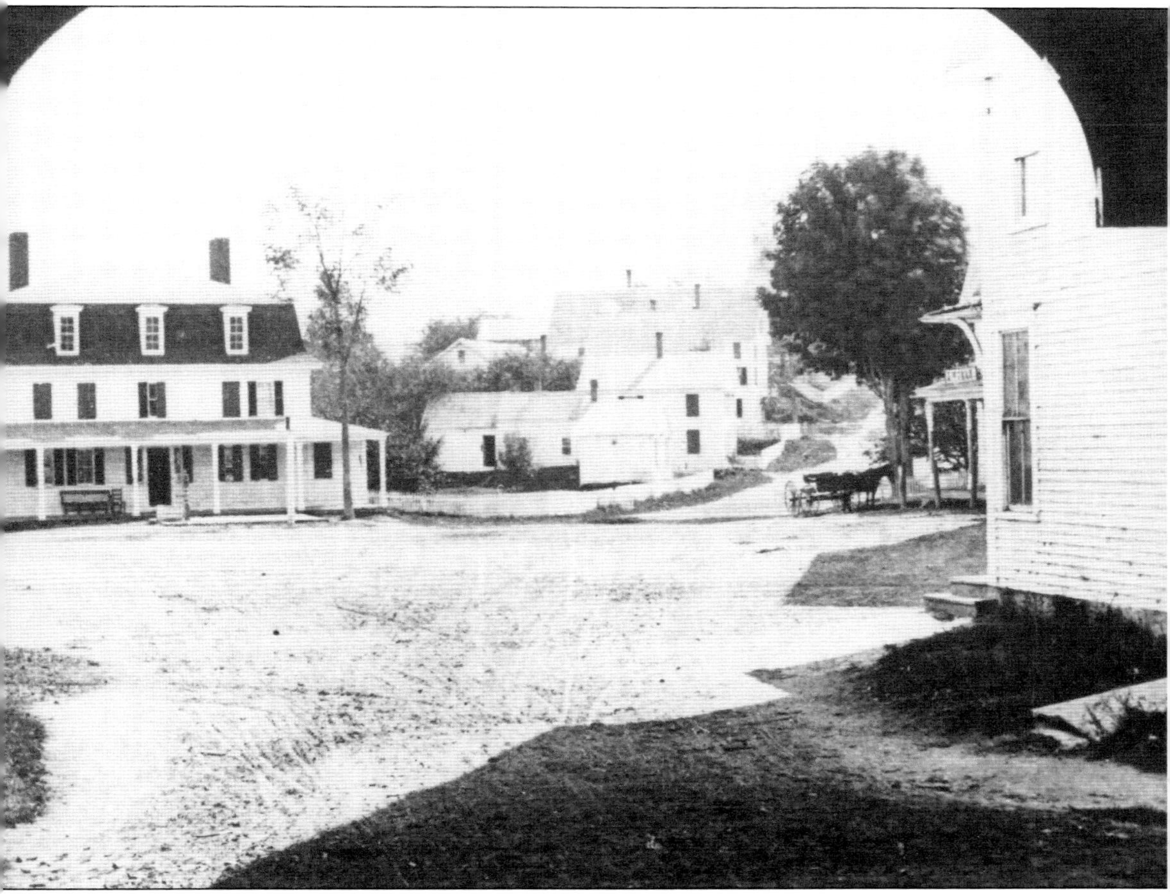

This pre-1878 photograph was taken from the covered highway bridge looking southeast towards the Contoocook Village Square and Maple Street. The building on the left was the second hotel in the village, built in 1831 by Mr. Sleeper and Mr. Wheeler. The two men were not successful in their efforts as proprietors, and the hotel was taken over by Herrick Putnam. It changed hands numerous times until 1872, when E.C. Bailey ran the hotel for six years before tearing it down to build a new hotel, the Central House, on what would be the western apex of the Walter S. Davis property. The venture was unsuccessful, and the unfinished hotel was moved to Cedar Street, where it became a two-family apartment house (and home to the Conant family). It would eventually become the Grange Hall. (Courtesy of Hopkinton Historical Society.)

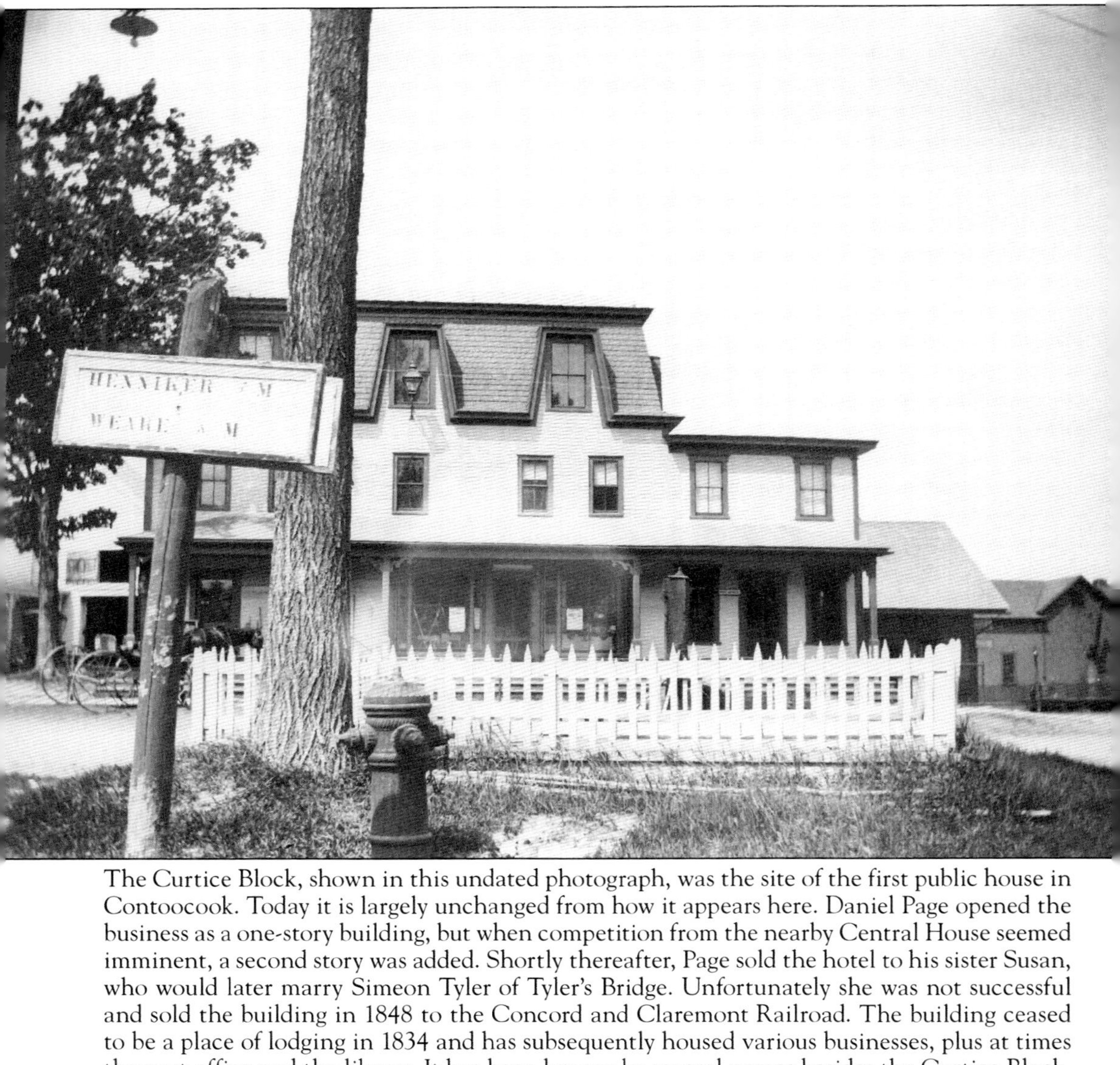

The Curtice Block, shown in this undated photograph, was the site of the first public house in Contoocook. Today it is largely unchanged from how it appears here. Daniel Page opened the business as a one-story building, but when competition from the nearby Central House seemed imminent, a second story was added. Shortly thereafter, Page sold the hotel to his sister Susan, who would later marry Simeon Tyler of Tyler's Bridge. Unfortunately she was not successful and sold the building in 1848 to the Concord and Claremont Railroad. The building ceased to be a place of lodging in 1834 and has subsequently housed various businesses, plus at times the post office and the library. It has been known by several names besides the Curtice Block, such as the Huntoon Block and the Kirk Block, named after different proprietors. John F. Kirk purchased the building in 1947 and the property remains in the Kirk family today. (Courtesy of Hopkinton Historical Society.)

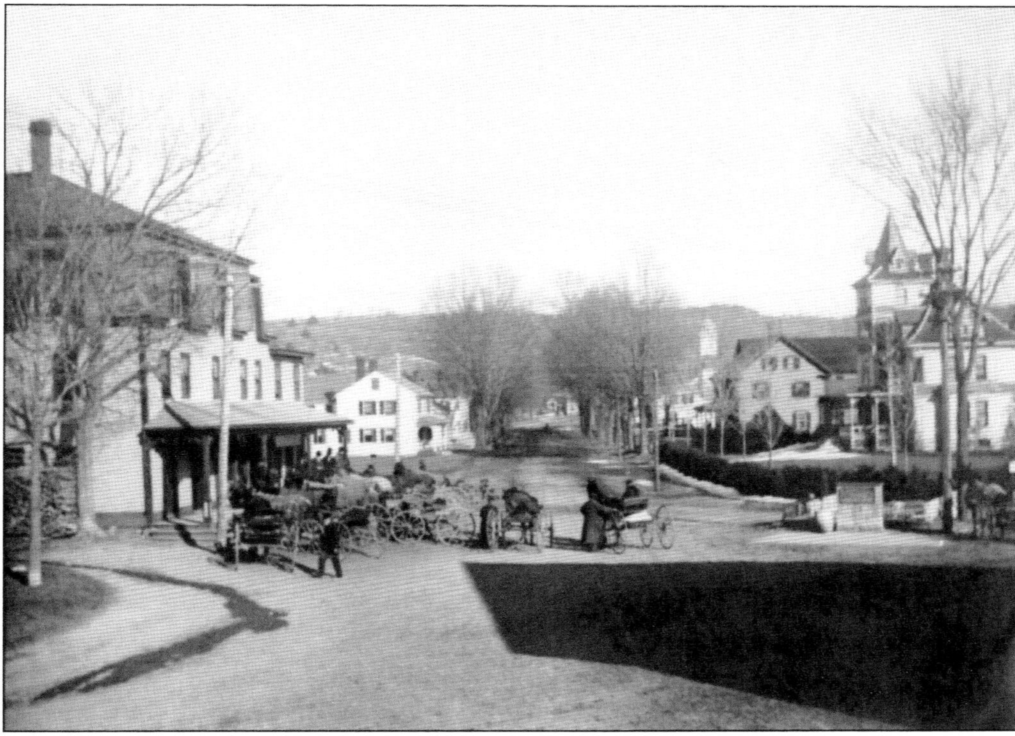

Horses and buggies gather in front of the Curtice Block in Contoocook Village in this undated photograph. The stately home of businessman and inventor Walter S. Davis is visible on the right. Next to the Davis residence stands the Highland House and just beyond that is the steeple of the Baptist Church. The old pump and trough can be seen in the center of the square. (Courtesy of Hopkinton Historical Society.)

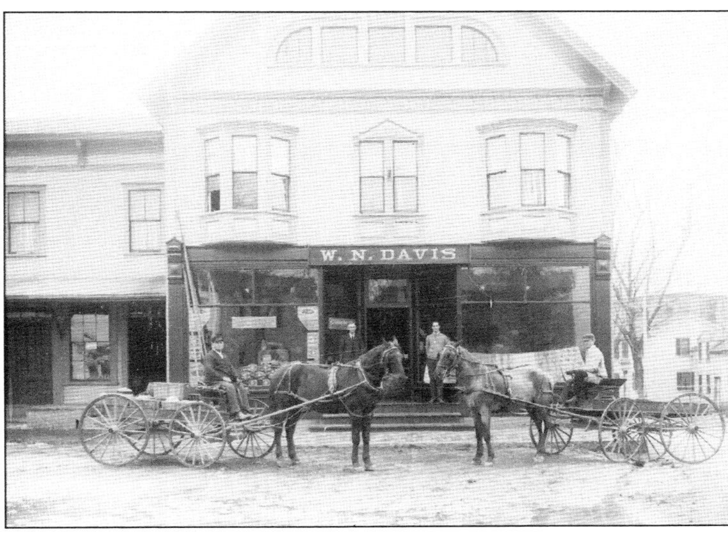

William Davis (left) and Erving Hicks (right) pose in front of the W.N. Davis store in Contoocook Village. The original Bailey Block, located here, was destroyed in a fire in 1900 and this building was constructed to replace it. The building has housed stores and businesses to this day. (Courtesy of Hopkinton Historical Society.)

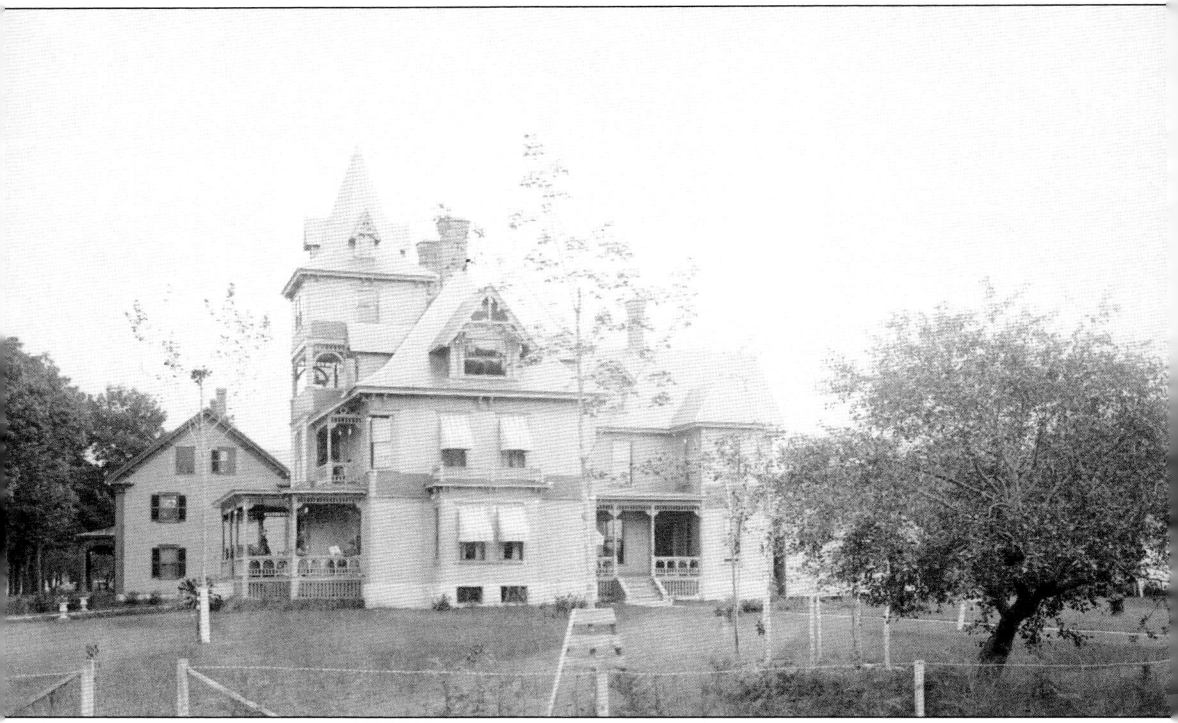

This undated photograph shows the home of Walter S. Davis, which still stands today just southeast of the village's square. Born in 1834, Davis spent much of his early career in the lumber business in Davisville with various business partners. In 1871, he started to manufacture strawboard in addition to his lumber endeavors. Davis moved his family to Contoocook in 1874, purchased the water power rights in 1887, and built this stunning residence the following year. As an inventor, he created the Davis Turbine Water-Wheel and a machine that produced paper boxes. Besides being a businessman, Davis also represented Hopkinton in 1878 and served as a state senator in 1885. (Courtesy of Hopkinton Historical Society.)

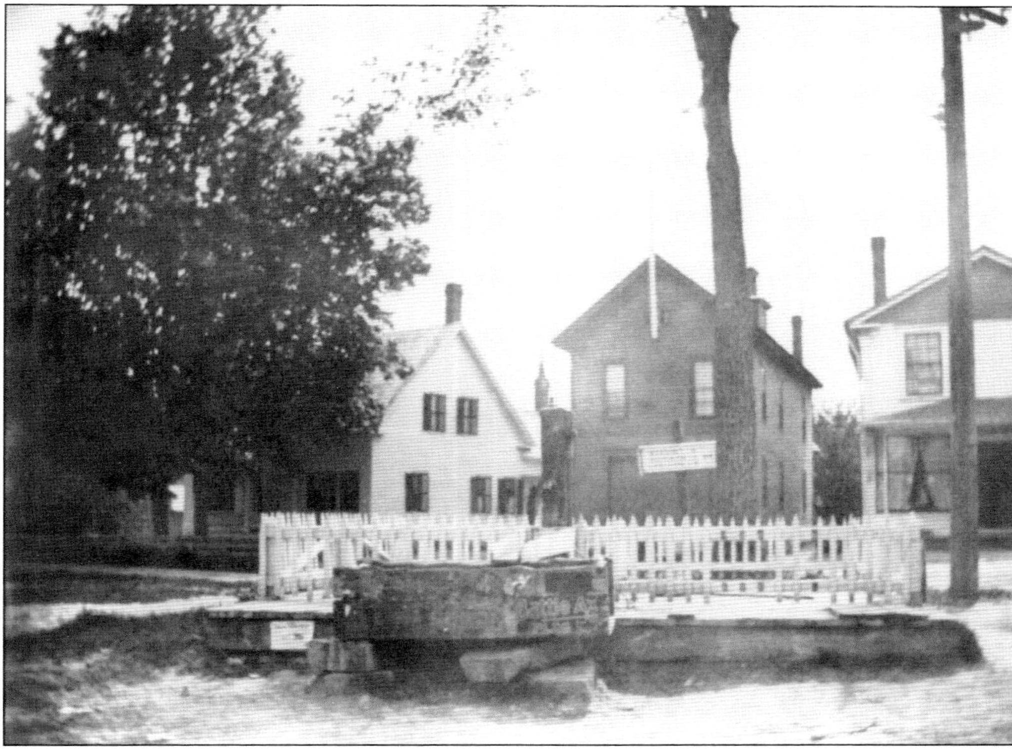

Early on, fresh water was provided in the village by a pump and trough. Behind the pump, the building in the middle, built in 1860, once served as the village's fire house. The house on the left has been Rusty's General Store for Pets for nearly three decades. The building on the right is part of the Bailey Block. All three buildings still stand today. (Courtesy of Hopkinton Historical Society.)

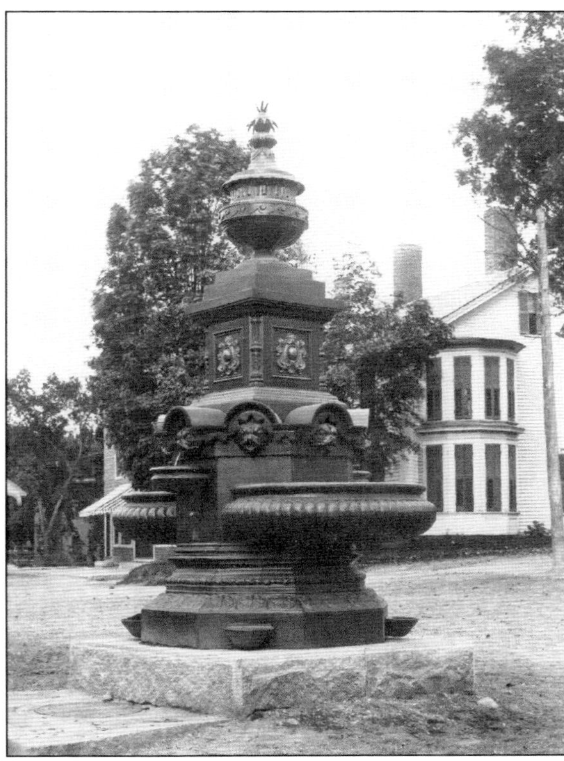

This large fountain, which sat in the middle of Contoocook's Fountain Square, was made of cast iron and elaborately detailed. The date of its installation is unknown but it replaced the old pump and trough sometime in the mid to late 1800s. Town records showed the fountain was sold to H. Lewis for $20, reportedly after it was hit by a truck and damaged beyond repair. (Courtesy of Hopkinton Historical Society.)

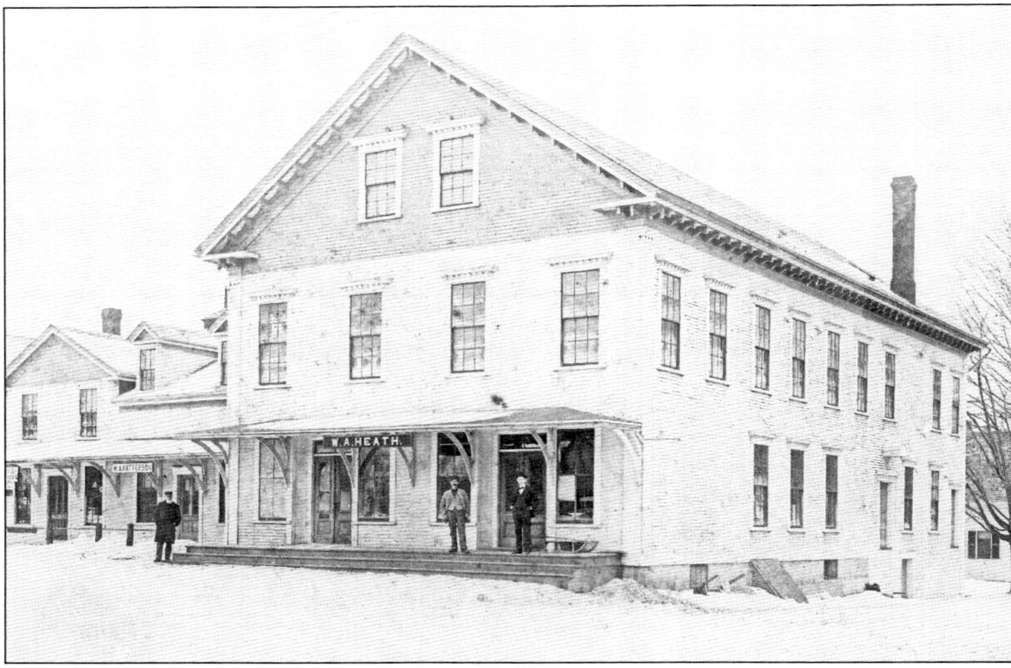

This photograph of the Bailey Block prior to the fire that destroyed it in 1900 shows two men standing in front of the store of W.A. Heath. On the left, a man stands in front of a door that reads "Undertaker." This building stood on the corner of Cedar Street and Route 103. (Courtesy of Hopkinton Historical Society.)

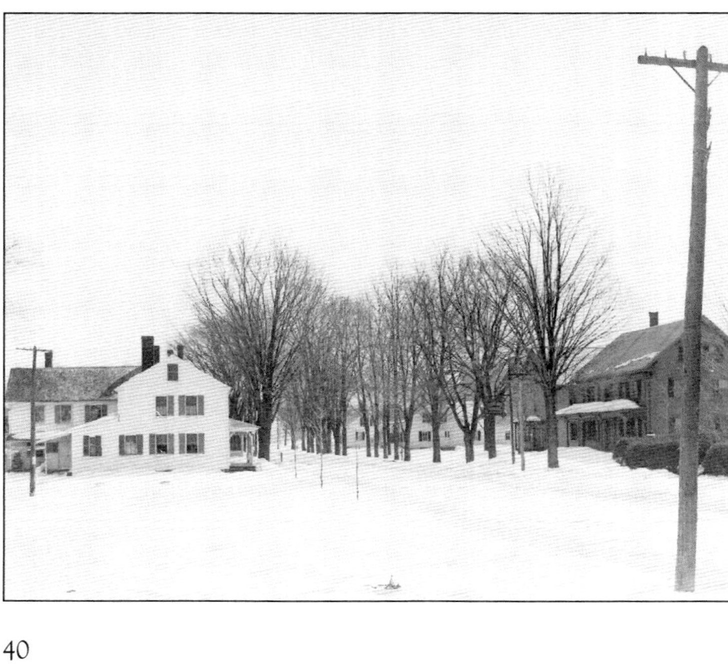

This photograph, looking east down Main Street from the area of the train depot and the Curtice Block, shows the Highland House on the right. It was once owned by Edwin C. Bailey, who owned the water power in the village and built the dam. Bailey also constructed the Bailey Block in Contoocook as well as one in Concord. (Photograph by Leown Kelley; courtesy of Hopkinton Historical Society.)

A horse pulls its load east on Main Street (Route 103) heading out of Contoocook Village near the intersection of Penacook Road. The brown house on the left was built in 1790 and was once home to photographer Leown Kelley. The small building on the right has a sign advertising "W.F. Fuller Rubber Stamp Job Printing." A nearly-treeless Gould Hill can be seen in the background. (Courtesy of Hopkinton Historical Society.)

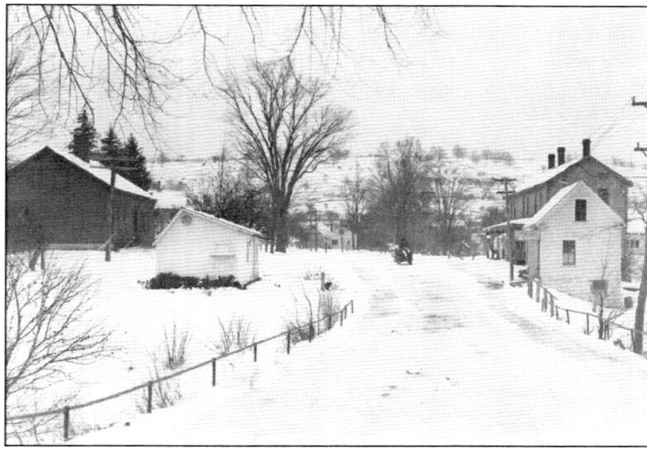

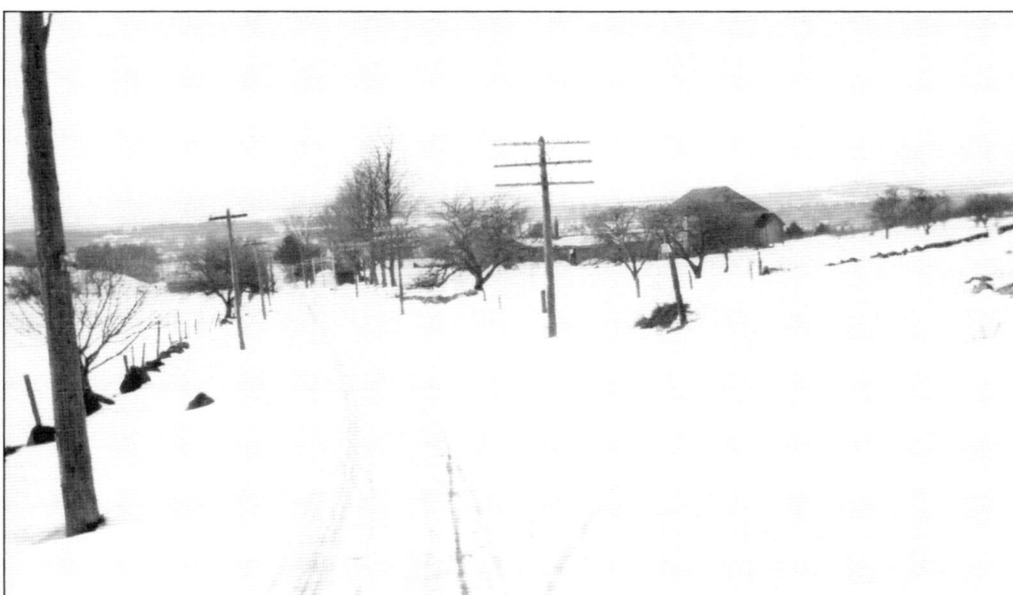

This undated photograph shows the view looking northwest towards Contoocook Village at the junction of Indian Ridge Road (right) and Main Street (Route 103). Not far from this spot was the location of Woodwell's Garrison, where eight early settlers were kidnapped by Indians on the morning of April 22, 1746, and marched to Canada to be ransomed or sold to the French. (Courtesy of Hopkinton Historical Society.)

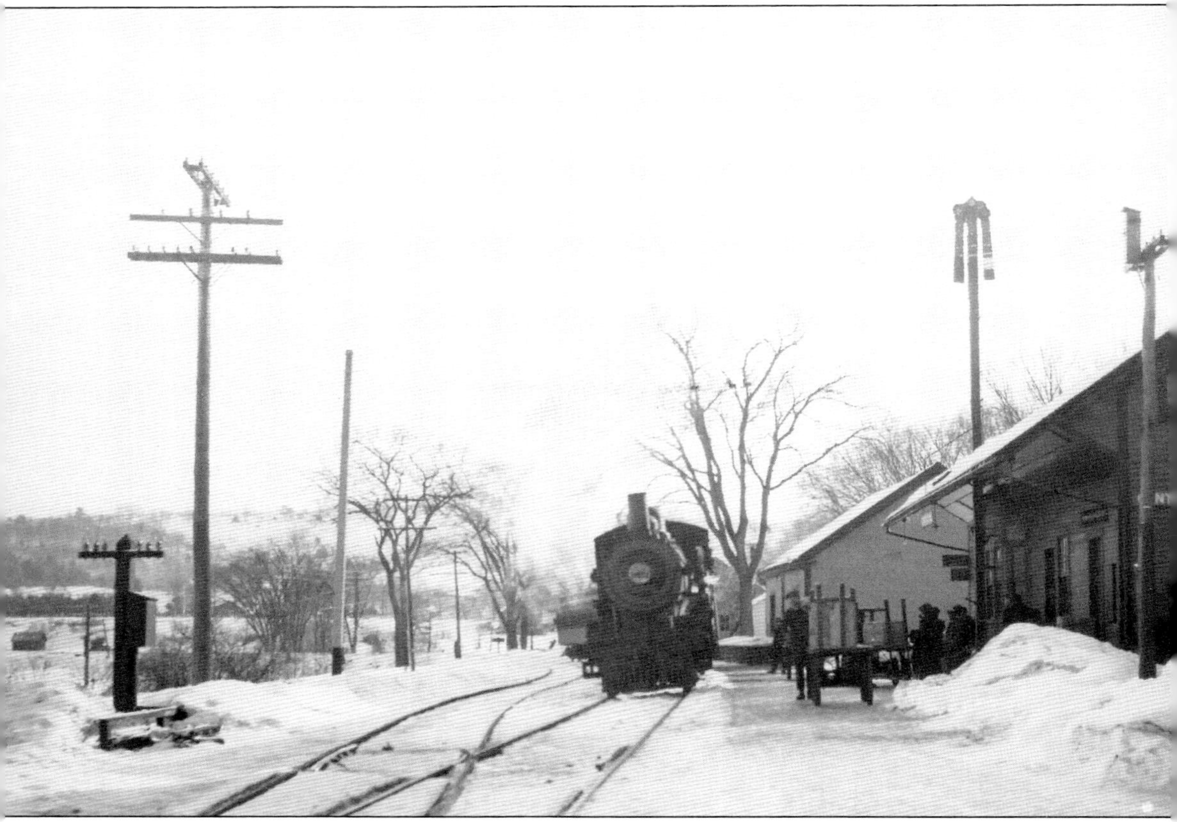

Despite fierce debate for many years, the first train steamed through Contoocook in 1849 as part of the Contoocook Valley Railroad, later known as the Boston and Maine. At this time, three train stations were built in Hopkinton: Contoocookville (as it was then called), Tyler, and West Hopkinton. Joseph Barnard, resident of Briar Hill Road in Hopkinton, was the railroad building agent from Contoocook to Hillsborough. It was reported by the *Boston Post* that the Contoocook Valley Railroad line was the most inexpensive line per mile built with the most beautiful views. Farther travel was made possible when the line was extended to Bradford and then Claremont; later, another line from Contoocook to Hillsboro Bridge and Peterborough opened. The town became a hub for traffic, with eight passenger and express trains running daily and numerous fast freight services aiding business and trade. (Courtesy of Hopkinton Historical Society.)

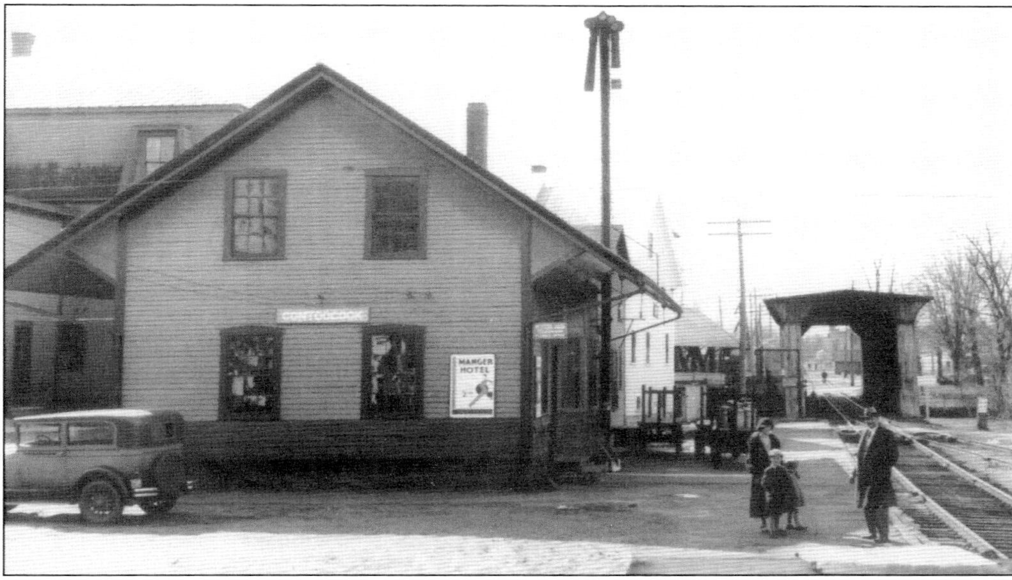

Until the early 1900s, several passenger trains and two freights went through the train depot in Contoocook Village. By 1950, when cars and trucks grew in popularity, only a single freight and one passenger train continued to travel these rails. After the last passenger train ran through town on December 31, 1955, the depot, which had been purchased in 1953 by Spencer Dodd, housed Dodd Insurance Agency, as seen below. The town library was also located in the building until 1959. The Contoocook Riverway Association purchased the depot from the town in 1999 for a silver dollar, and in 2002 the group began a $400,000 renovation project to restore the train depot to its 1910 condition. (Above, courtesy of the Contoocook Riverway Association; below, courtesy of Hopkinton Historical Society.)

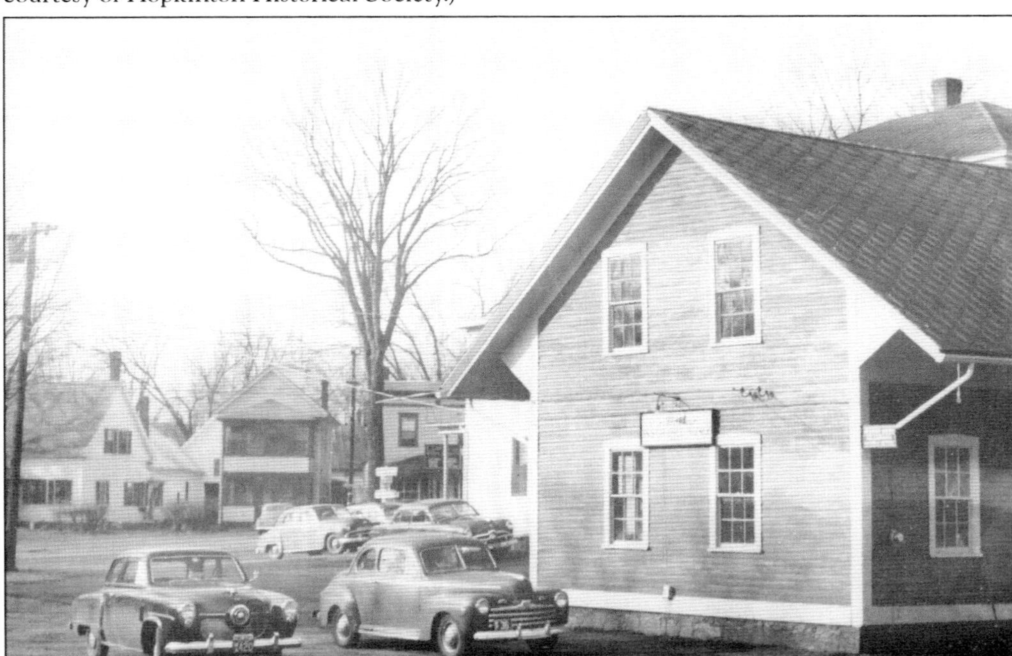

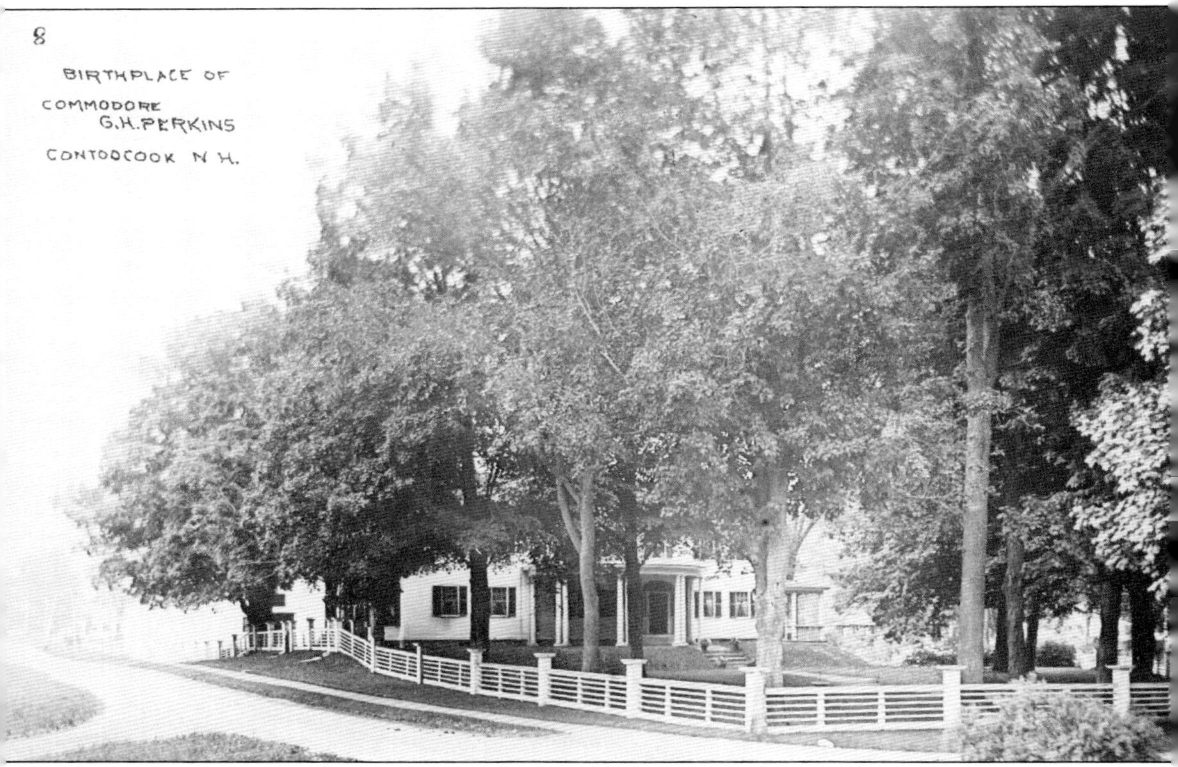

The grand building known as Perkins Manor is located at the northern end of the Main Street bridge in Contoocook Village. Built in 1825 by Roger Eliot Perkins, it was the birthplace of his grandson, George Hamilton Perkins (October 20, 1836–October 28, 1899) who was a noted officer in the US Navy during the Civil War. Perkins graduated from the US Naval Academy in 1856. He served the first several months of the Civil War on the steamer *Sumpter* on anti-slavery patrols. Later he became commanding officer of the gunboat *Cayuga*, which was instrumental in the 1862 capture of New Orleans. Perkins continued to serve in the Navy until 1891, and five years later he received a congressionally-authorized promotion to the retired rank of commodore. The Navy has named three destroyers *Perkins* in honor of him: destroyer No. 26, later DD-26 of 1910–1935; DD-377 of 1936–1943; and DD-877, later DDR-877 and DD-877 of 1945–1973. Commodore Perkins's daughter, Isabel Weld Perkins Anderson, sold the property to Stewart Astles in 1948 and the home was renovated into apartments and remains an apartment house today. (Courtesy of William Stevens.)

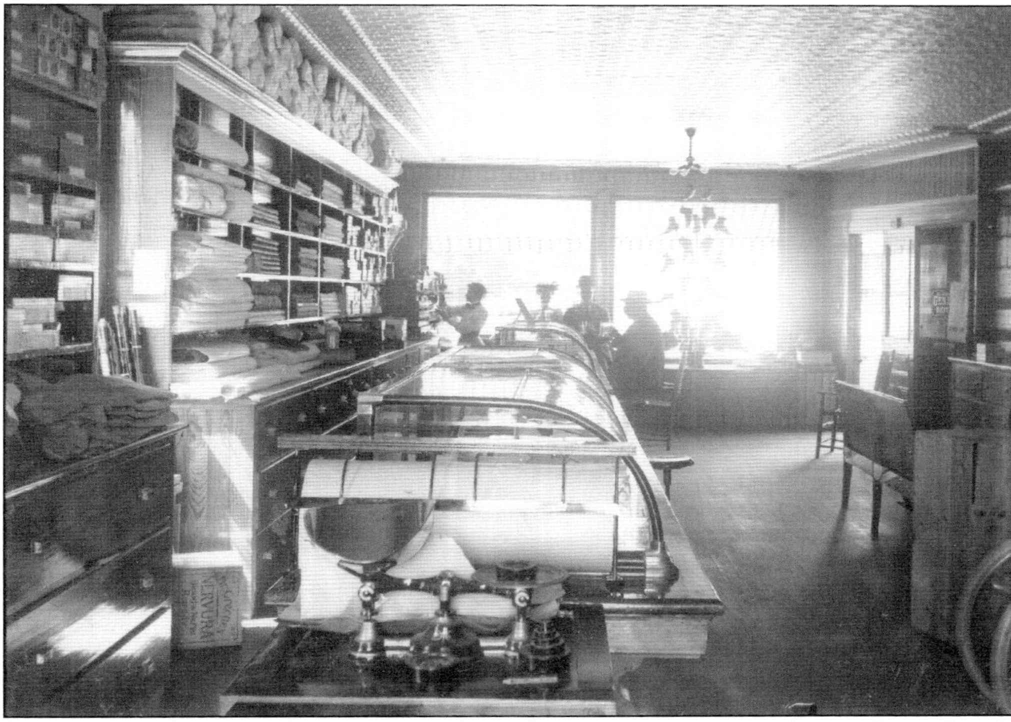

Customers enjoy a beverage at the soda fountain at Warren (Ward) Rand's store located at the southeast corner of the bridge on Main Street (Route 103). Rand had been a partner in Curtice, Rand and Company next door in the Curtice Block before starting his own store. Rand was the first shop owner in this building and there have been many since. (Courtesy of Hopkinton Historical Society.)

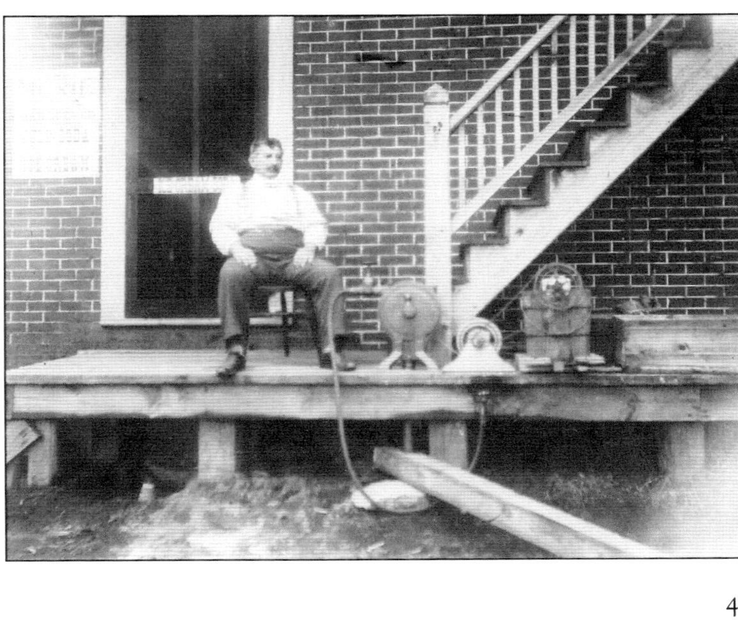

Warren (Ward) Rand sits on the back steps of his shop next to his water-powered ice cream freezer. After the Rand Store, William Davis had a hardware store in the building and Nettie Woodard ran a dry goods store on one side. Later it would become Reddy's Market and for years was known as the Center Store. (Courtesy of Hopkinton Historical Society.)

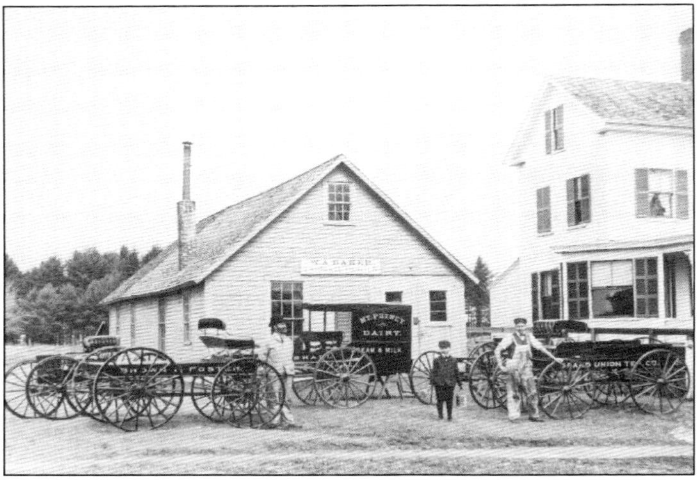

William Baker, Lee Steven, and an unidentified child pose in front of the W.A. Baker carriage painting shop on Pine Street in Contoocook. Baker painted carriages and signs in the early 1900s and, in this undated photograph, proudly displays his work on the Brown and Foster, Mt. Putney Dairy, and Grand Union Tea Company carriages. (Courtesy of Hopkinton Historical Society.)

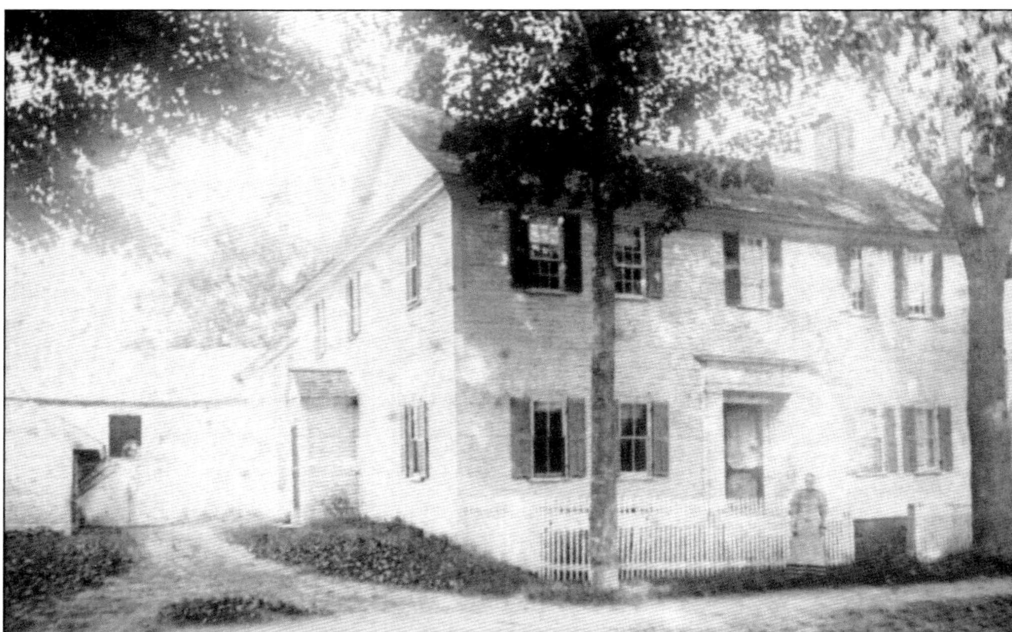

Martha G. Chase (Gus Ordway's wife) poses in front of a home in September 1896. The home is believed to have been built prior to 1800 and still stands next to the former Bates Library (now the town clerk's office) on Main Street. Most of the land in that area of Main Street was part of this original property. At one time it was the home of a Dr. Wilson who ran his dental practice in a front room. (Courtesy of Hopkinton Historical Society.)

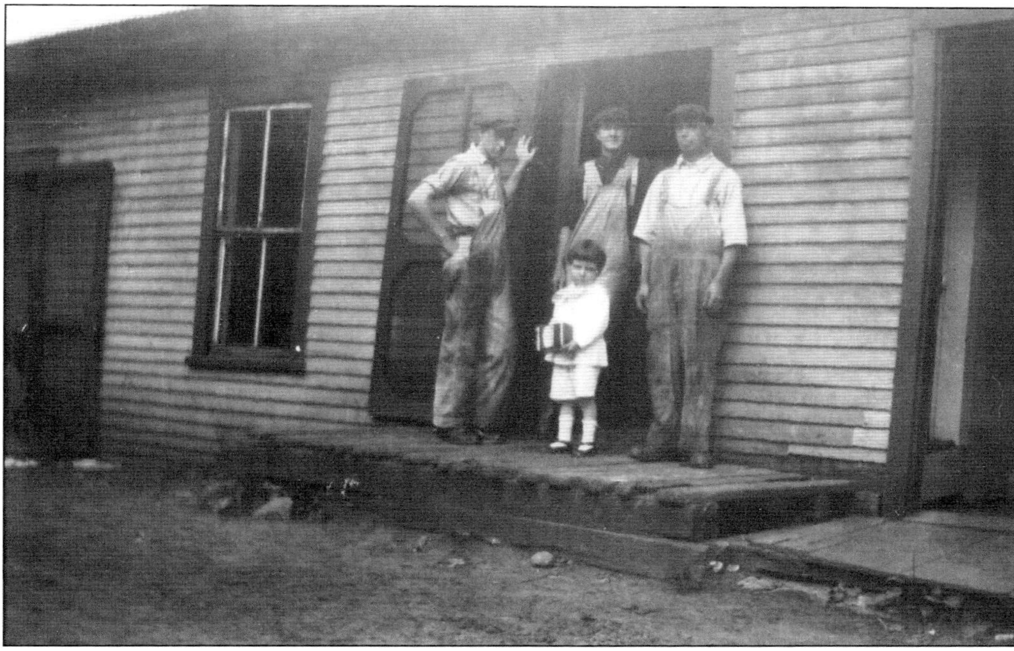

Local farmers brought their milk to be separated and bottled at the local creamery located on Cedar Street, just past the southern bend of the road. The Deerfoot Farm operated the creamery from 1890 to 1900. Crowell Processing Company then purchased it and for the next nine years developed new methods of processing the milk. However, these new methods were too costly and the creamery was sold to William L. Montgomery in 1909. In 1913 Harry Sedgell operated the creamery, when milk began to be collected more often by trucks and hauled to Concord and other areas for processing. In the photograph above, from left to right, an unidentified man, Martin Robinson Jr. (child), Harry Sedgell, and Martin Robinson stand in the doorway of the dairy's sterilization room. Below, Marcelene and Martin Robinson Jr. sit on the steps of the creamery, which still stands today. (Courtesy of Hopkinton Historical Society.)

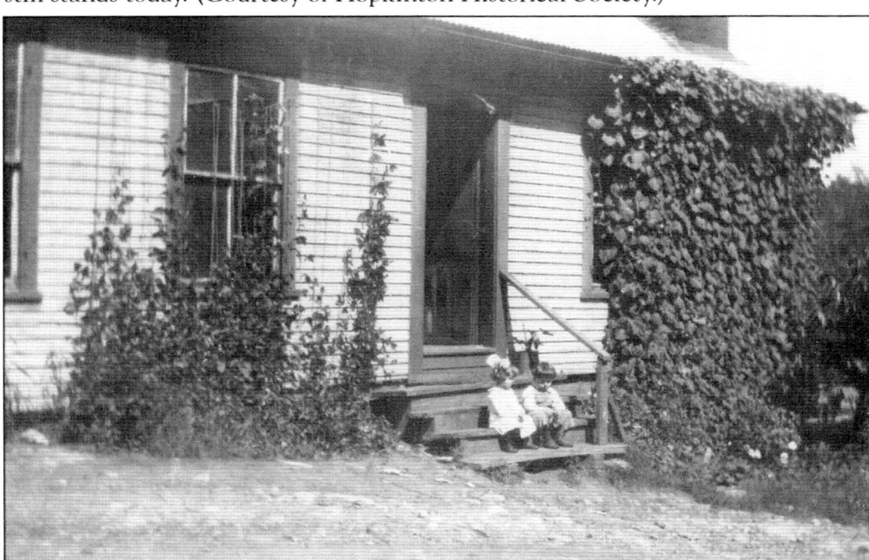

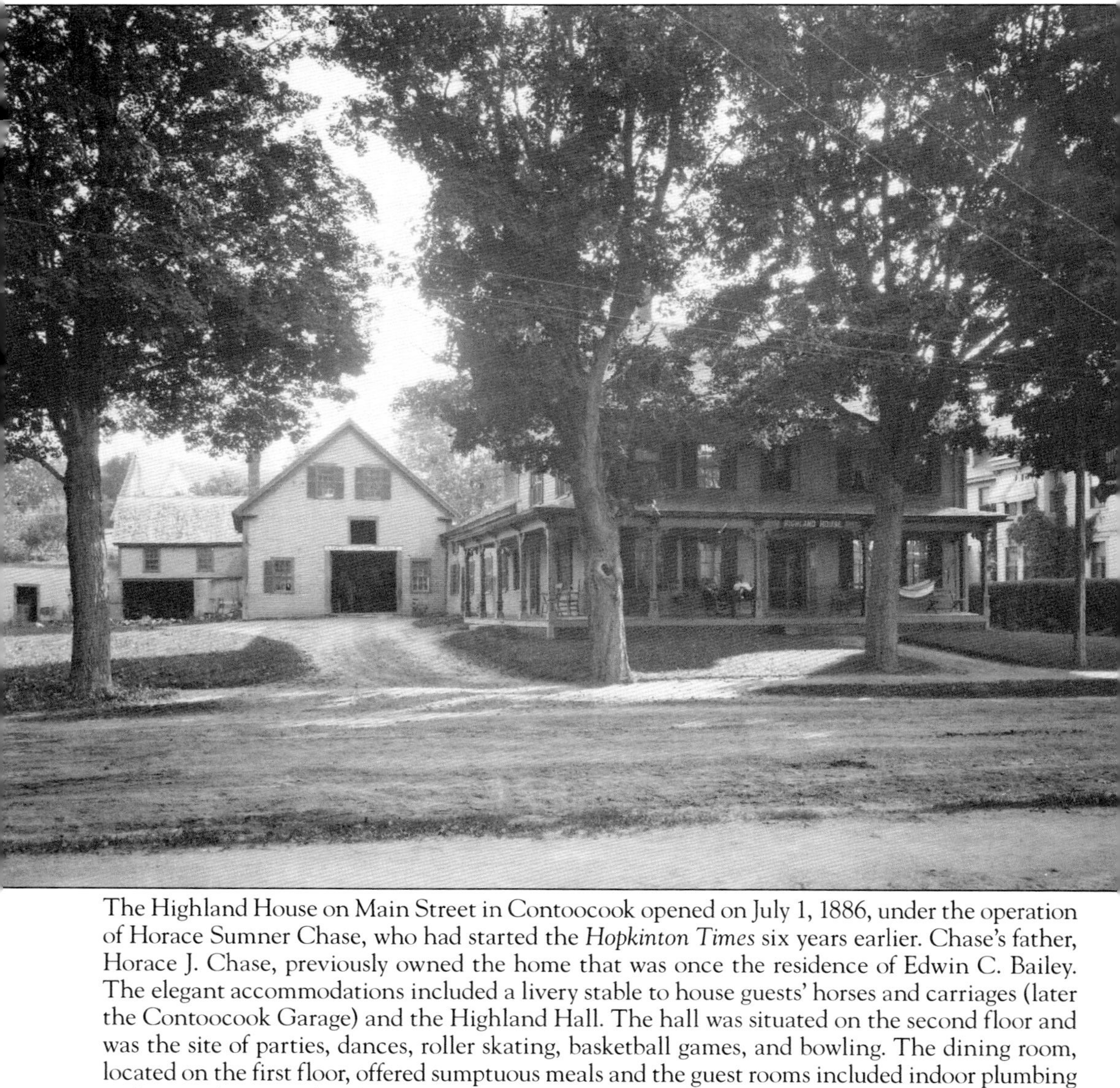

The Highland House on Main Street in Contoocook opened on July 1, 1886, under the operation of Horace Sumner Chase, who had started the *Hopkinton Times* six years earlier. Chase's father, Horace J. Chase, previously owned the home that was once the residence of Edwin C. Bailey. The elegant accommodations included a livery stable to house guests' horses and carriages (later the Contoocook Garage) and the Highland Hall. The hall was situated on the second floor and was the site of parties, dances, roller skating, basketball games, and bowling. The dining room, located on the first floor, offered sumptuous meals and the guest rooms included indoor plumbing and steam heat. Under the proprietorship of L.L. Claflin, the hotel offered rooms for $2 a day. In 1951, the Highland House was remodeled into apartments and renamed Contoocook Manor. (Courtesy Hopkinton Historical Society.)

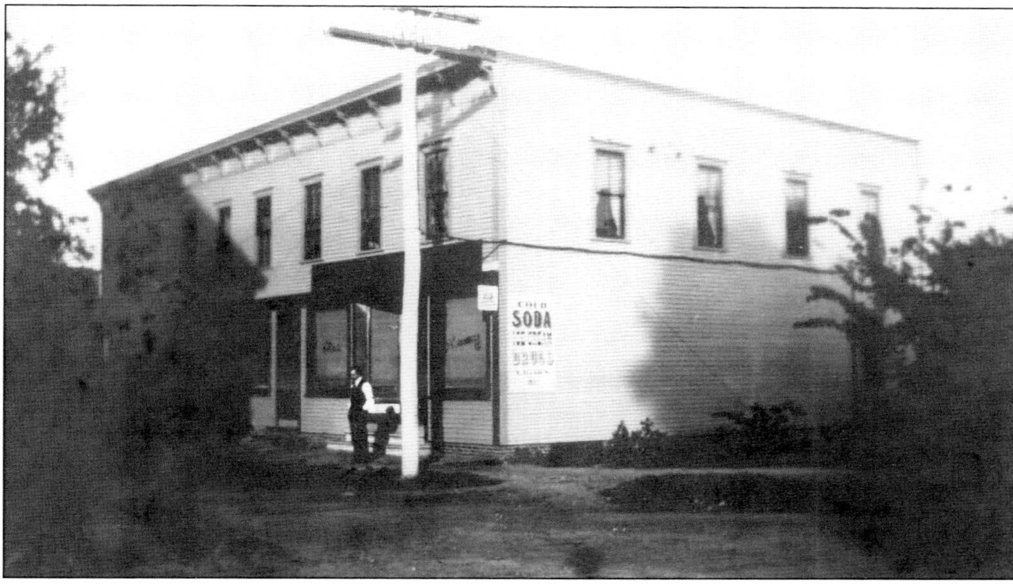

This building, located on Cedar Street, was built by Harry Clifford in 1900 after a fire devastated the surrounding block and destroyed the store and house that sat at this location (see pages 96–99). Frank H. Reed opened his drug store here on January 1, 1901, and Dexter Ladd occupied another portion of the building for his plumbing and heating business. Two years later it was sold to Charles C. David, who was a manager of the Kingsbury & Davis Machine Company located on the same street. It was said he also lived on the second floor during the winter. Robert G. Reed bought the building later and sold it to brothers Robert M. Bean and George W. Bean in 1967. In January 1974, the store was sold to the partnership of David Story, Richard Lord, and Bayard Pope. It has since changed hands, and Reed's Store, a staple in the village for generations, closed its doors in the 1990s. (Courtesy of Hopkinton Historical Society.)

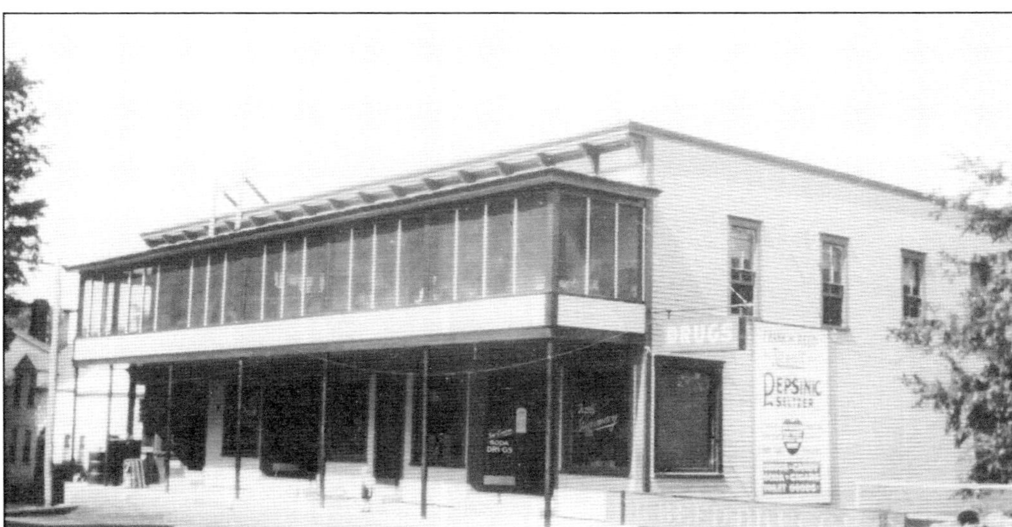

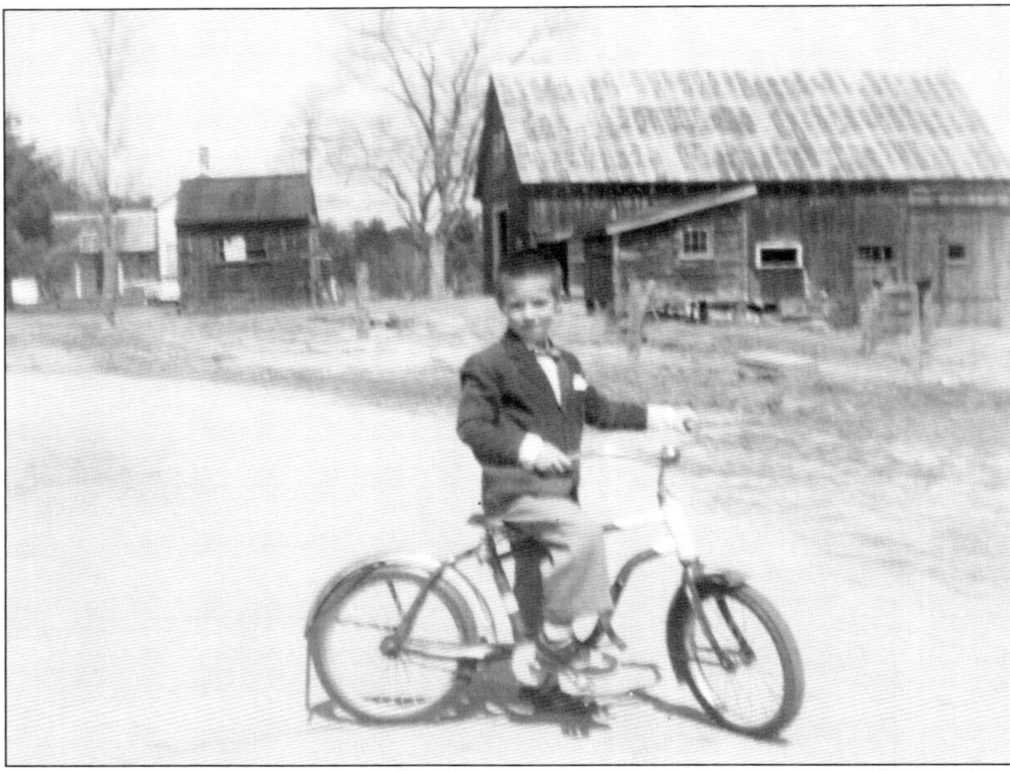

Robert J. Duclos Jr. pauses in front of his family's farm on Burham Intervale in 1955. This land, southwest of Contoocook Village, was once owned by Benjamin Wiggin, early tavern keeper from Hopkinton. In 1816, the area was hit with four inches of snow on June 4, inauguration day, followed by a summer drought and an unusually early frost. These events damaged or destroyed many crops, including corn—the staple for both people and livestock. However, the fertile lands of this farm along the Contoocook River were spared severe damage and Wiggin graciously made his corn available for nominal prices, or donated it to the most needy. Below, the Bergstrom family, previous owners of the same farm, gather for a ride in the hay rig to the Hopkinton Fair in 1916. (Above, courtesy of Marion Duclos; below, courtesy of Edith Carr.)

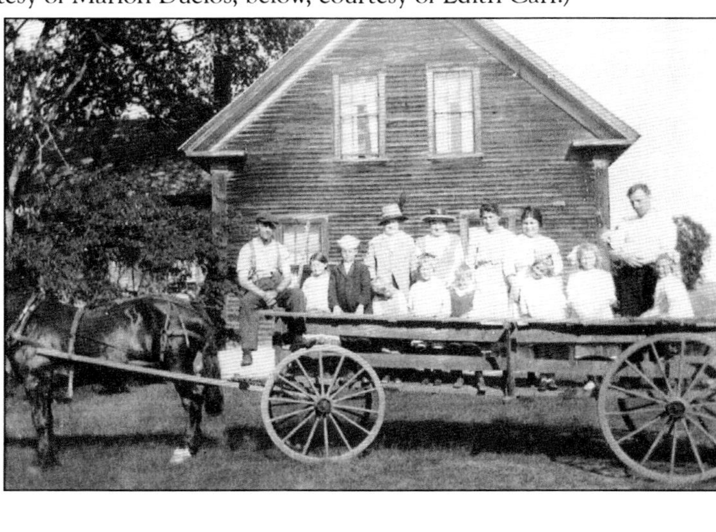

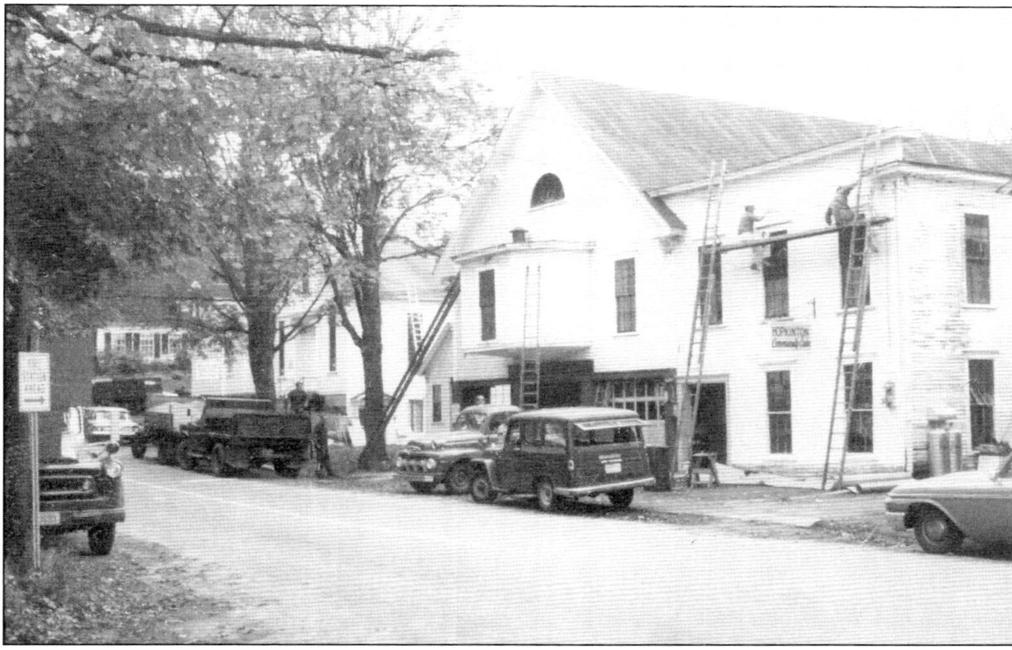

Columbia Hall was originally the stables of the Walter S. Davis family and was donated in 1926 to Contoocook Fire Precinct. The second floor had a stage for productions (shown below) as well as a basketball court. For years it hosted graduation ceremonies, local social functions, sporting events, and Saturday evening movies. At various times, the first floor housed offices, a shoe repair shop, car parking, and the town's fire department. Columbia Hall would later be called the community center, and for decades remained a hub of social activity in town. Eventually the building succumbed to the effects of time and was auctioned off in 2009 and demolished in 2010 when the building was found to be beyond repair. (Above courtesy of Barbara Brown Carpenter; below Courtesy of Hopkinton Historical Society.)

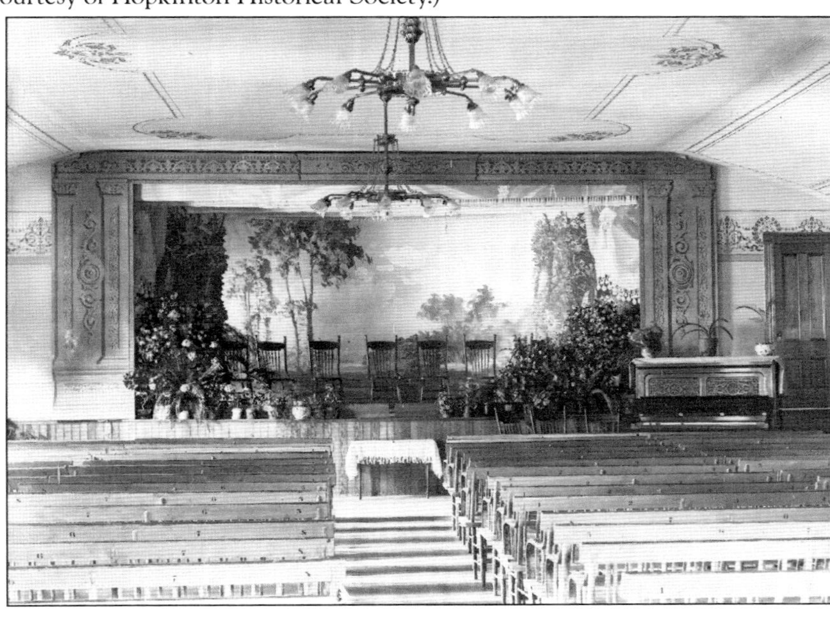

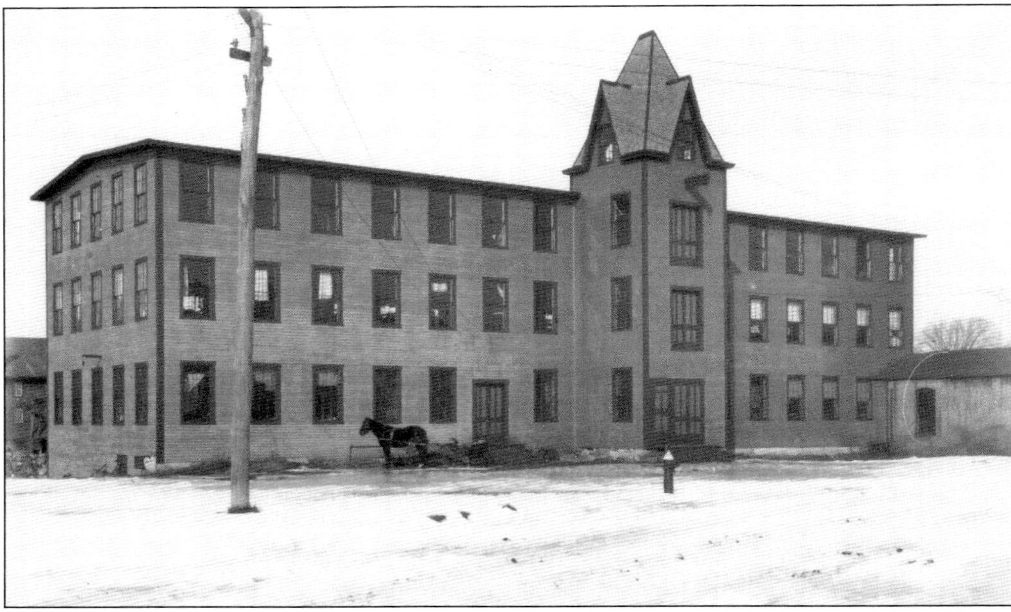

Walter S. Davis purchased the water power in Contoocook Village in 1887. After inventing the Davis turbine water wheel and the first box-making machine, he went into business with Addison Kingsbury to form Kingsbury & Davis Machine Company. In 1892, the partners built this three-story wooden building on Cedar Street. The building included a water wheel that powered the mill. Here, Kingsbury & Davis manufactured the Leader shoe box–making machine, Quadruple Staying Machine, Stacker, and a cigar box–making machine. The second floor housed the Conant Manufacturing Company and the third floor was occupied by the Contoocook Needle Company. The photograph below shows an addition to the first floor. (Photographs by Leown Kelley; courtesy of Hopkinton Historical Society.)

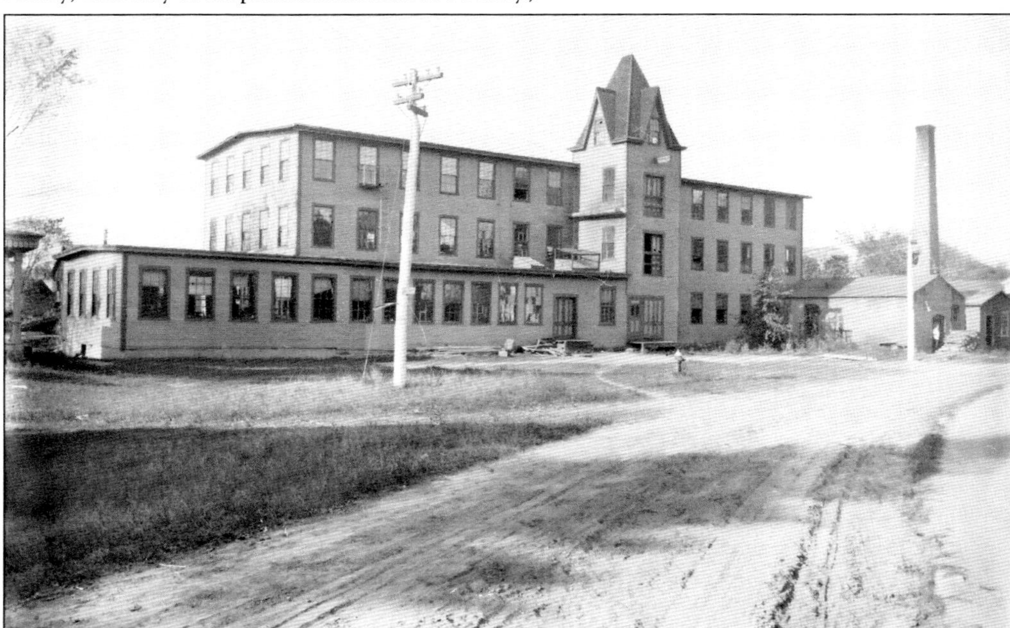

In 1835, there was a push to produce silk locally. Silk worms and mulberry trees were obtained and silk thread and cloth were manufactured. However, the production costs couldn't compete with the cheaper European labor and the local silk industry failed. But in 1901, Hiram E. Conant opened a silk mill in the Kingsbury & Davis Machine Shop where his company Conant Manufacturing, pictured here, produced 100 pounds of silk organzine a day. (Courtesy of Hopkinton Historical Society.)

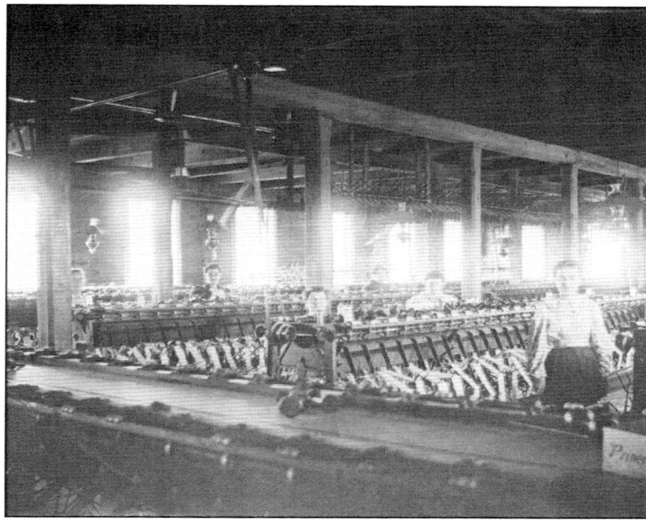

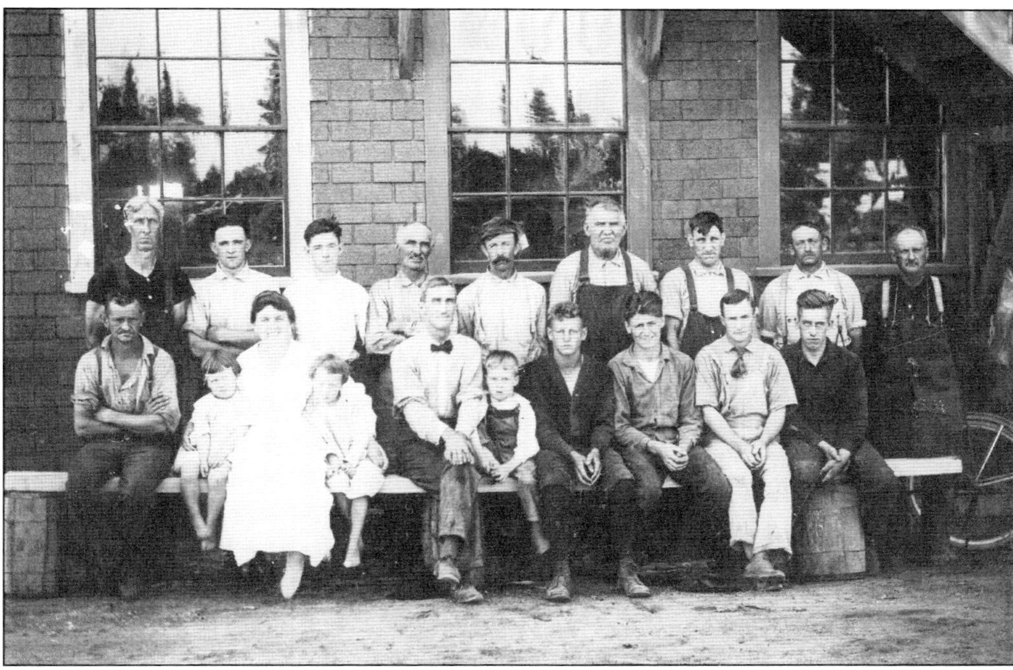

This photograph, taken around 1919, shows employees of the Kingsbury & Davis Machine Company. From left to right are (first row) Delbert Cooper, Barbara Pipler, Mabel (Harty) Emerson, Rae Pipler, Harry Bunnell, Paul Bunnell, Tige (?) Mitchell, Leo Lessard, Alvah Bunnell, and Harold Smart; (second row) Leown Kelley, Gilman D. Brown, Harold E. Brown, unidentified, Reuben Brown, Chase Stanton, Frank Glanville, Frank Heseltine, and Fred Chase. (Courtesy of Barbara Brown Carpenter.)

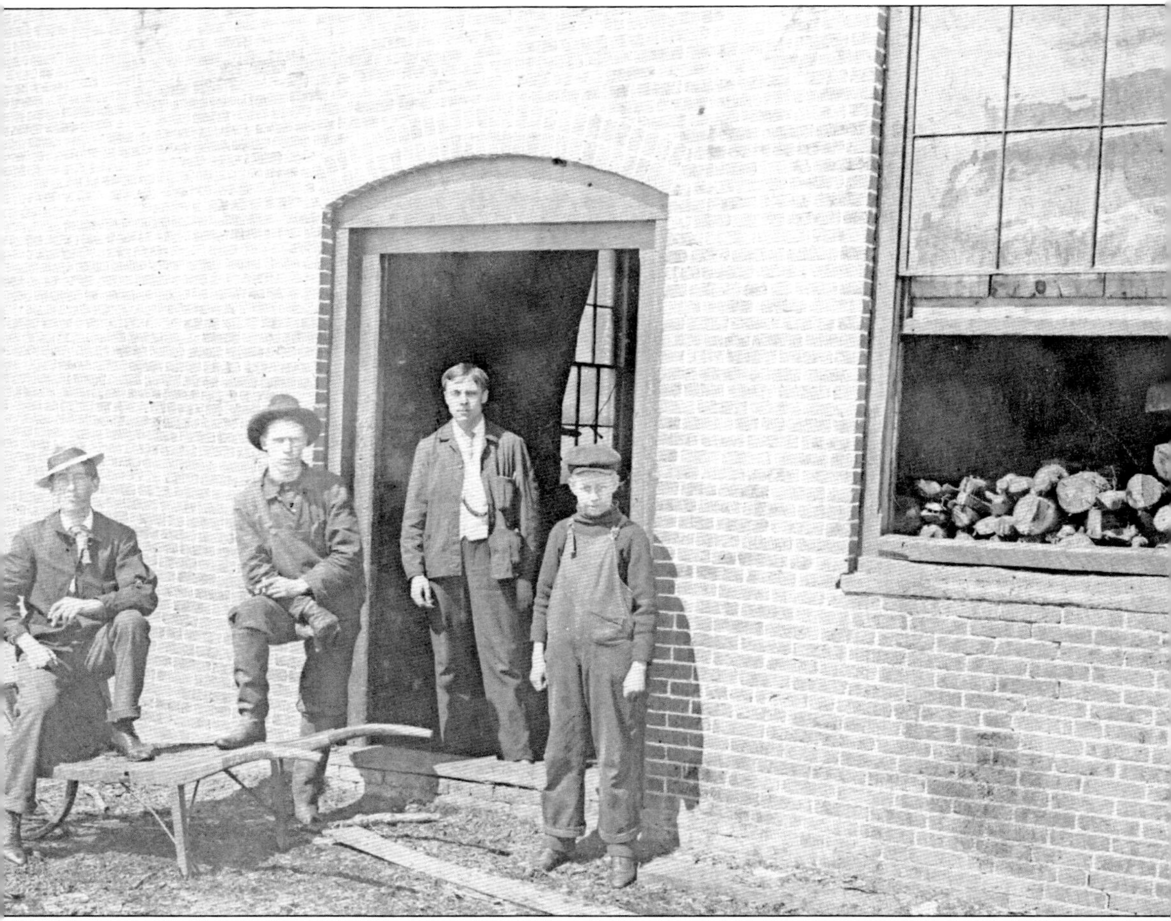

In 1891, Hiram B. Conant and his wife, Lena (Shattle) Conant, along with their two sons, Dwight and Frank, came to Contoocook from Petersburg, Virginia, where they had been silk throwsters by trade, twisting silk into yarn. The Conants lived in a building located at the southern end of the Kingsbury & Davis mill that had been built to be a hotel in Fountain Square, but was later moved to this location and used as a two-family dwelling. This building would years later become the Grange Hall and still stands today. In 1901, the family ran Conant Manufacturing on the second floor of the Kingsbury & Davis building, producing silk organzine. The family operated their silk mill until 1925, when the rayon industry made the business too costly to continue. This undated photograph shows Dwight Conant standing in the doorway of the mill. (Courtesy of Hopkinton Historical Society.)

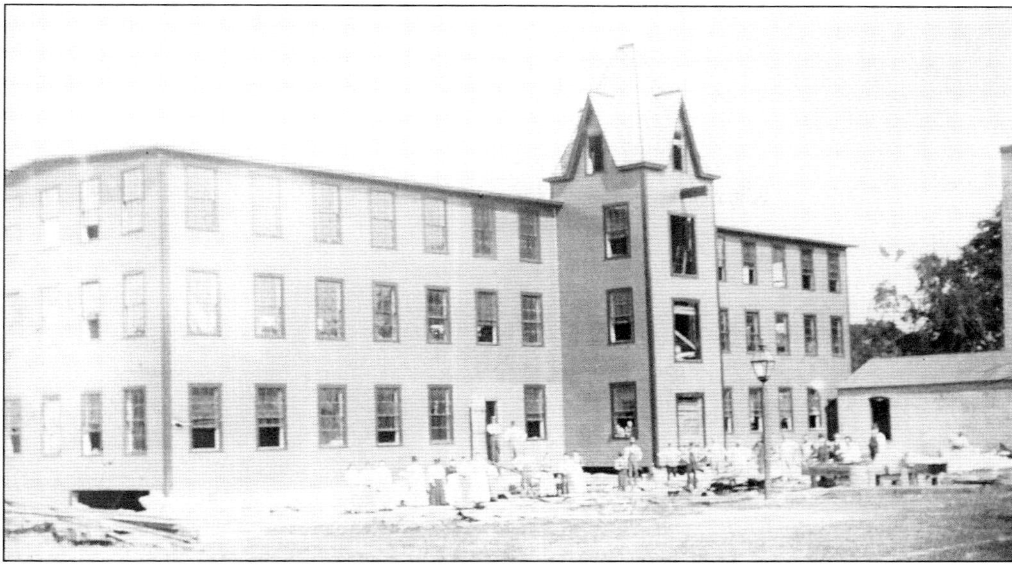

The three-story building constructed by Kingsbury & Davis housed the Kingsbury & Davis Machine Company on the first floor. Hiram E. Conant's Conant Manufacturing produced silk organzine on the second floor, and the third floor was occupied by the Contoocook Machine Needle Company. The silk mill and the needle shop employed about 40 workers. (Courtesy of Hopkinton Historical Society.)

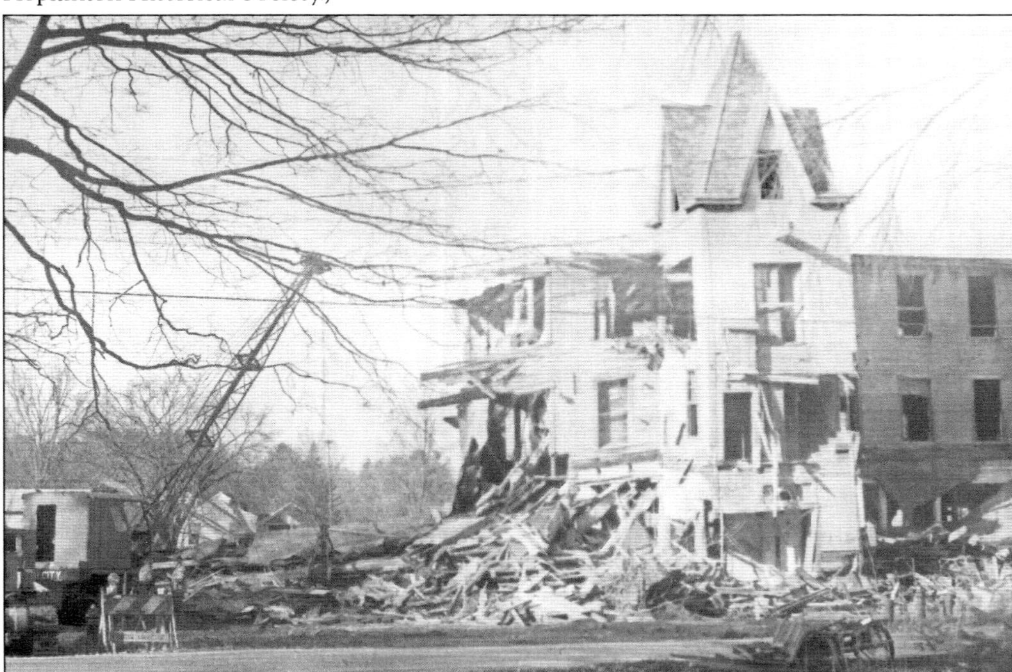

The Kingsbury & Davis mill was purchased by Merle Patenaude from the Davis estate in 1951. The large wooden structure was converted into a chicken coop. The property was sold to the town in April 1969 and the building was demolished on November 25, 1969. (Photograph by James P. Hargrove; courtesy of Hopkinton Historical Society.)

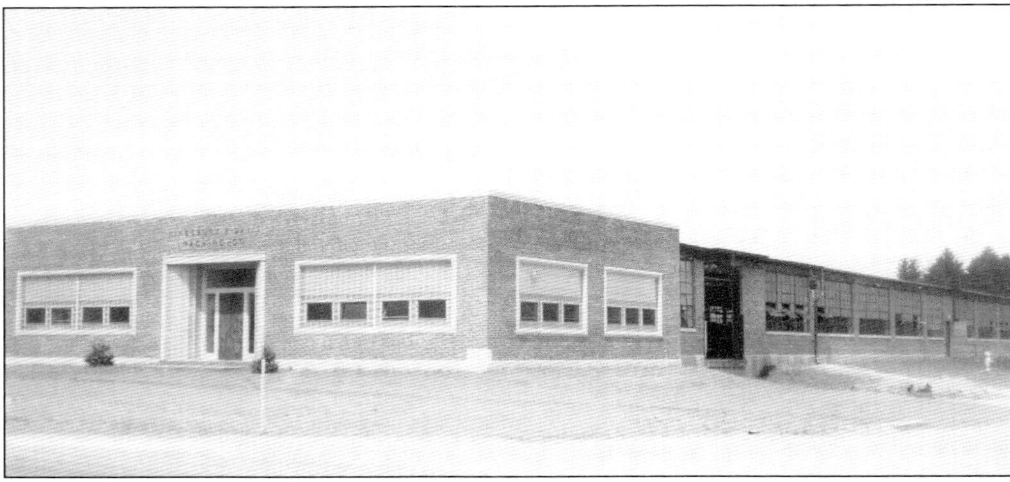

In 1947 Kingsbury & Davis built a new modern facility on Park Avenue about half a mile northwest of Contoocook Village. Among their products was the Transparent Lid Machine for forming and heat-sealing acetate lids and corrugated cookie boxes used in packaging Girl Scout cookies and other baked goods. In 1952, FMC Corporation (formerly Food Machinery and Chemical Company) acquired the Kingsbury & Davis Company, and the company employed around 100 people. After FMC closed this plant in 1971, National Northeast Fiberglass Corporation operated in the facility but eventually it too ceased business here and the building was demolished. River Grant Condominiums now occupy the land. (Courtesy of Hopkinton Historical Society.)

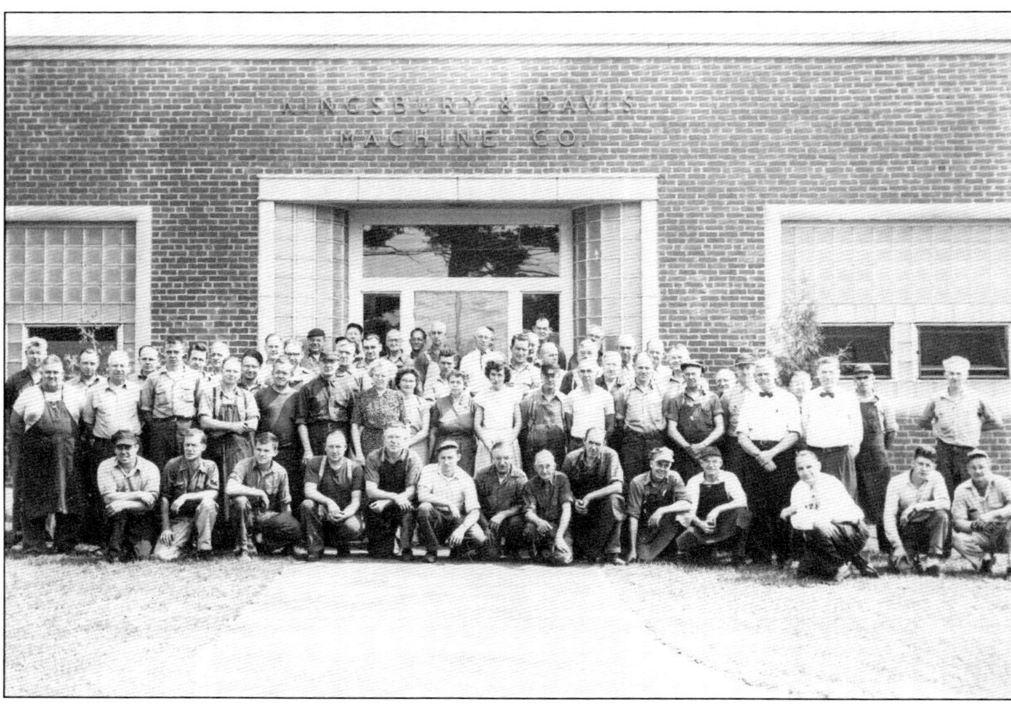

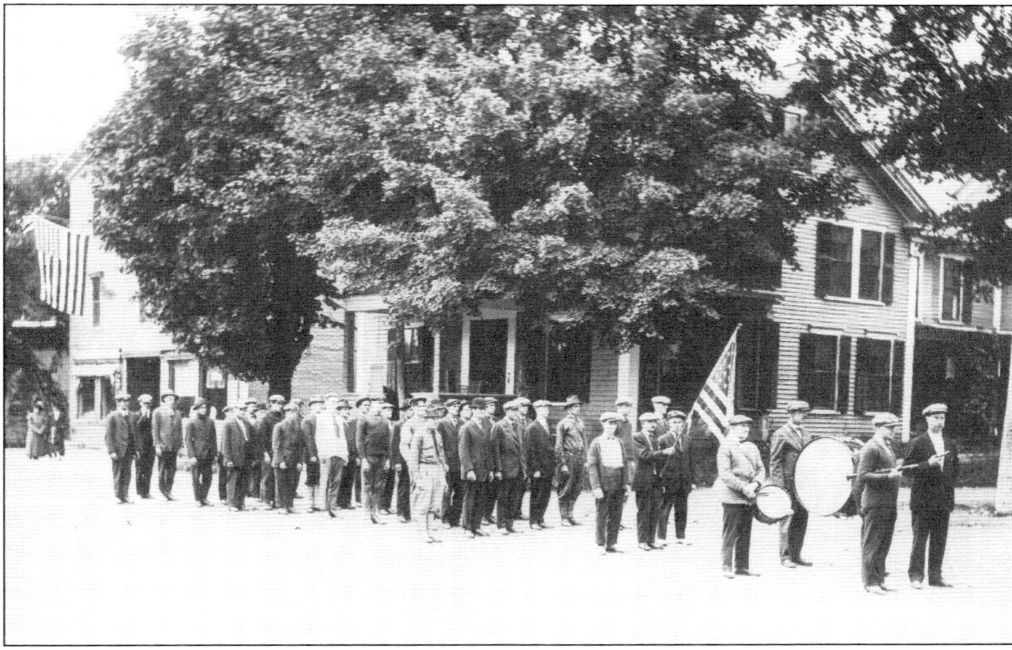

Young men march down Main Street in Contoocook Village to register to serve in World War I. Hopkinton men served in the 103rd Regiment, which was primarily composed of National Guard troops from the 2nd Maine Infantry and the 1st New Hampshire Infantry. The regiment was key to stopping the German drive on Chateau Thierry. Wendell Clough was the first New Hampshire soldier sent home wounded after losing a leg. The sole casualty from Hopkinton was E. Roger Montgomery, and it is in his honor that the American Legion formed the E. Roger Montgomery Post Number 81. (Courtesy of Hopkinton Historical Society.)

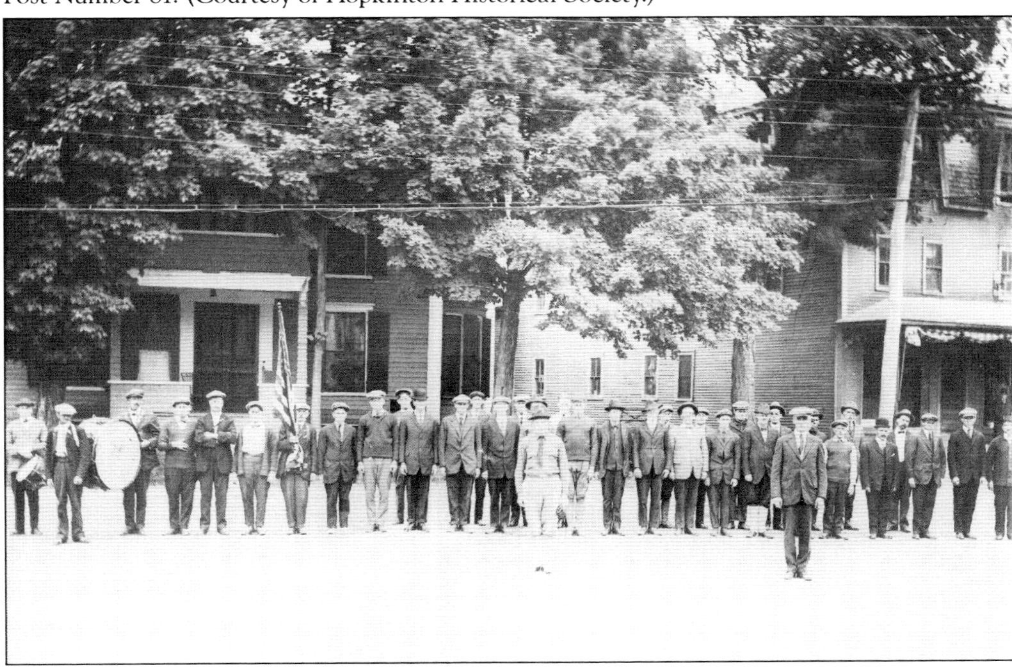

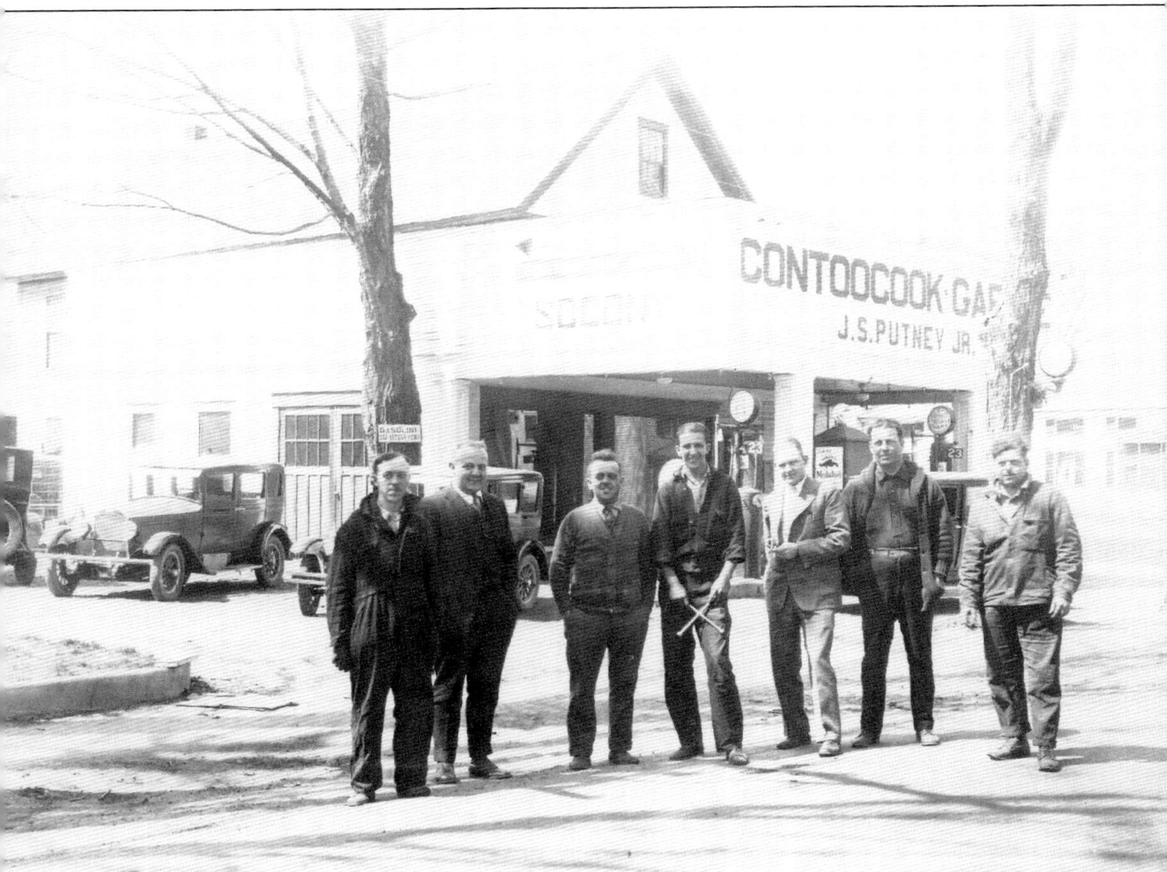

The large back portion of the Contoocook Garage once served as the livery stable for the Highland House Hotel. However, with the growing popularity of the automobile, the stables were converted into a garage and repair shop. In 1908, gas pumps were added and the front portion was constructed as a showroom. Jack Putney bought the garage in 1921. When Putney passed away in 1934, Hiram Conant—who had worked at the garage since graduating from mechanics school—ran the shop until Putney's estate was settled and he could purchase the business with Lewis Nelson. In 1958, the garage was sold to Richard Coen and George Barnard. This building was demolished in 1972 and replaced with a more modern facility. Pictured from left to right are Hiram Conant, Jack Putney, Lucius Conant, Les Coburn, Carl Oslund, B. Billings, and Dan Griffin. (Courtesy of Hopkinton Historical Society.)

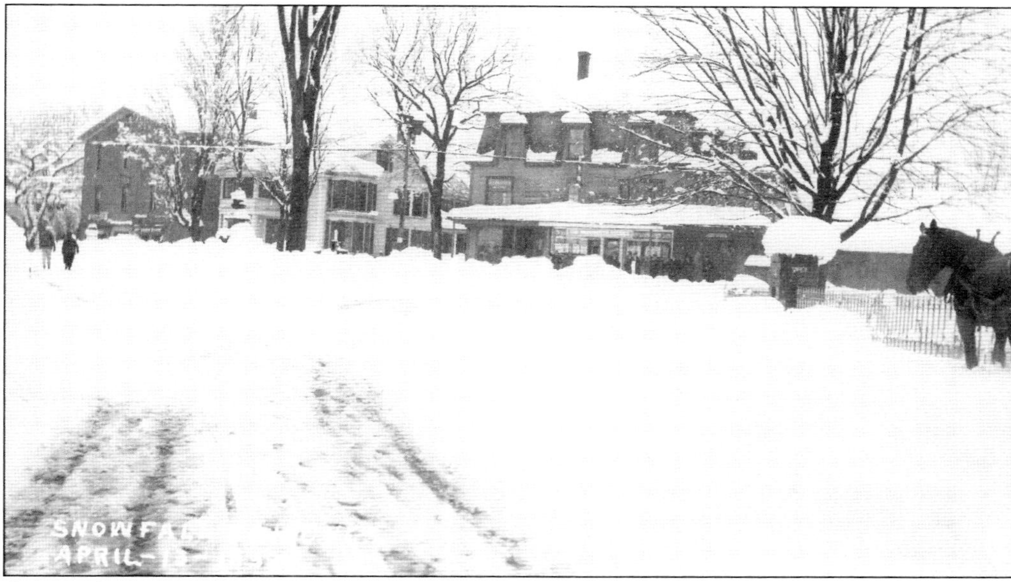

On April 13, 1933, a snowstorm dumped 30 inches of snow on Hopkinton. A crowd of people have gathered under the cover of the Curtice Block in front of the Woodworth Store. At this time, the post office was located in the same building and the building itself was owned by storekeeper Arthur C. Huntoon. (Courtesy of Hopkinton Historical Society.)

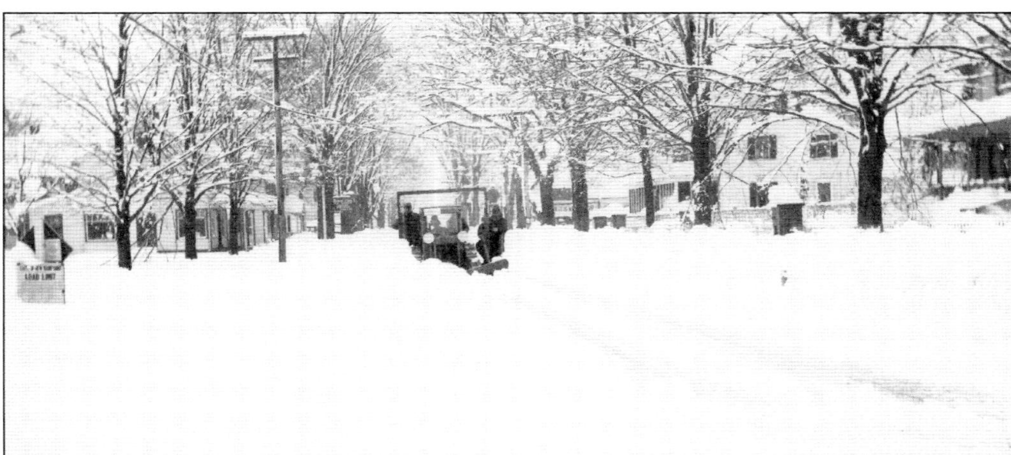

After the same storm of April 1933, the town plow vehicle helps to clear the road, heading west on Main Street in Contoocook Village. At that time trucks were not powerful enough to move such heavy loads of snow, so tractors fitted with "v" plows were employed for the task. (Courtesy of Hopkinton Historical Society.)

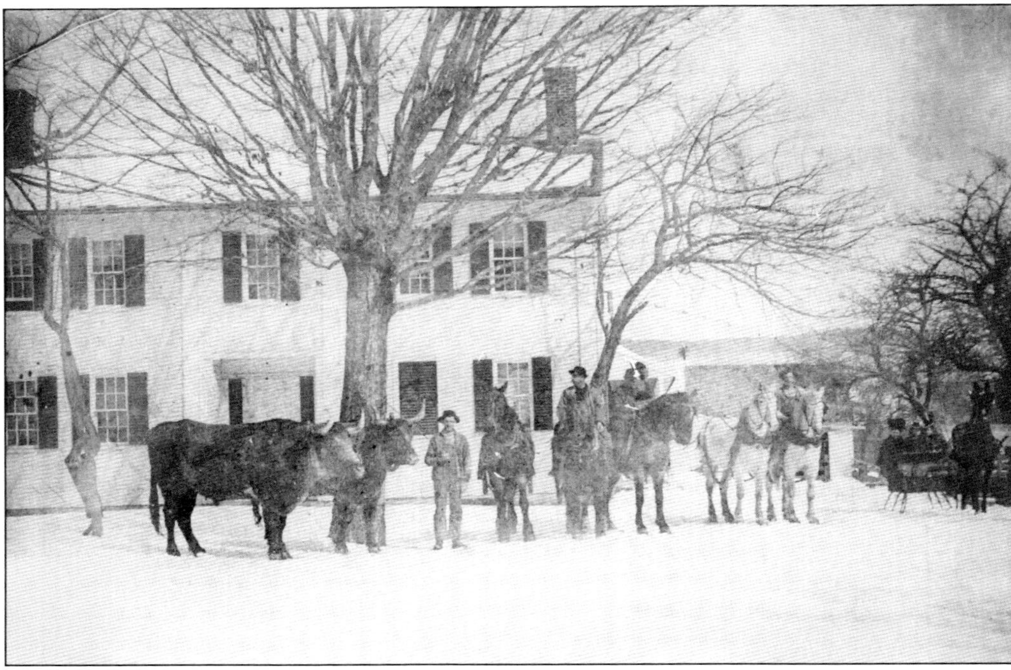

Horace Chase Stanley built this house on Maple Street in the mid-1800s. Stanley was a carpenter and farmer, and was involved in many local interests. He was a direct descendant of Matthew Stanley, an early resident of Hopkinton. This photograph, taken around 1900, shows Stanley's grandson Clinton J. Stanley standing with a team of oxen, and his mother Mary Clough Stanley in the sleigh. (Courtesy of Hopkinton Historical Society.)

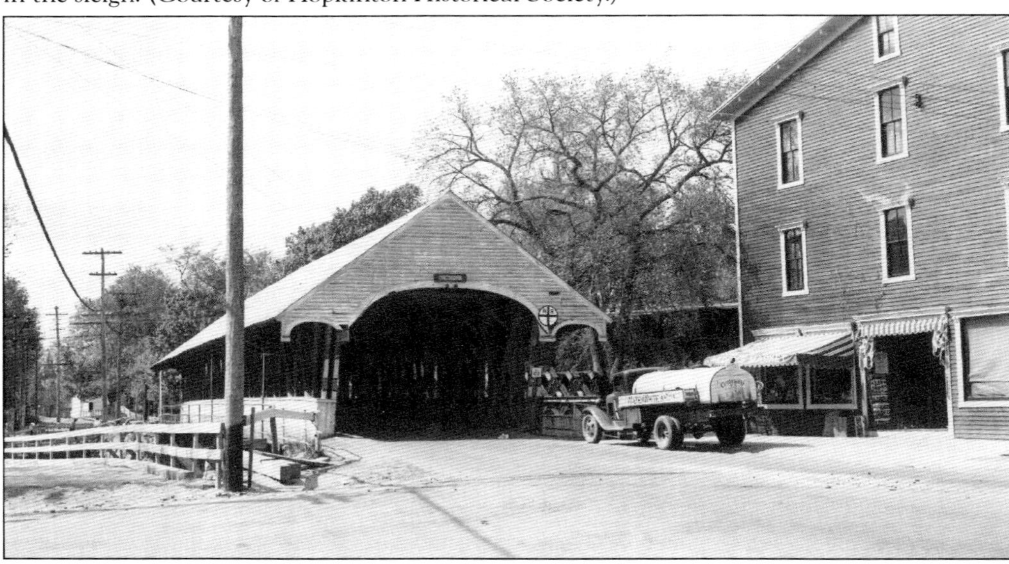

This pre-1935 photograph shows the covered highway bridge that spanned the Contoocook River just northwest of Fountain Square. On March 2, 1853, the town voted to construct this bridge in the same style as Rowell Bridge in West Hopkinton. This bridge remained in service until 1935 when it was torn down and replaced by "the stone bridge." (Courtesy of Hopkinton Historical Society.)

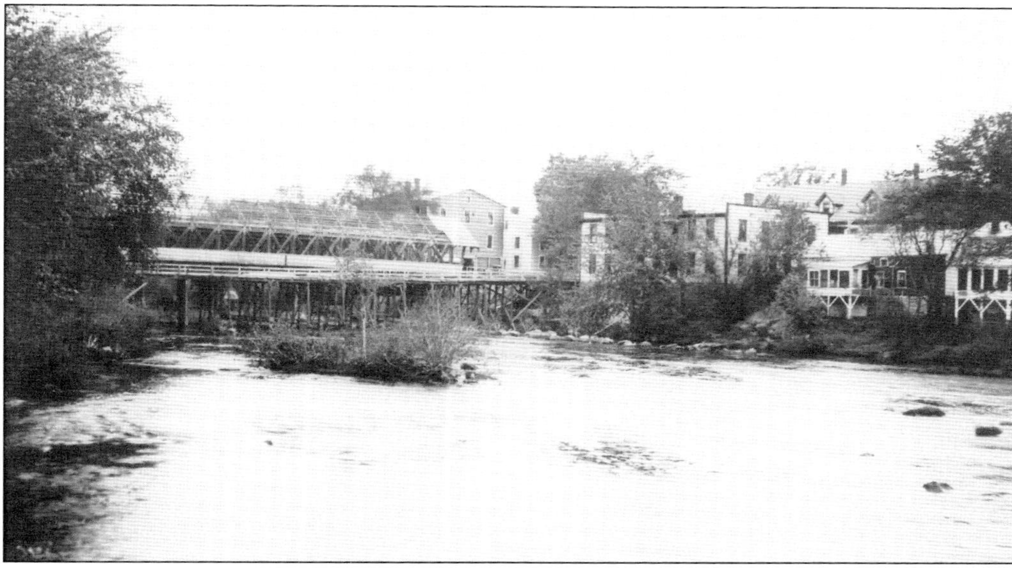

In 1935, the 82-year-old wood-covered highway bridge was dismantled and a new stone-faced concrete bridge was built in its place. The bridge construction, which lasted from May 1 to October 1, cost approximately $50,000 and employed 30 to 40 workers. A temporary bridge was built just west of the spot to divert traffic during the construction. In 1985, the state legislature dedicated the bridge to 91-year-old Hopkinton resident Leroy Kimball, who had worked on the project. During construction, Kimball had placed a copper box as a time capsule into the southeast corner of the bridge. Within the capsule were details of the bridge's construction, a photograph of the old highway bridge, and notes about life in Contoocook at that time. Above, workers begin to tear down the old wooden bridge. Below, some of the 71 tons of steel are put into place in the new bridge. (Courtesy Hopkinton Historical Society.)

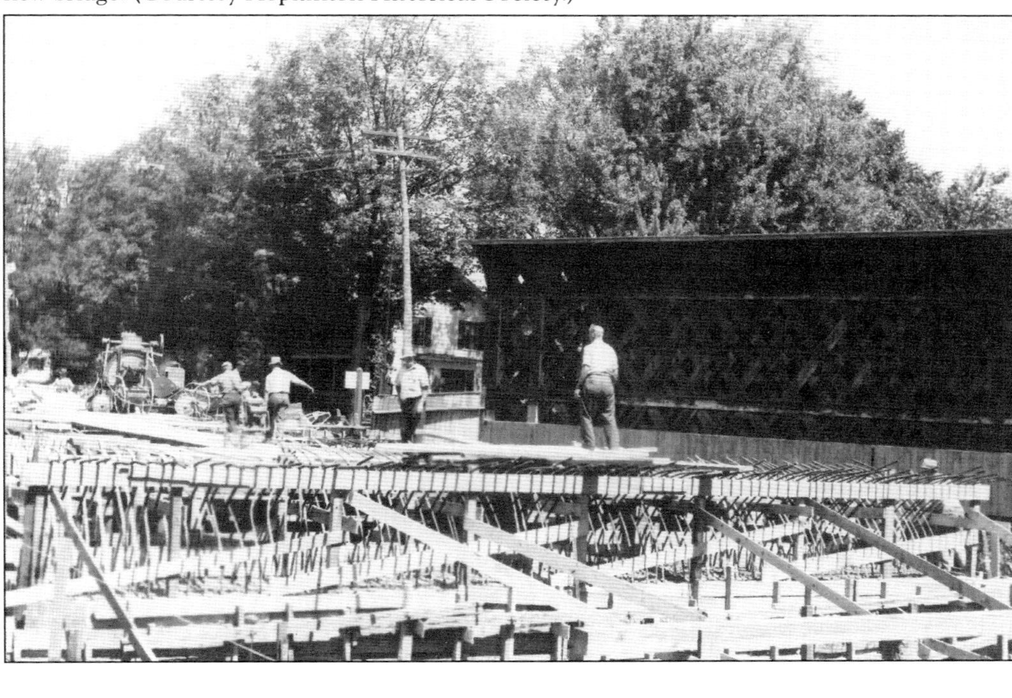

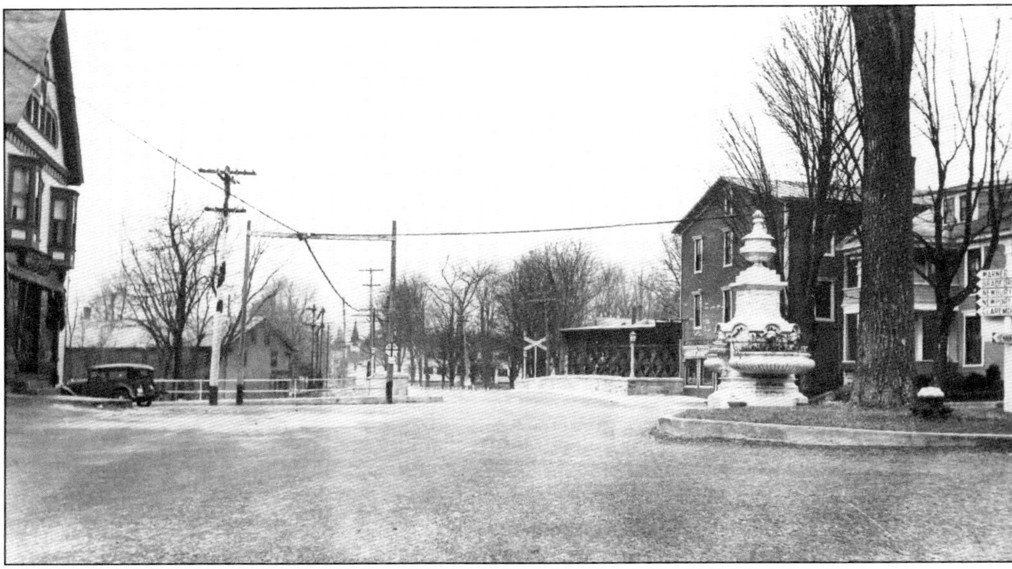

The current stone bridge that spans the Contoocook River in the village replaced the covered highway bridge in 1935. This photograph, probably taken shortly after the new bridge's completion, shows Lewis A. Nelson's grain mill on the far side of the bridge (left). Perkins Manor can be seen to the right of the mill, and the covered railroad bridge and Reddy's Market are on the right. (Courtesy of Hopkinton Historical Society.)

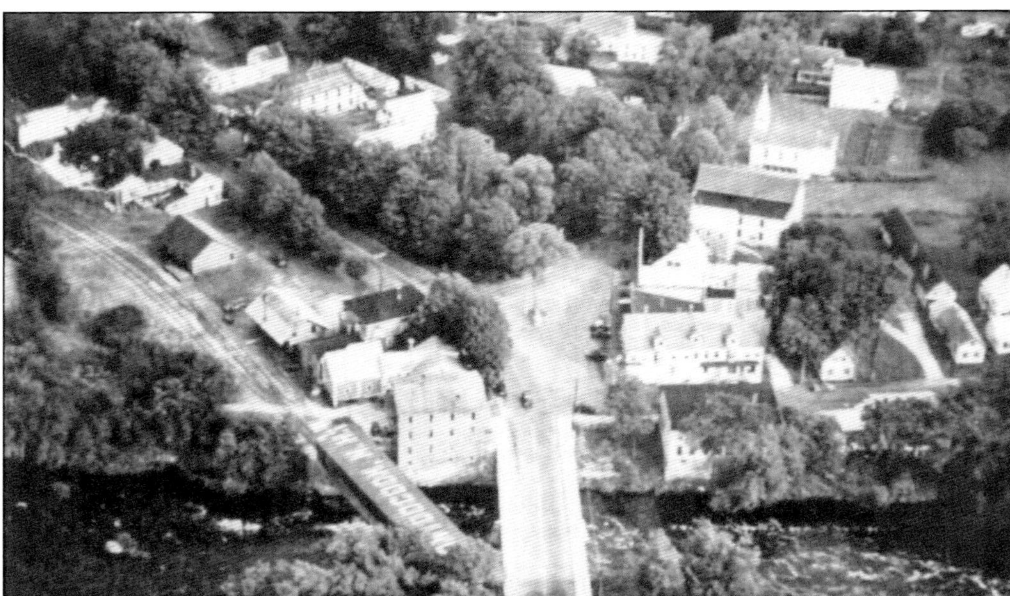

This aerial view looking southeast at Contoocook Village was published as a postcard by Reed's Drug Store. The photograph shows the covered railroad bridge and the 1935 stone bridge. The roof of the railroad bridge no longer has "Contoocook, NH" painted on it. (Courtesy of Hopkinton Historical Society.)

Three

WEST HOPKINTON

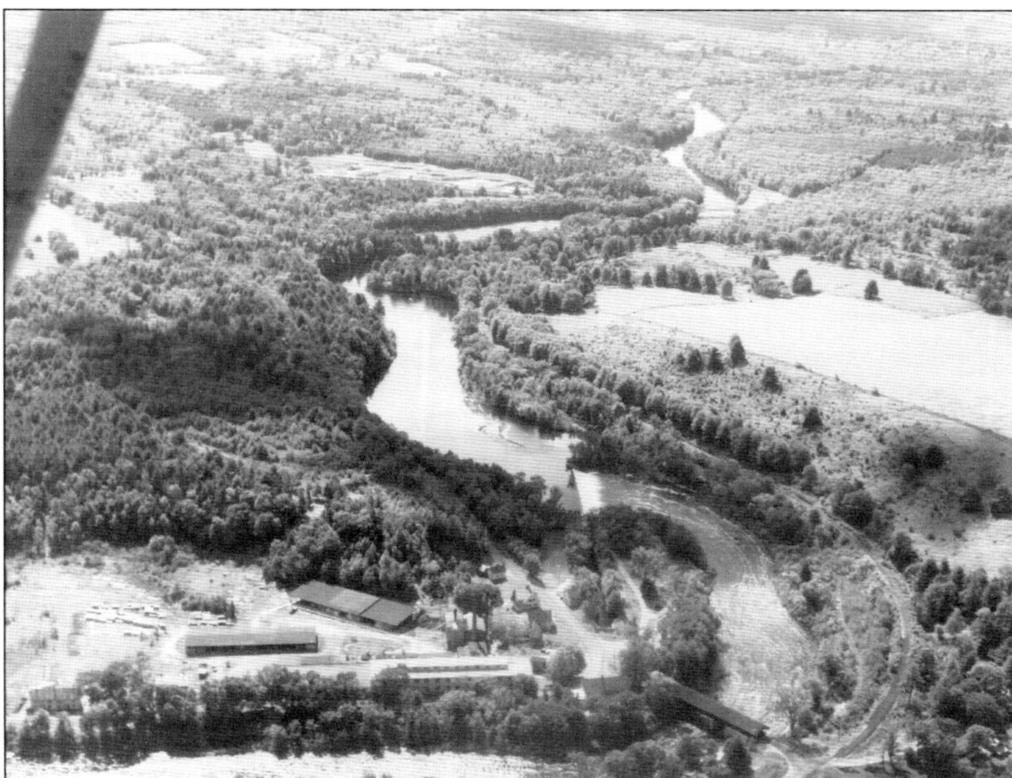

This aerial photograph, taken on September 15, 1954, shows West Hopkinton before the construction of the Hopkinton-Everett Lakes Flood Control Project, which permanently changed the landscape. The Davis Paper Company and Rowell Bridge can be seen in the lower portion of the photograph. (Photograph by Cyrus R.G. Phelps; courtesy of Hopkinton Historical Society.)

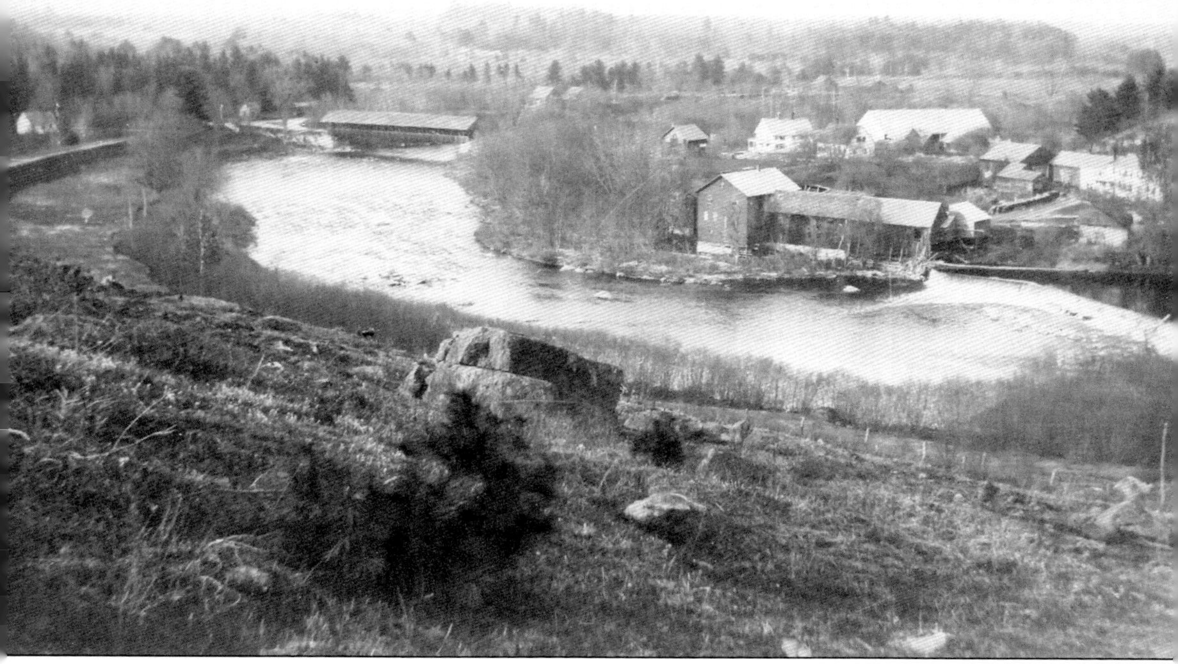

An early view of West Hopkinton from Kast Hill shows the site of the old Rowell Mill and farm. Between 1835 and 1865, John Smiley operated a popular grinding mill here. Frank H. Carr purchased the site for a saw mill after the Civil War. In 1899, the true potential of the water power at this location was realized by Henry C. and Horace J. Davis, who previously operated a business in Davisville. The two men took over the farm belonging to Charles S. Rowell and obtained the water rights of Carr's saw mill, although Carr retained first water rights and continued to saw lumber until his death in 1918. The Davis brothers built a leather board and fiber board mill on the site and created the Davis Paper Company. (Courtesy of Hopkinton Historical Society.)

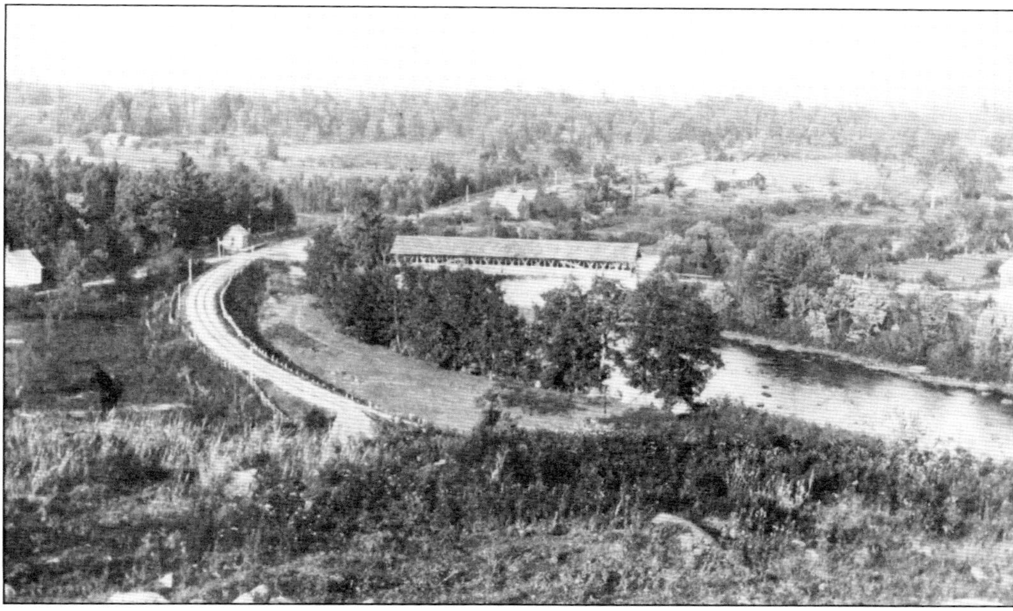

This photograph, taken between 1870 and 1880, shows the railroad tracks heading northeast towards Contoocook. At the time, there were three railroad stations in Hopkinton: Contoocookville, Tyler, and West Hopkinton. In the center is Rowell Bridge, named after the Rowell Family, whose farm was located nearby and remained in the Rowell family for around 100 years. (Courtesy of Hopkinton Historical Society.)

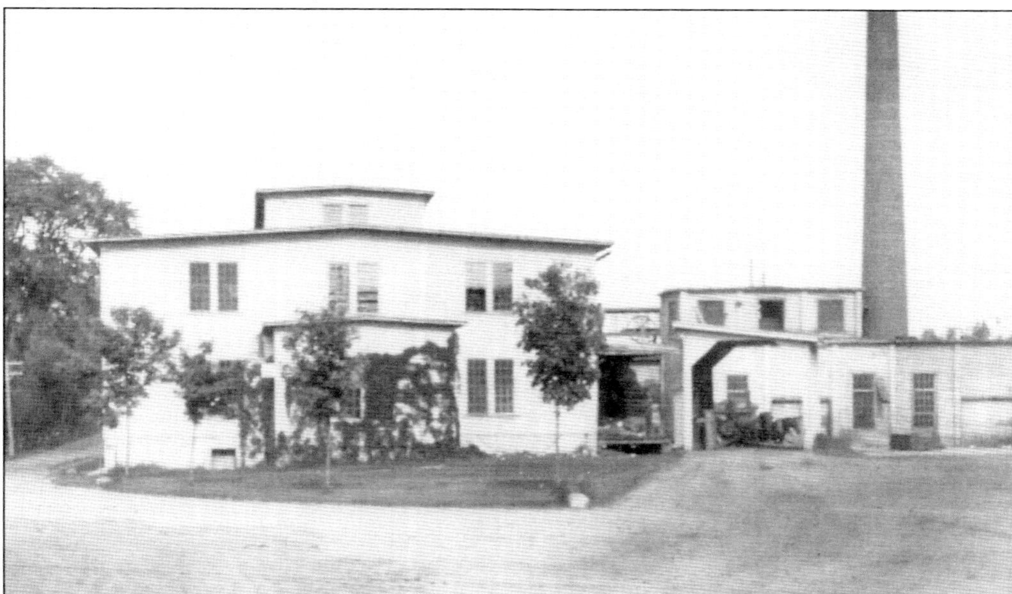

This photograph from 1916 shows part of the Davis Paper Company in West Hopkinton. Built by Henry C. and Horace J. Davis, it was reported to have cost a quarter of a million dollars to build. The business included a leather board mill with a concrete foundation and a connected strawboard mill built entirely of concrete. They also built a new dam that spanned the Contoocook River. (Courtesy of Hopkinton Historical Society.)

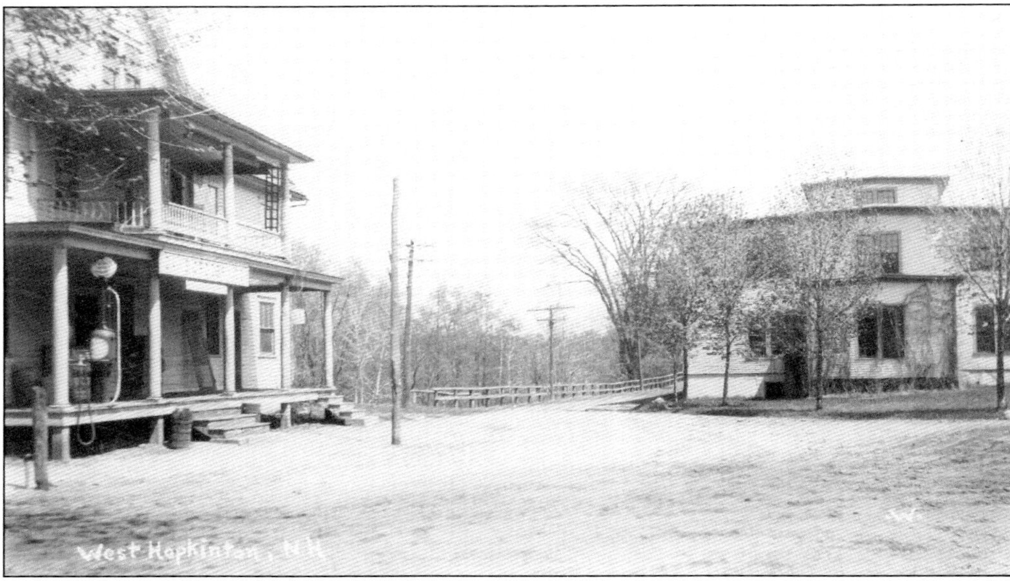

With the creation of the Davis Paper Company, a village of 18 tenement buildings and the Davis Grocery Company also sprang up in West Hopkinton. The Davis Grocery Store was located across the street, northwest of the mill. The building later housed the West Hopkinton Post Office from around 1918 until it closed in 1972. The early-1900s photograph above is looking east on Route 127. The Davis Grocery store is seen on the left and a mill building is on the right. The building has changed owners many times since and has most recently been used for storage and office space. (Courtesy of Hopkinton Historical Society.)

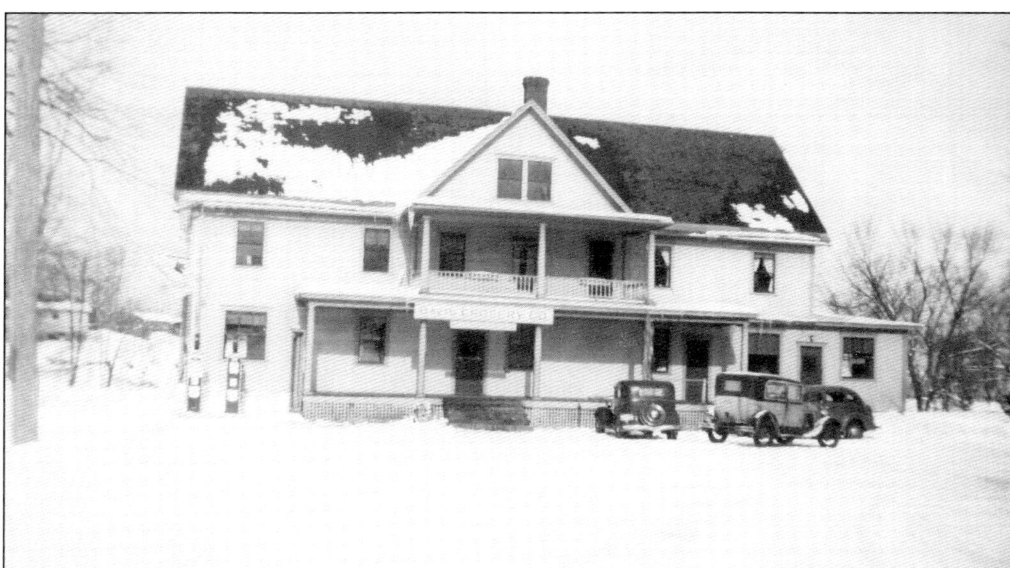

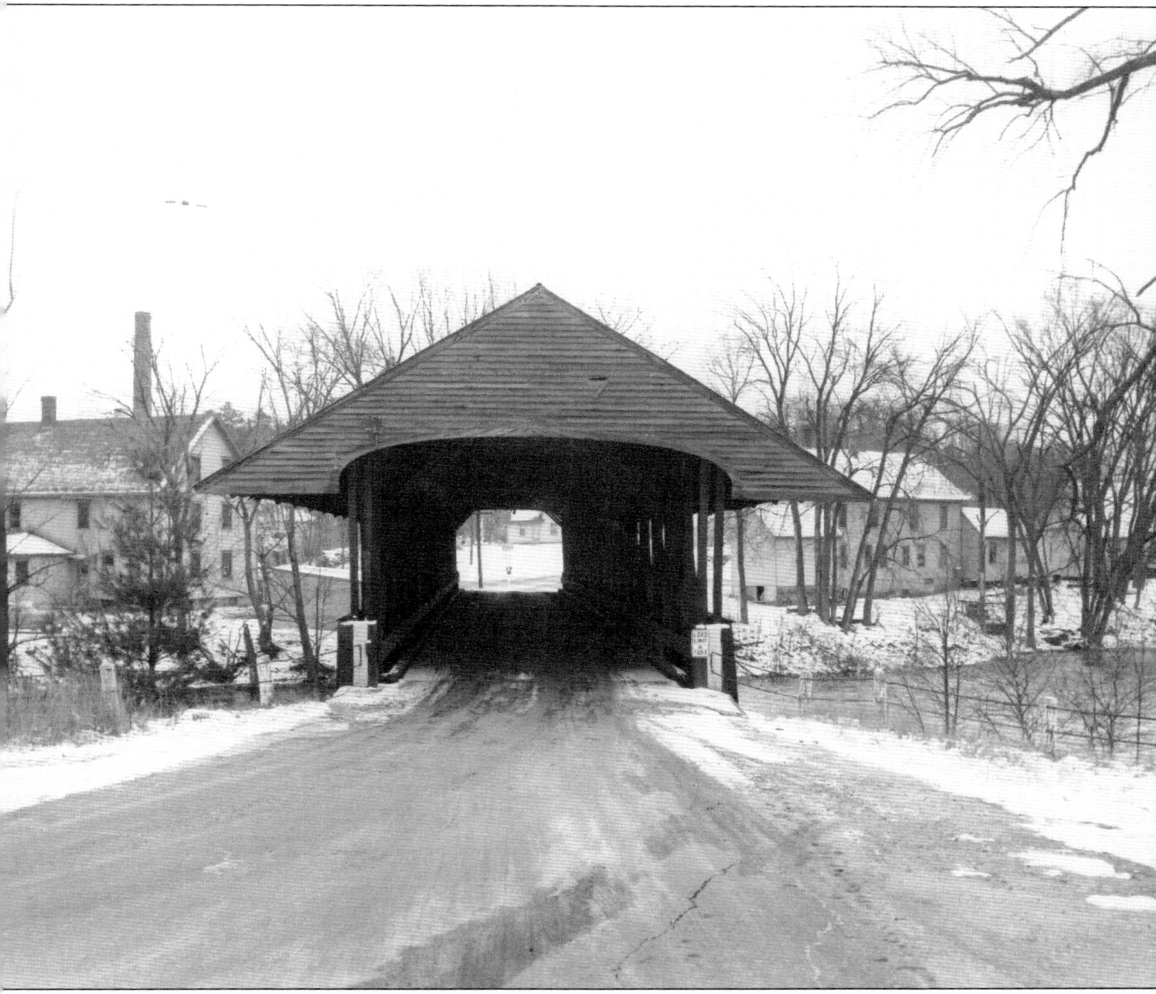

Rowell Bridge is located north of New Hampshire Route 127 on Clement Hill Road over the Contoocook River in West Hopkinton. It was built in 1852 by Horace Childs of Henniker at a cost of $300.25 using a truss design patented by Hopkinton native Col. Stephen Harriman Long. Born in 1784, Long was a US Army explorer, topographical engineer, railway engineer, and inventor. He spent many years leading government explorations between the mouth of the Mississippi River and the Great Plains Mountains, and Longs Peak in Colorado is named for him. The Burr-type construction is unusual in that solid timber arches are fitted end-to-end and bolted to the side timbers to form the basic design, while most arches in other designs are laminated. Shortly after its construction, the bridge came off its abutments when a herd of cattle was driven too quickly over it. The structure was put back in place and reattached to its abutments. A central pier was added in the 1930s under the middle of the bridge in an effort to provide additional support; however, this caused the bridge to teeter under heavy loads, so the top of the pier was removed. The bridge proved to be strong enough without the additional support. Rowell Bridge is listed in the National Register of Historic Places. (Courtesy of Hopkinton Historical Society.)

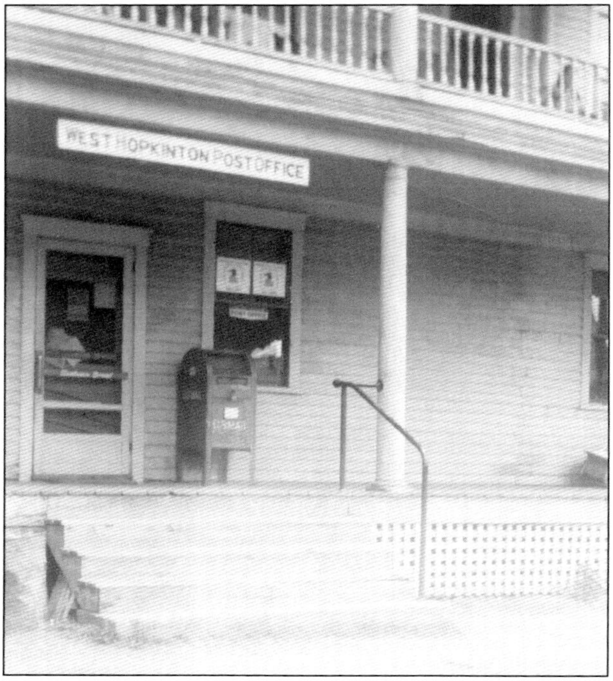

The first post office in West Hopkinton was established on May 29, 1857, with Joseph P. Dow as postmaster. It was located in the Rowell home from 1867 to 1899, when the Davis Paper Company bought the Rowell farm for their paper mill. The post office was then located in the home of Frank H. Carr until his death around 1918. The Davis Grocery Store was the West Hopkinton post office's final home. With Horace Stanley as its longtime postmaster, the post office closed on August 18, 1972. The picture below shows Contoocook postmaster Albert Hankins (left) and retiring postmaster Horace Stanley (right) burning the unused money orders at the closing of the post office. (Courtesy of Hopkinton Historical Society.)

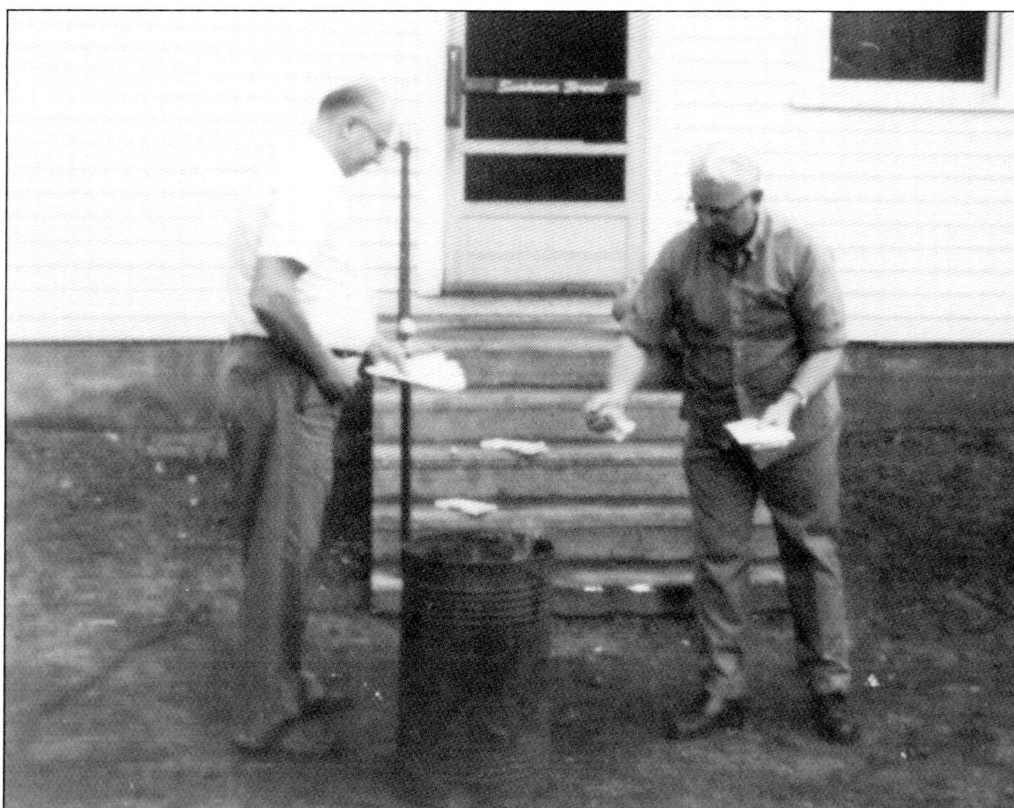

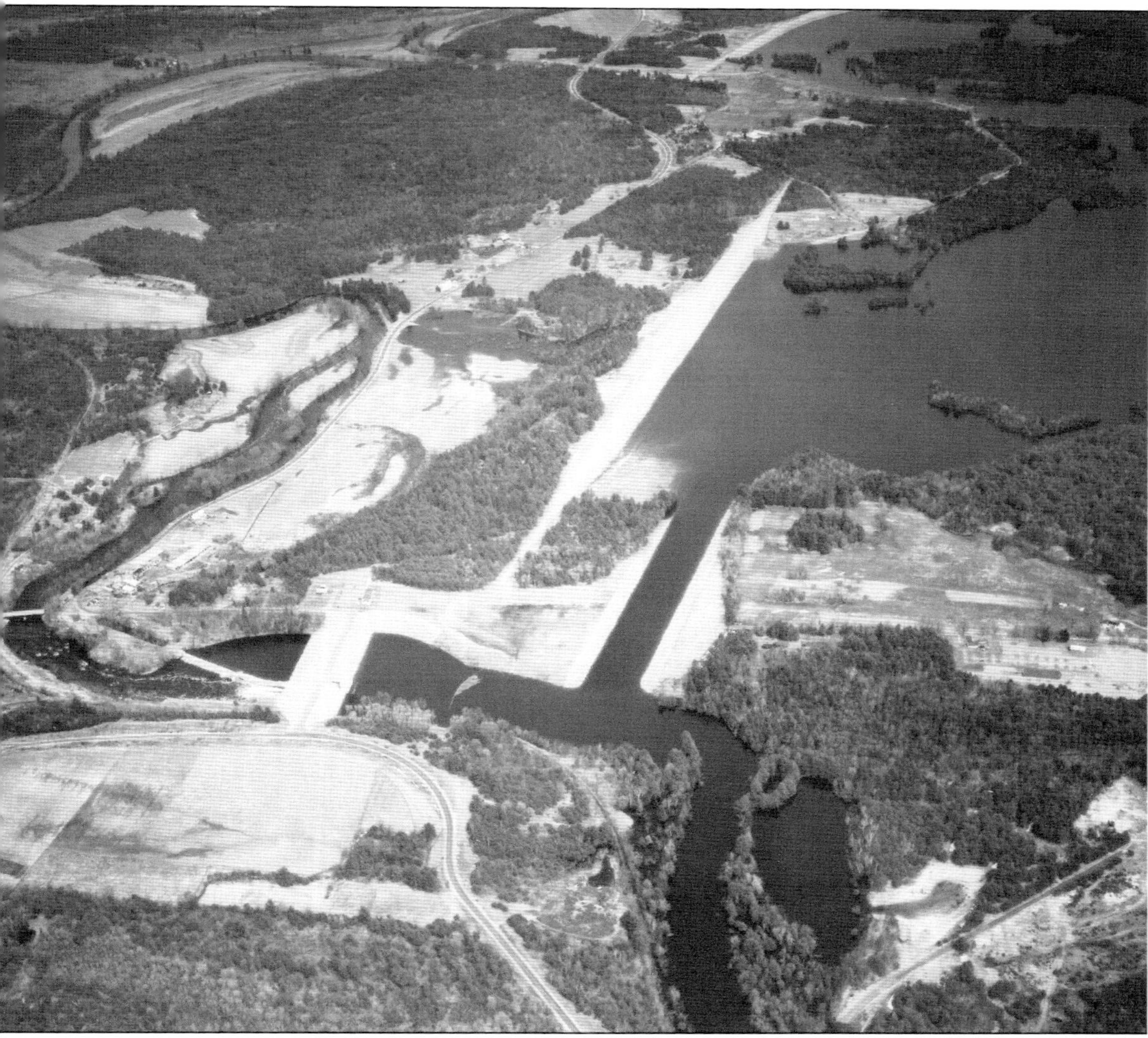

The devastating effects of the 1936 flood and the 1938 hurricane led to the creation of a flood control system for the Contoocook River, a tributary of the Merrimack River. The general concept of protecting towns and cities located downriver through flood control projects on the Merrimack's tributaries was supported by New Hampshire and Massachusetts, but it took nearly 20 years to resolve the allocation of costs between the two states. The New Hampshire state senate gave its approval to the Hopkinton-Everett Flood Control Project in 1957 and the Army Corps of Engineers broke ground on September 26, 1959. Vice President Richard Nixon was among the dignitaries attending the ground breaking ceremony. The project involved the construction of two dams, the Hopkinton Dam in West Hopkinton and the Everett Dam in Weare, both built with rolled-earth fill and rock slopes. These dams are located on two tributaries of the Merrimack River and the project consists of a two-reservoir system divided into three storage areas. Two of these storage areas are located on the Contoocook River, and one on the Piscataqua River. The storage areas are connected by two canals that act as a separate reservoir during minor flooding; the entire area serves as a single reservoir during periods of moderate or major flooding. The cost of the project was about $21.4 million and it has successfully protected the town from catastrophic flooding. (Courtesy of Hopkinton Historical Society.)

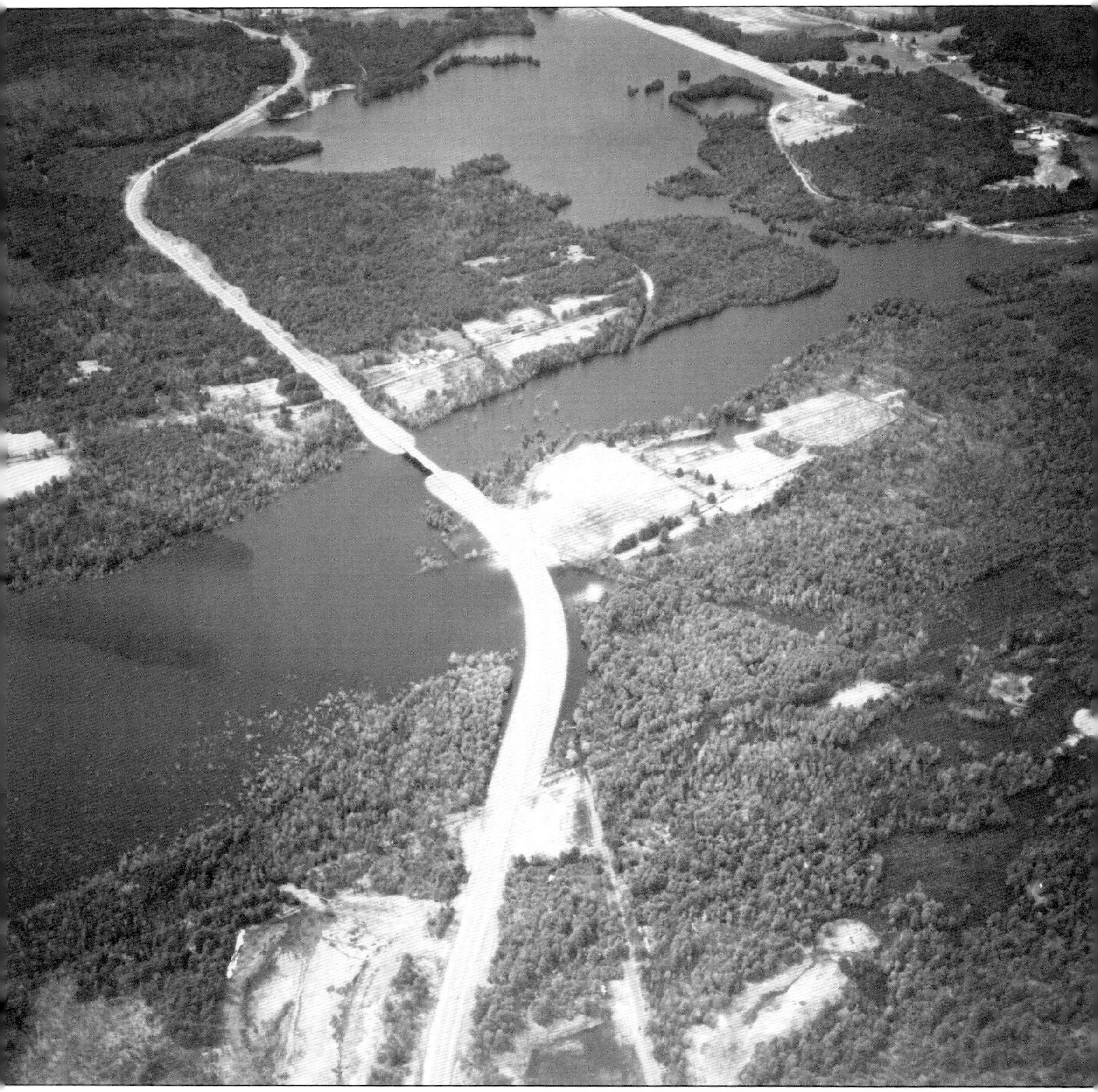

The creation of the Hopkinton-Everett Flood Control Project had a great impact on West Hopkinton. Farms and homes that stood in the path of the dam and its reservoirs and canals were purchased by the government and demolished to make way for the project. The Stumpfield area was flooded and new roads needed to be constructed or altered. The project changed the village's population and how a traveller got from here to there. Overpasses were necessary on Routes 202 and 9 and at the same time a new interstate, General Frank D. Merrill Highway (Interstate 89), was being constructed. The project also made it necessary to move Stumpfield Cemetery, which dated from the 1700s. In 1959, workers spent weeks carefully relocating the cemetery to an area in the back of the Contoocook Village Cemetery, naming the new burial ground the New Stumpfield Cemetery. This 1969 aerial photograph of the Stumpfield area (looking west) and Routes 202 and 9 shows how the old roads lead into and out of land now covered by water. (Courtesy of Hopkinton Historical Society.)

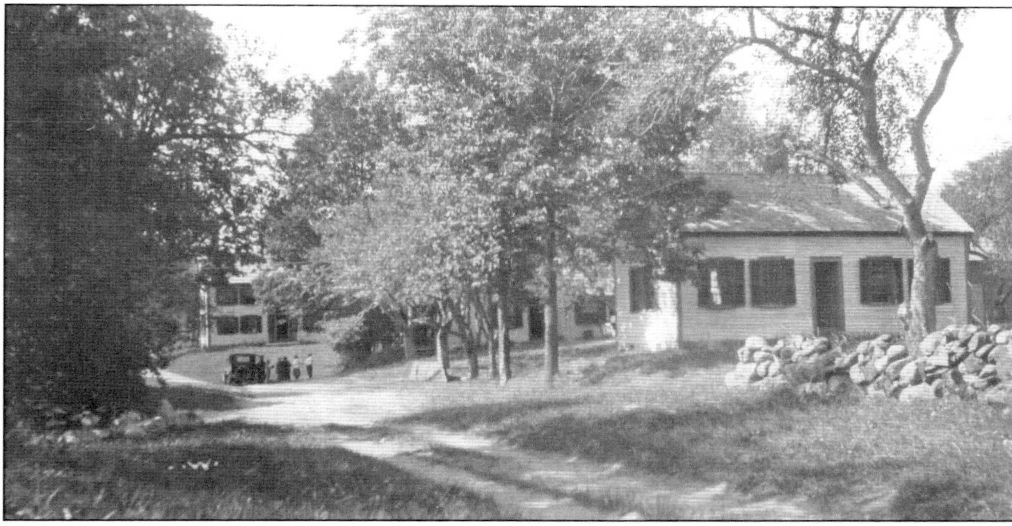

In 1806, James Clough IV and his son William Clough V purchased 360 acres of forest land and a lake in the northwest area of Hopkinton. They built a cabin and a mill and later cleared land for a homestead. Cloughville, as it would become known, was home to generations of the Clough family and their friends. It was a thriving community of carpenters, millers, shoemakers, and farmers. The large house in the background above was home to siblings Sylvia and Joseph Clough. They were the last residents of Cloughville and the source of the name for Lake JoSylvia. The photograph below shows the original Clough descendants' cottage in the background on the east side of Lake JoSylvia, which is also known as Clement Pond. (Courtesy of Hopkinton Historical Society.)

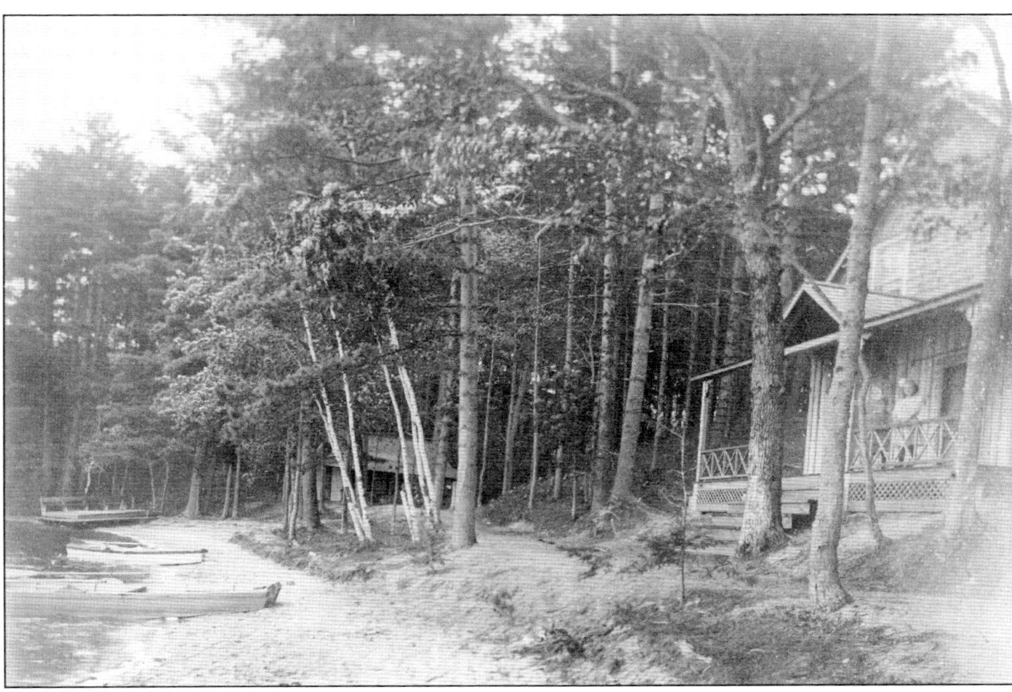

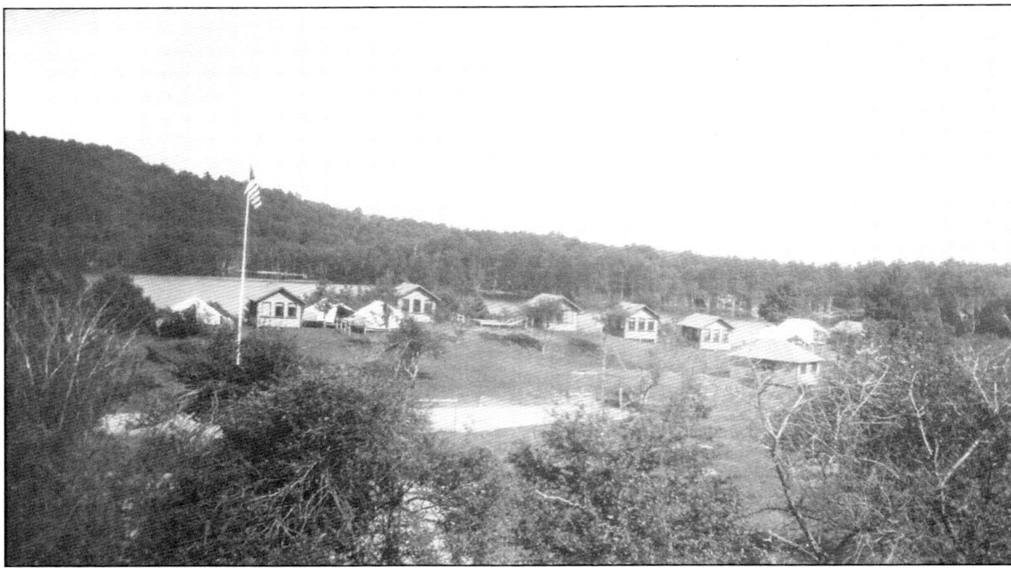

In 1917, after the death of Joseph Clough, his sister Sylvia moved from Cloughville and the property was sold to two men from New York, Mr. Price and Mr. Pick. The men started a Jewish boys camp named Camp Merrimac and ran it until the mid-1950s. Mr. Werner Rothchild and Mr. Robert Martin then purchased the property and continued to operate the camp with a general camp program. In September 1998, the Greek Orthodox Metropolis of Boston purchased the property and renamed it the St. Methodios Faith and Heritage Center. The organization made many renovations to update the facility so that it could be used year round. The property still hosts summer camps as well as retreats and conferences. (Courtesy of Hopkinton Historical Society.)

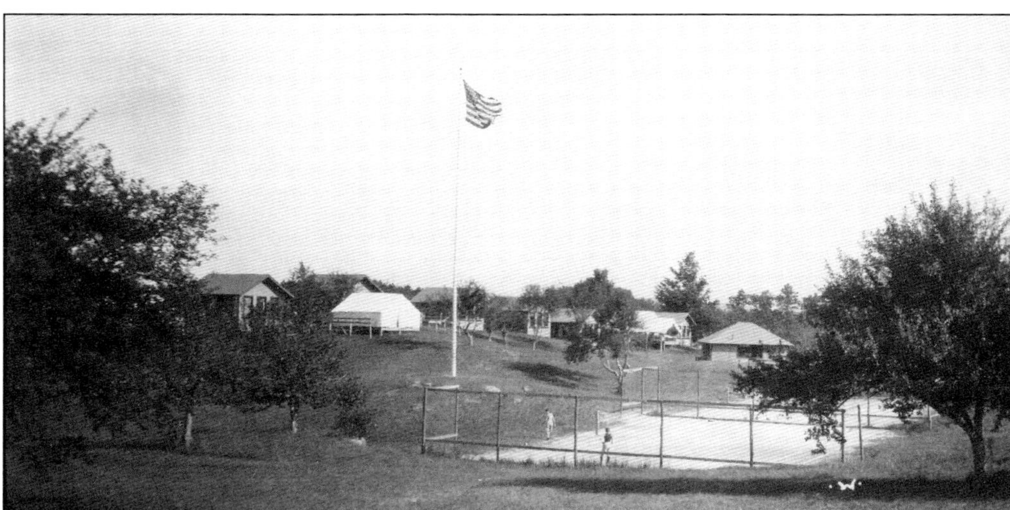

Four

FIRES AND FLOODS

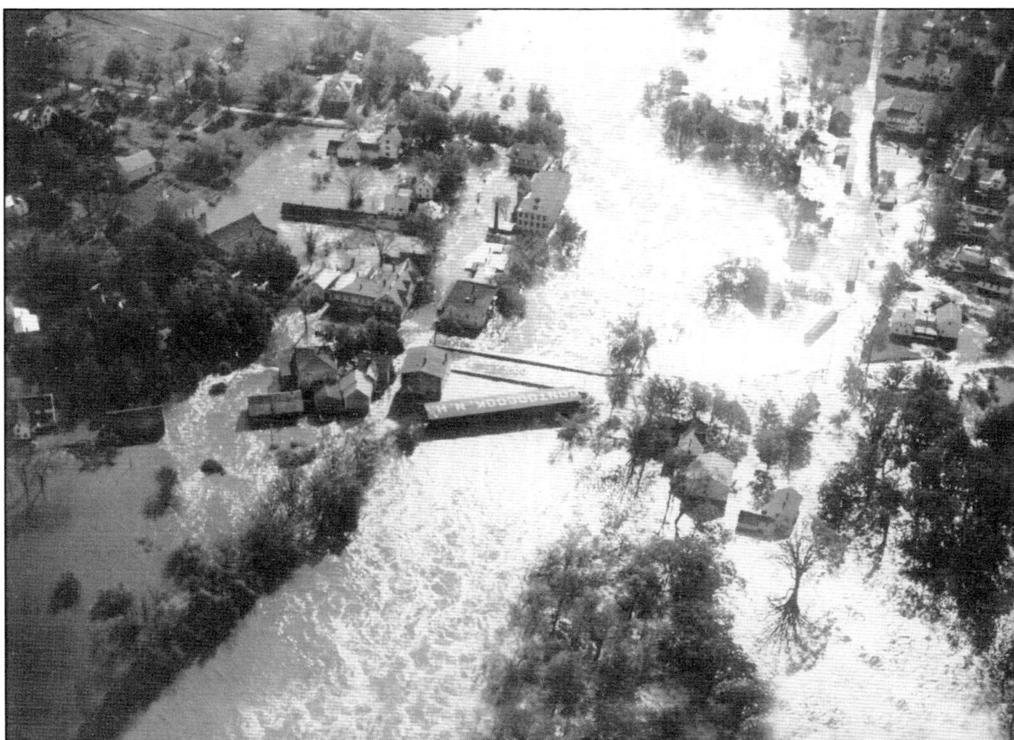

On March 9, 1936, a moisture-laden front stalled over New England, bringing with it increased temperatures and three days of heavy rain from March 11 to 13. The melting snow and the reported five inches of rainfall caused the worst flooding in three centuries. The Contoocook River spilled over its banks and caused damage in Contoocook Village and West Hopkinton. (Courtesy of the Contoocook Riverway Association.)

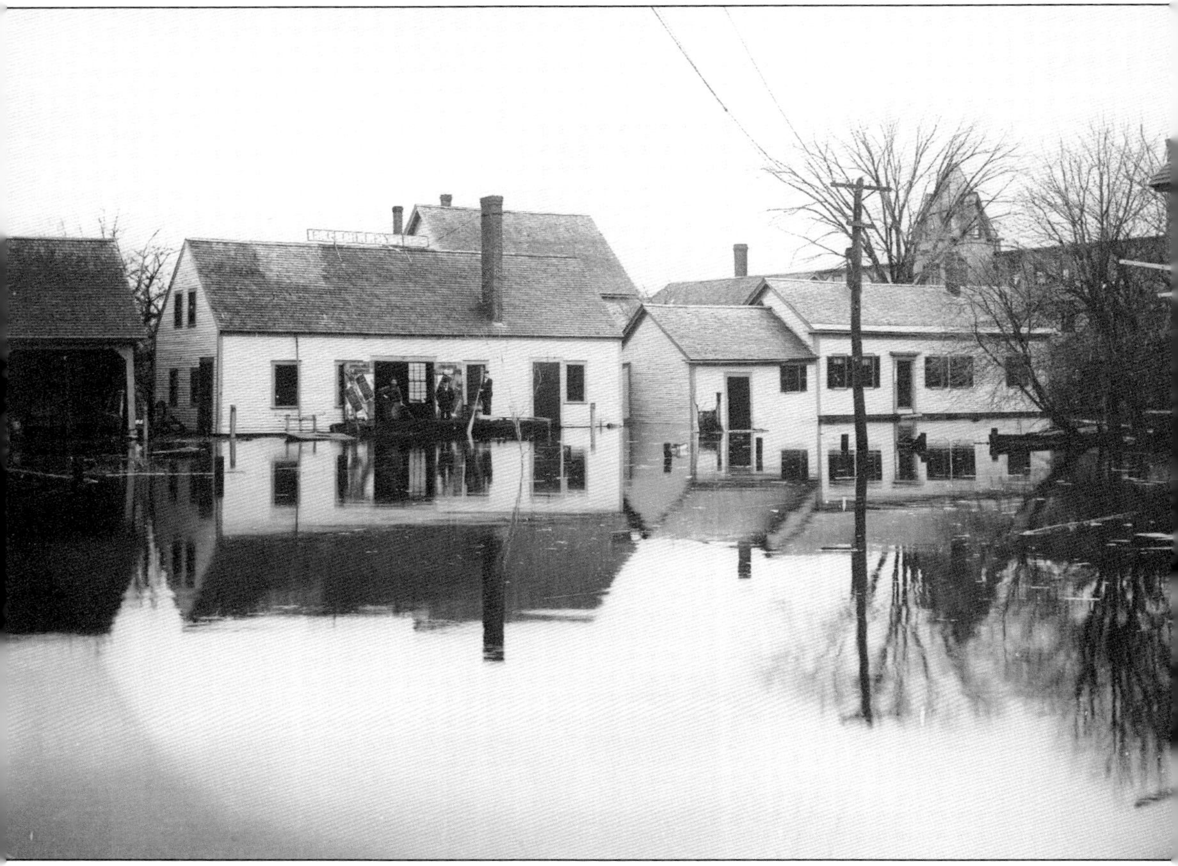

Contoocook Village owed its development to the Contoocook River and was no stranger to floods. On October 23, 1785, the Contoocook River had its greatest discharge ever. The next reported flood was March 24–30, 1826. Due to heavy snowmelt, the river overflowed again April 19–22, 1862. On October 3–5, 1869, a tropical storm that lasted 36 hours and saturated the area with 6–12 inches of rain caused the river to rise over its banks once again. This photograph, taken around the turn of the 20th century, shows the blacksmith shop of E.G. Cilley on Cedar Street. A man stands in a boat that he likely used to navigate the flooded roads. In the background the Kingsbury & Davis building can be seen; under normal conditions, the river flows behind it. (Courtesy of Hopkinton Historical Society.)

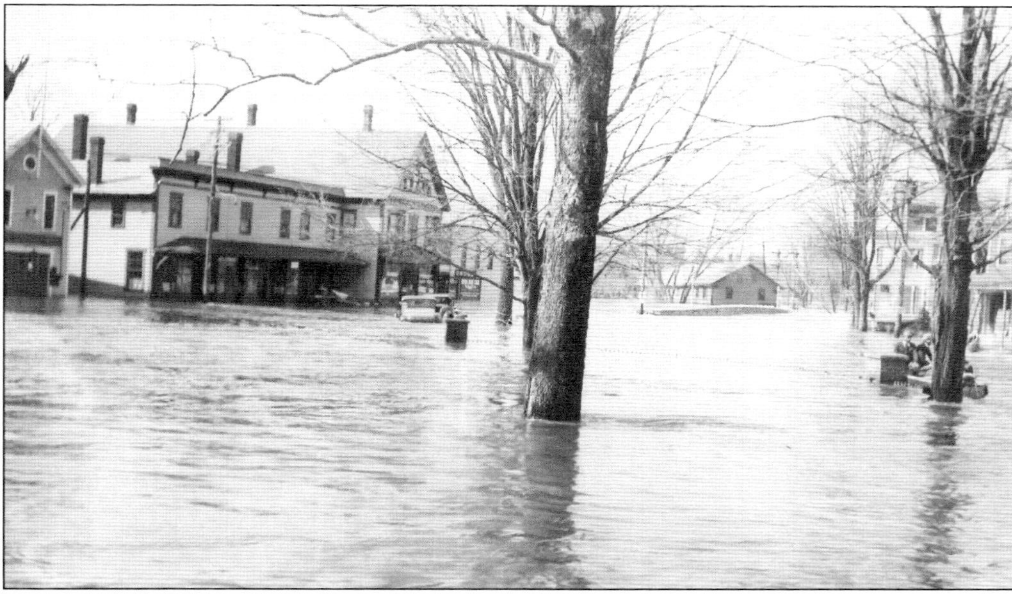

This photograph, taken near the Walter S. Davis home looking northwest, shows Contoocook Fountain Square completely submerged in several feet of water during the 1936 flood. Barely visible are the tips of the iron fence around the perimeter of the Davis property. (Courtesy of Hopkinton Historical Society.)

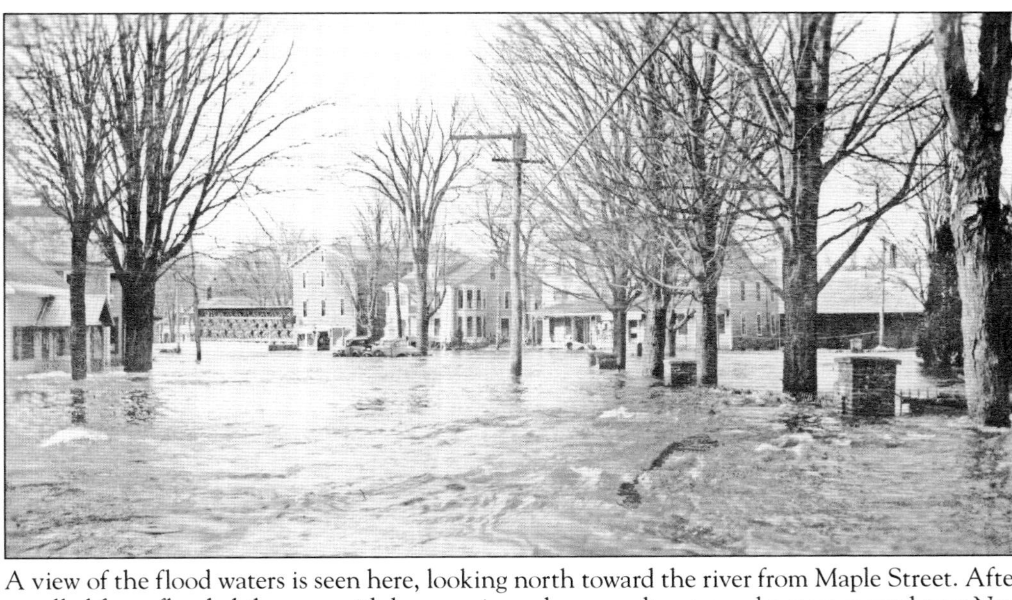

A view of the flood waters is seen here, looking north toward the river from Maple Street. After a stalled front flooded the area with heavy rain and snowmelt, a second system moved over New England a few days later with additional rainfall. A third system, although less severe, hit the area shortly after. Although it didn't cause additional damage, it did prolong the effects of the original flooding. (Courtesy of Hopkinton Historical Society.)

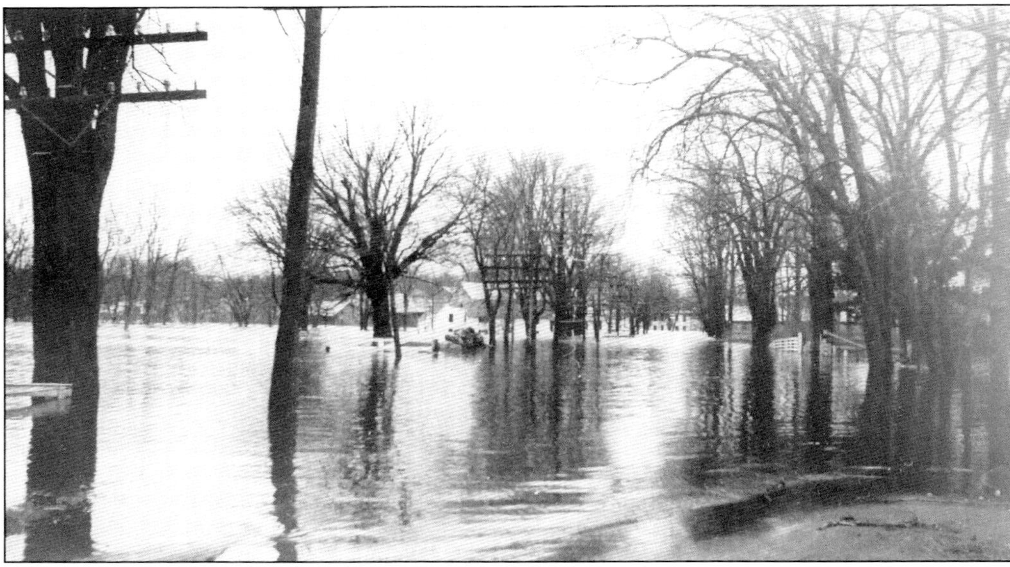

The flood waters in March 1936 made their way up Park Avenue in Contoocook as shown in this photograph that looks south toward the village. The open fields on the left, once a part of the farm belonging to Capt. Paul Rolfe George, would later be the site of the "new" A&P market and today is a business plaza. In many areas of New England—including Contoocook—the flood of 1936 is still the worst on record. (Courtesy of Hopkinton Historical Society.)

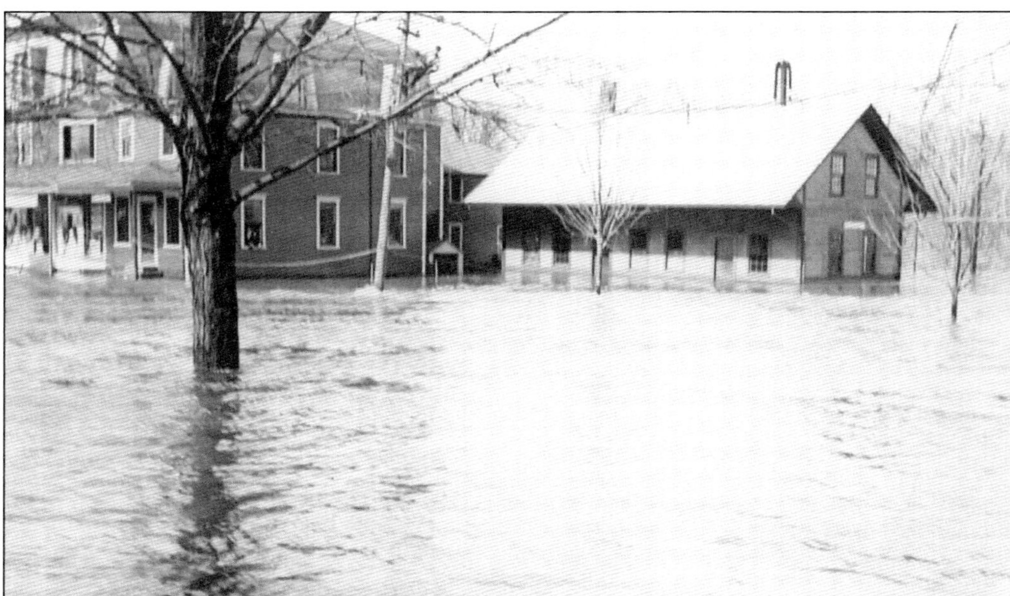

The Curtice Block (left) and the train depot (right) in Contoocook Village are partially submerged in the flood waters of 1936. During the two-week period, the majority of New England was affected by the flooding caused by snowmelt and rainfall totalling over 10 inches, with some estimates at 30 inches. This rain was compounded by snowmelt from an estimated snowpack of about seven and a half inches. (Courtesy of Edith Carr.)

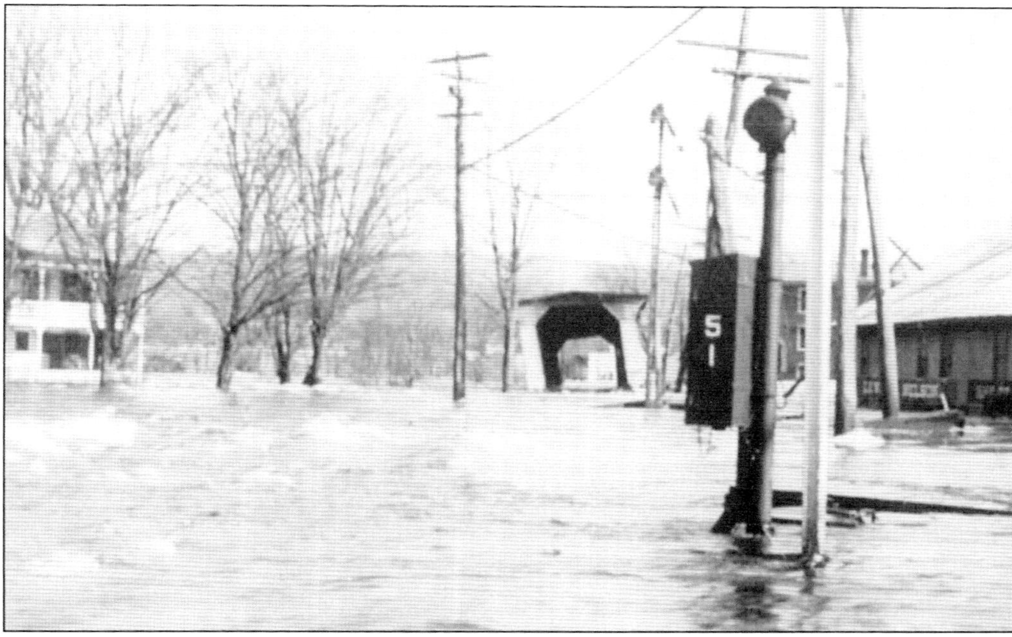

The 1936 flood waters race over the railroad tracks at the intersection of Pine Street and Kearsarge Avenue. A significant amount of damage during the flood was caused by ice moving down the river and the ice jams this caused. The rushing water and ice caused the covered railroad bridge in Contoocook to be pushed off its abutments. (Courtesy of Edith Carr.)

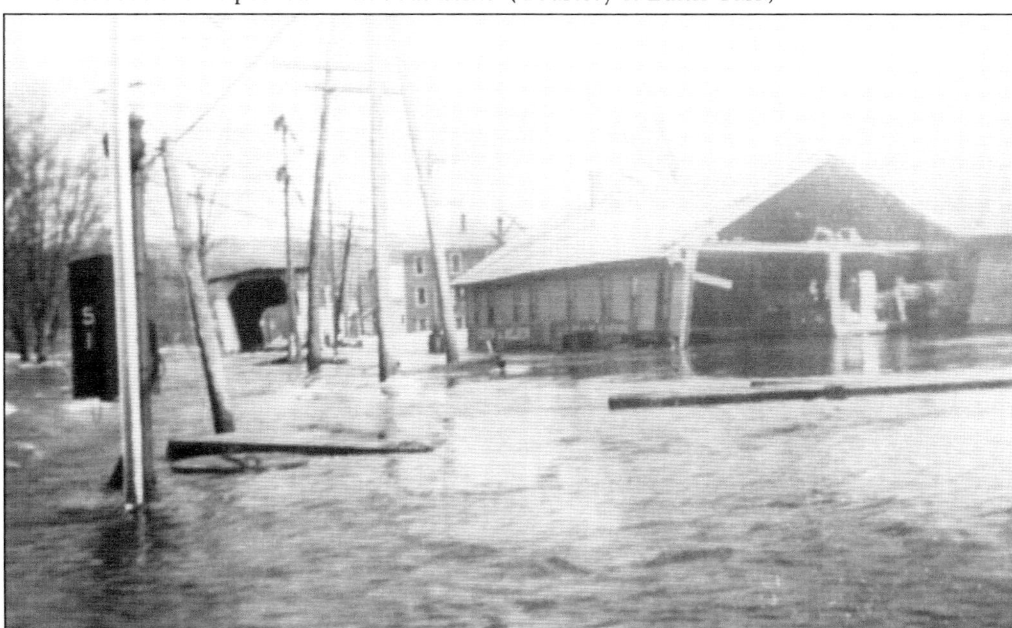

The untamed force of the raging waters left a path of destruction through Contoocook Village. This photograph shows the covered railroad bridge (left) listing to the side as the water forces it off its abutments. On the right, the Lewis A. Nelson grain mill has been sheared in two. (Courtesy of Edith Carr.)

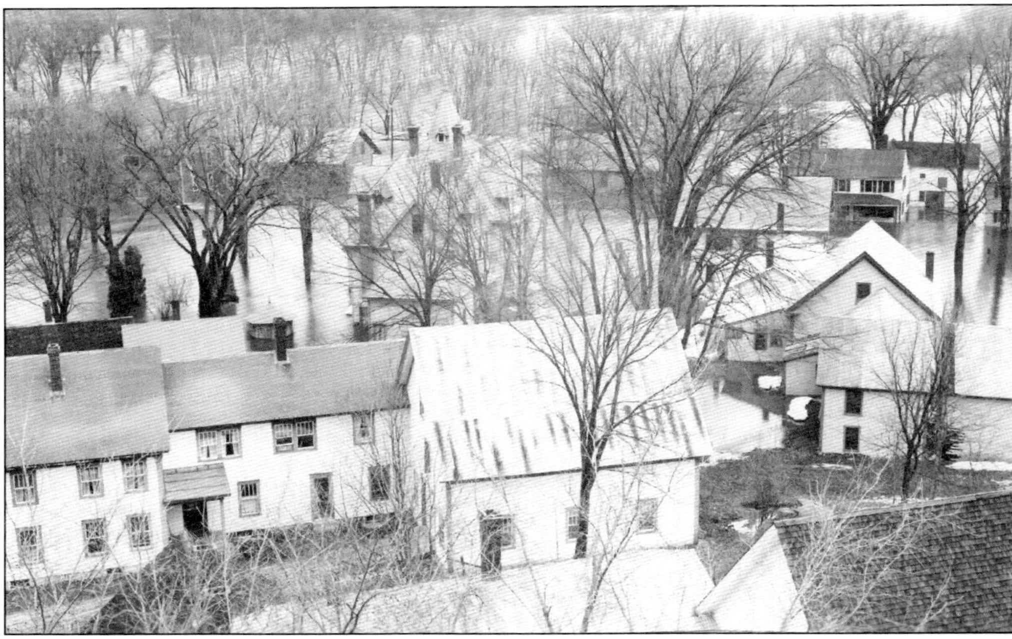

A view from atop the Swedenborgian New Jerusalem Church on Maple Street looking north shows the flood waters over Main Street. The numerous chimneys and peaks of the Walter S. Davis home can be seen at center; the house itself is completely engulfed by the flood waters. (Courtesy of Hopkinton Historical Society.)

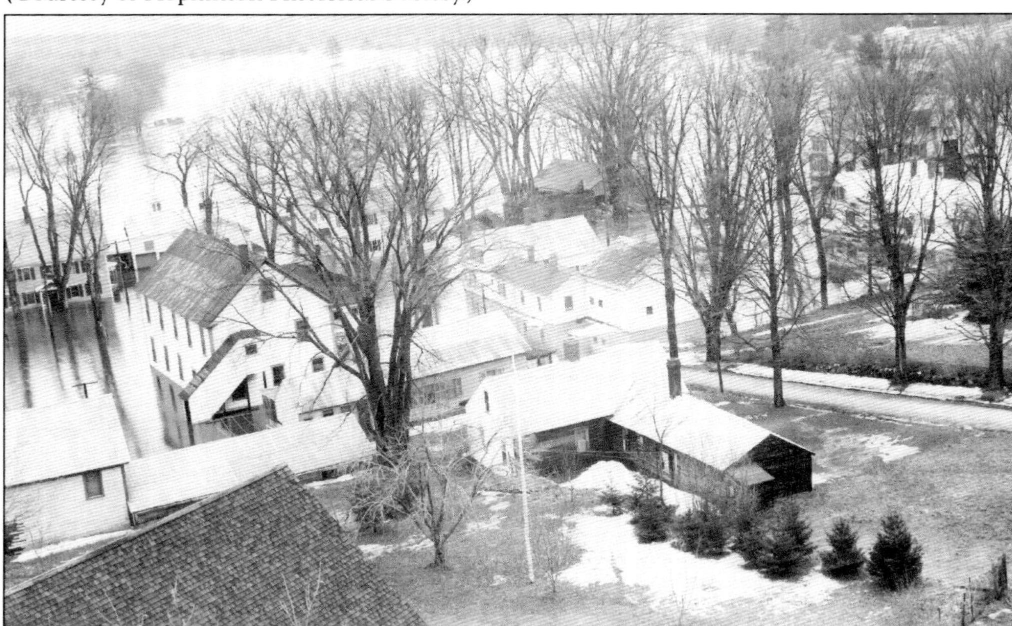

Another view from atop the Swedenborgian New Jerusalem Church looking north towards Main Street shows the incredible amount of water that overtook the village. The fields north of Main Street are completely submerged and only the roof of a building on that farmland is visible. (Courtesy of Hopkinton Historical Society.)

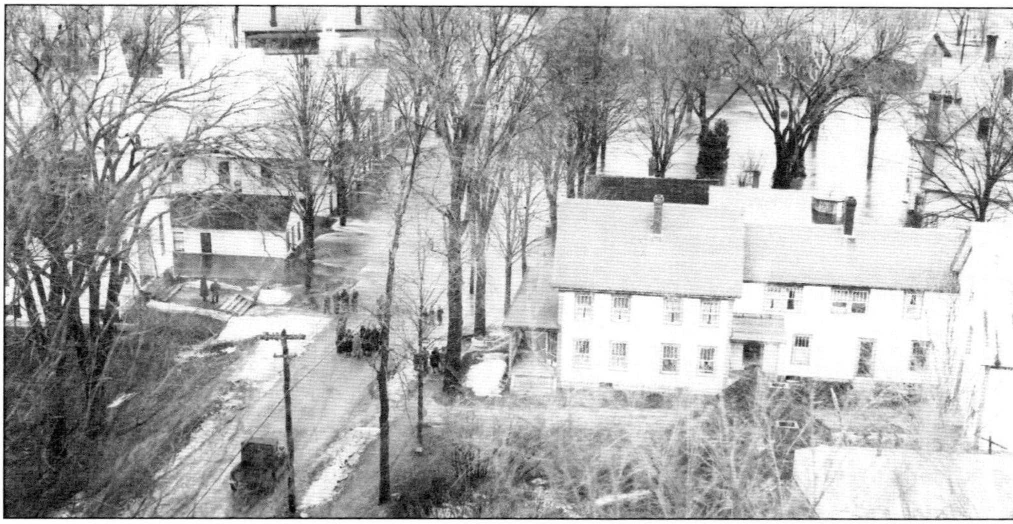

Looking down from the steeple of the Swedenborgian New Jerusalem Church towards Maple Street, the flood waters can be seen reaching the steps of the Methodist church. The photograph above shows curious townspeople gathering to witness the record-breaking flood waters that have submerged the entire Fountain Square. Below, the photograph shows that the river has turned the village into one large body of water stretching all the way from Maple Street to Pine Street. In the upper right, the Lewis A. Nelson grain mill can be seen torn in half by the raging water. (Courtesy of Hopkinton Historical Society.)

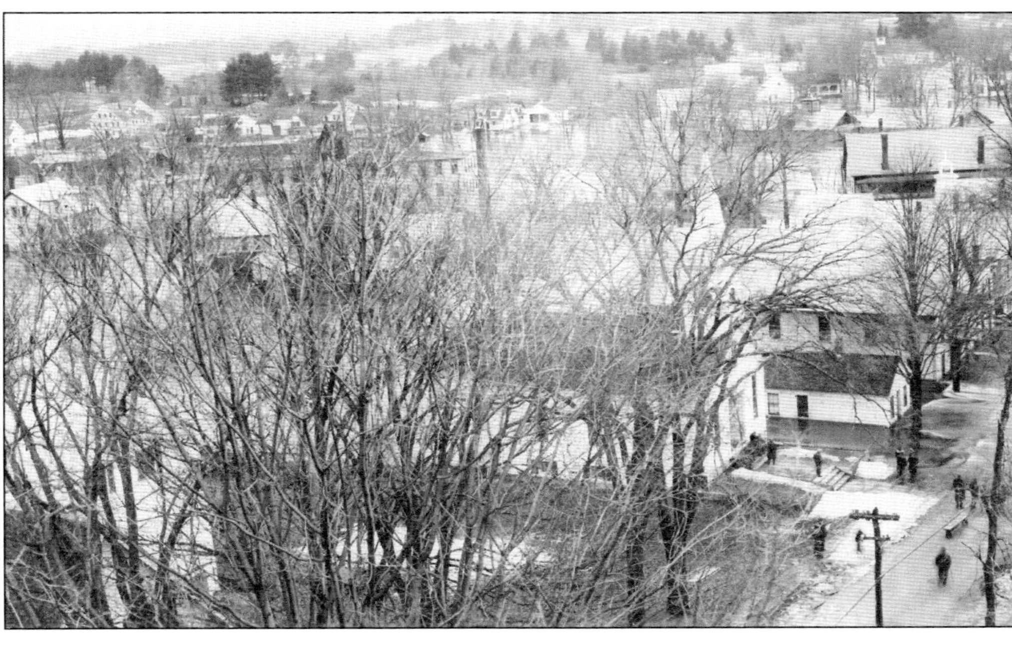

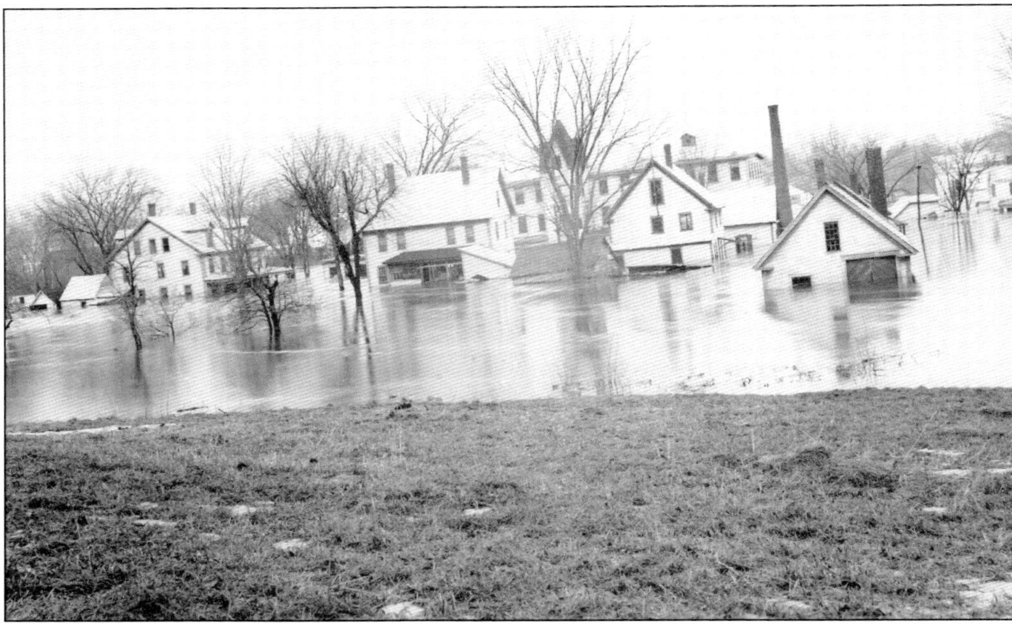

This photograph, taken from behind the Methodist Church looking northwest, shows the flood waters on Cedar Street. Many people living along the Contoocook River had to be rescued from their homes as flood waters reached the second floors of houses. Churches and public buildings became emergency shelters for those whose homes were underwater. (Courtesy of Hopkinton Historical Society.)

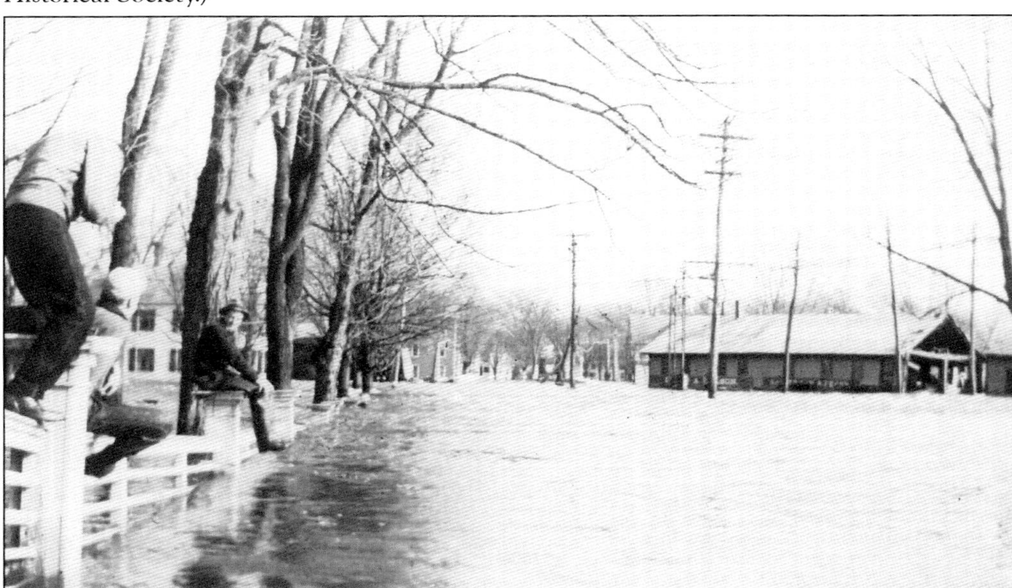

Men sit on the fence of Perkins Manor to view the massive amounts of water and destruction caused by the 1936 flood. The water covers Kearsarge Avenue looking south towards the village. The damage to the Lewis. A. Nelson grain mill is clearly shown on the right and the covered railroad bridge on the left continues to tilt at an even more dangerous angle. (Courtesy of Hopkinton Historical Society.)

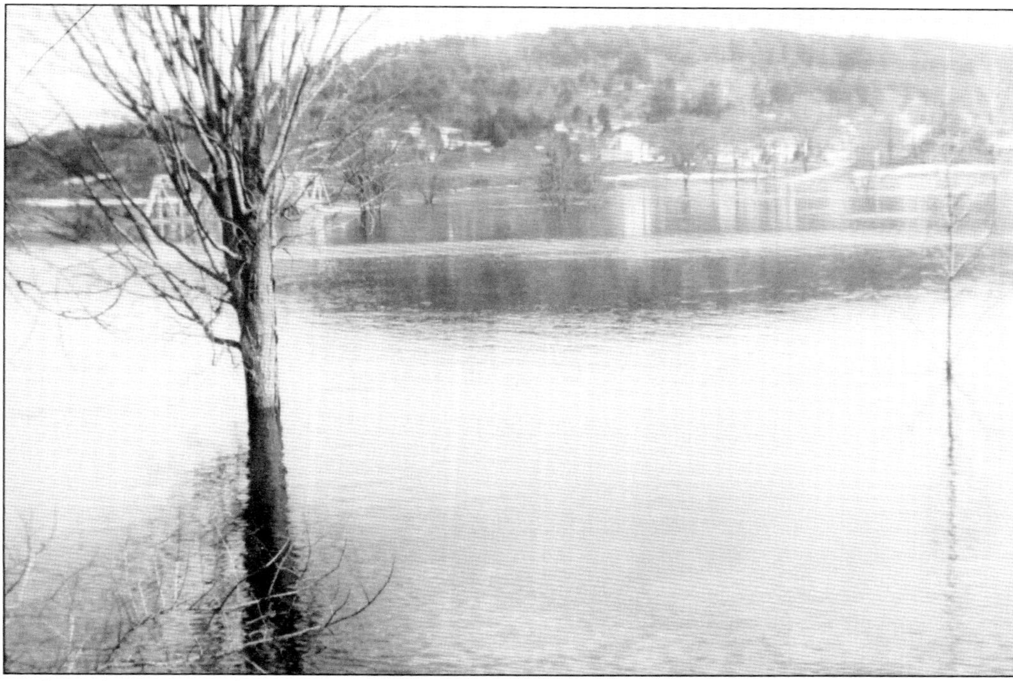

In the Tyler section of town, northeast of Contoocook Village, the flooding was no better. This photograph, taken from the front porch of the Bohanan Farm house, shows the river taking over the farmland and submerging the bridge on Penacook Road. A closer look at the bridge shows that a cottage belonging to the Lovells has been washed downstream and is lodged against it. (Courtesy of Hopkinton Historical Society.)

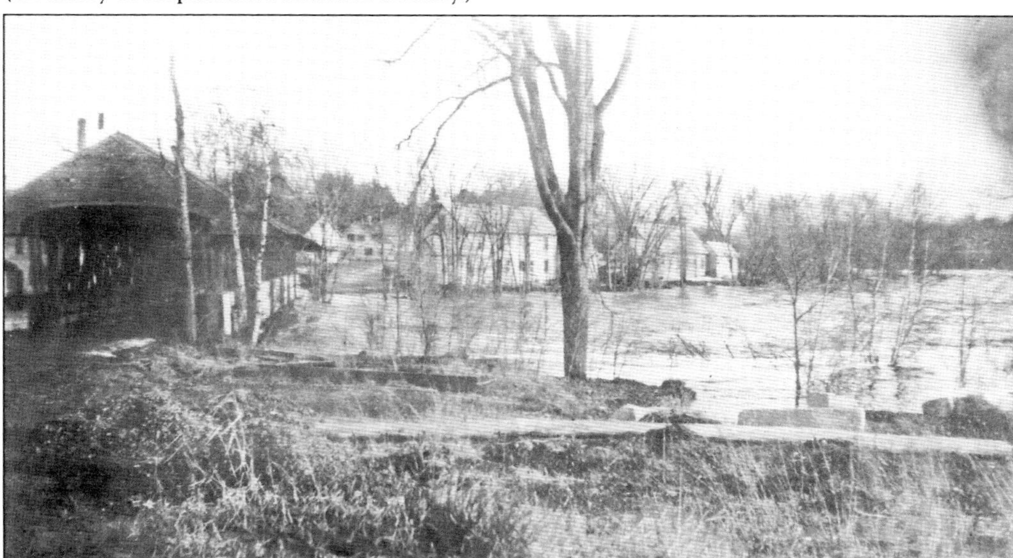

The 83-year-old Rowell Bridge in West Hopkinton stands strong against the powerful flood waters in 1936. Due to geographic advantages, the village of West Hopkinton fared better than Contoocook during the flooding. The houses around the Davis Paper Company, on the north side of the river, were largely spared. (Courtesy of Hopkinton Historical Society.)

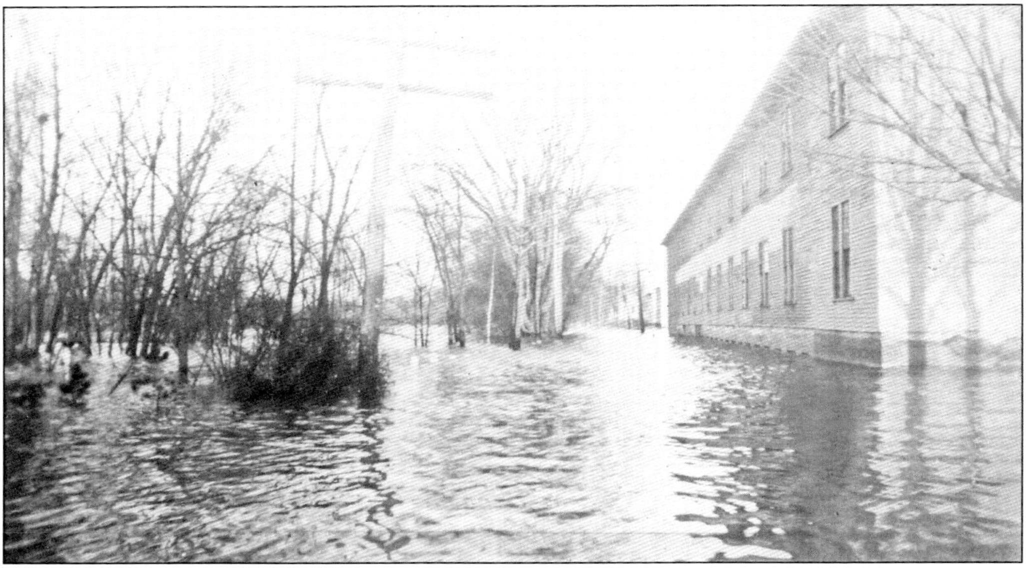

The photograph above shows one of the Davis Paper Company mill buildings on Route 127 enveloped as the water spills over the banks of the Contoocook River. The water was so deep it nearly submerged the fence along the left side of the road. Below is a photograph of the Davis Grocery Store surrounded by the river's water. (Courtesy of Hopkinton Historical Society.)

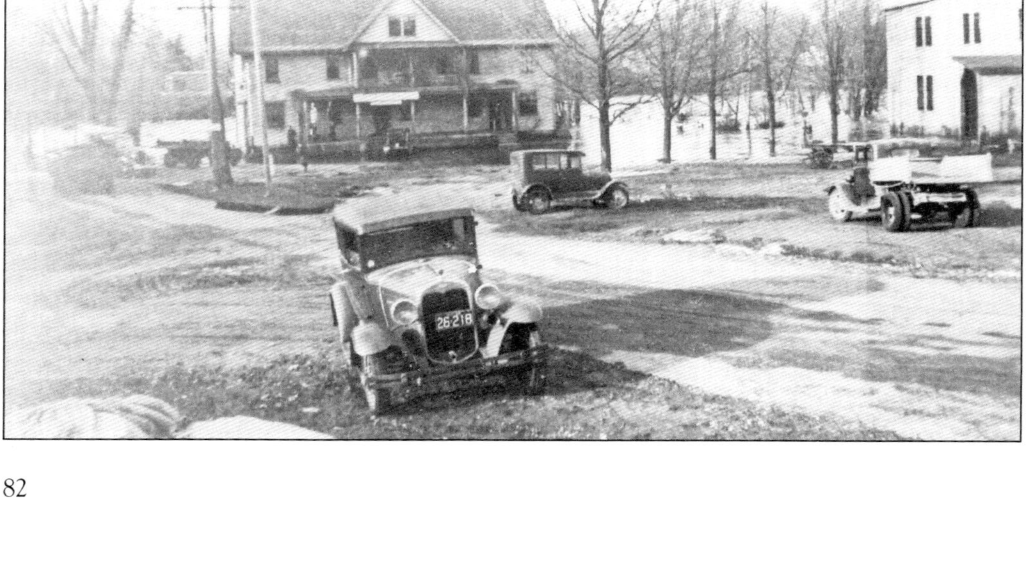

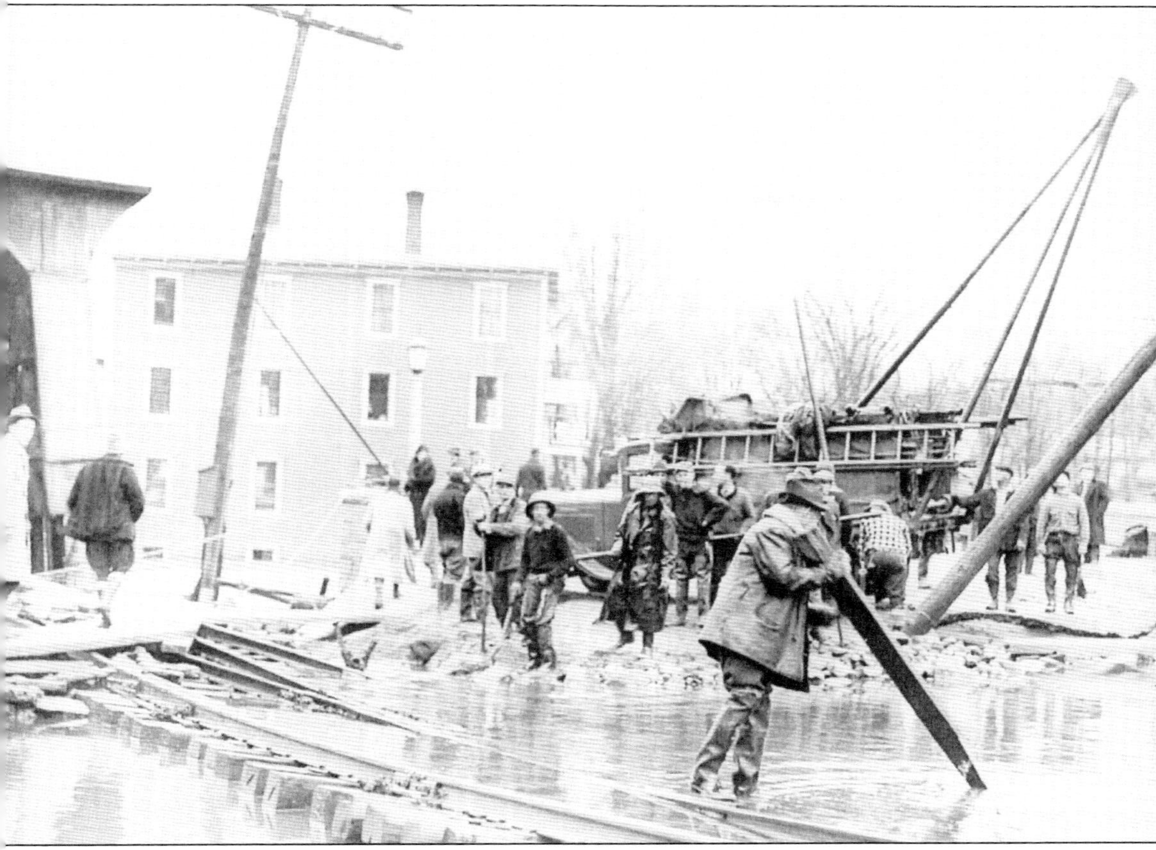

Once the 1936 flood waters receded, damages could be assessed and government crews sent to help with the cleanup and recovery. It was reported that 24 people in the Northeast perished in the flood and 77,000 were rendered homeless. In New Hampshire, countless bridges were washed away and miles of railroad tracks were lifted from their beds, making travel extremely difficult. Homes were washed away, businesses suffered heavy damages, and lives were changed forever. It is estimated that the flood caused damages of nearly $140 million in today's dollars in New Hampshire alone. In the picture above, crews assess the damage on the railroad tracks just north of the railroad bridge in Contoocook as the water levels begin to return to normal. (Courtesy of Edith Carr.)

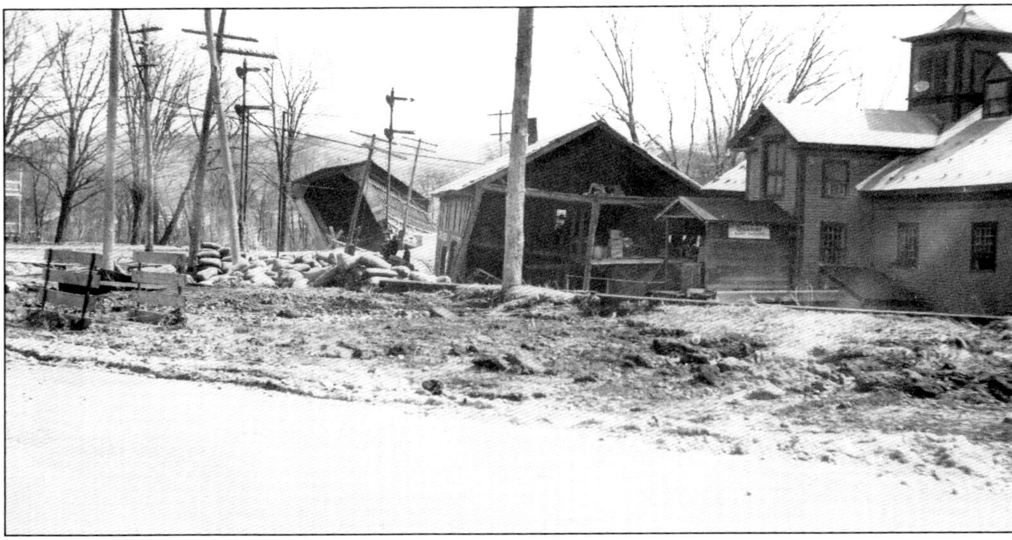

Above, the effects of the flood are visible in this photograph taken from Pine Street looking toward the village. The covered railroad bridge sits at a precarious angle, being nearly washed away by the quick moving water. Lewis A. Nelson's grain mill was cut in half and a portion of the building was carried yards from its foundation by the force of the waters. Below, bags of grain from Nelson's grain mill can be seen strewn around the ground. (Courtesy of Hopkinton Historical Society.)

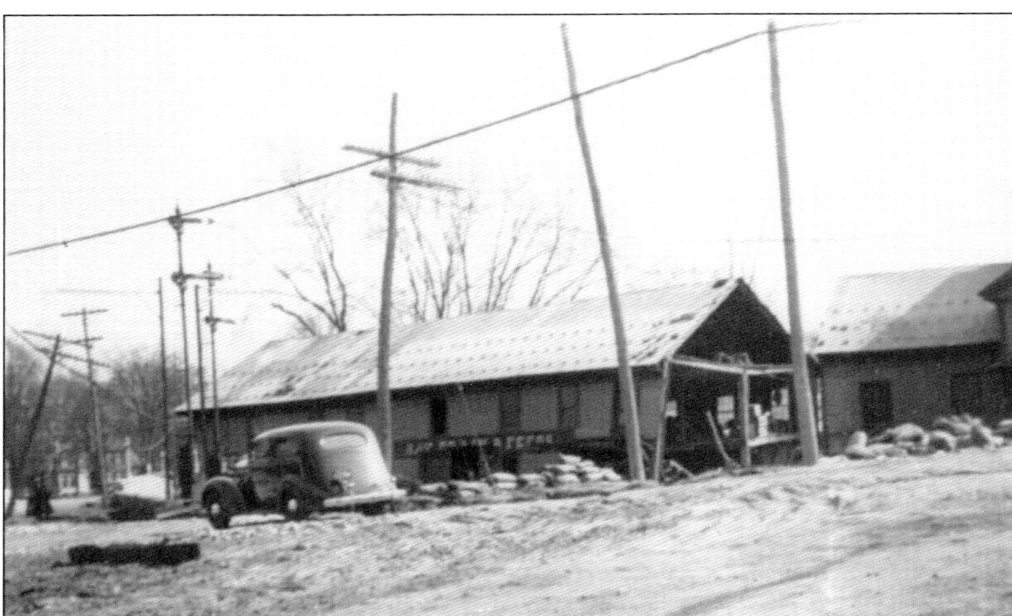

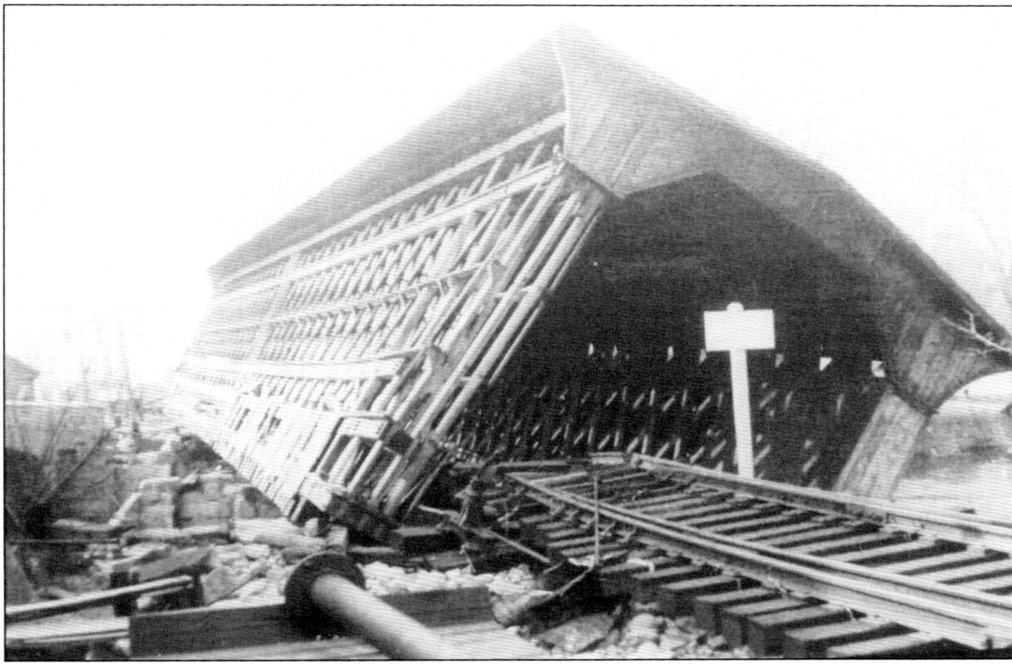

It was a fortunate decision to replace the old covered highway bridge with the current stone bridge in 1935, just months before the flood waters of 1936. Had the 82-year-old covered wooden bridge remained at the time of the flood, there is little doubt that it would not have held against the flood waters and would have crashed against the covered railroad bridge. The water and ice alone nearly sent the railroad bridge downstream; the impact of the covered highway bridge would have surely destroyed it. (Courtesy of Hopkinton Historical Society.)

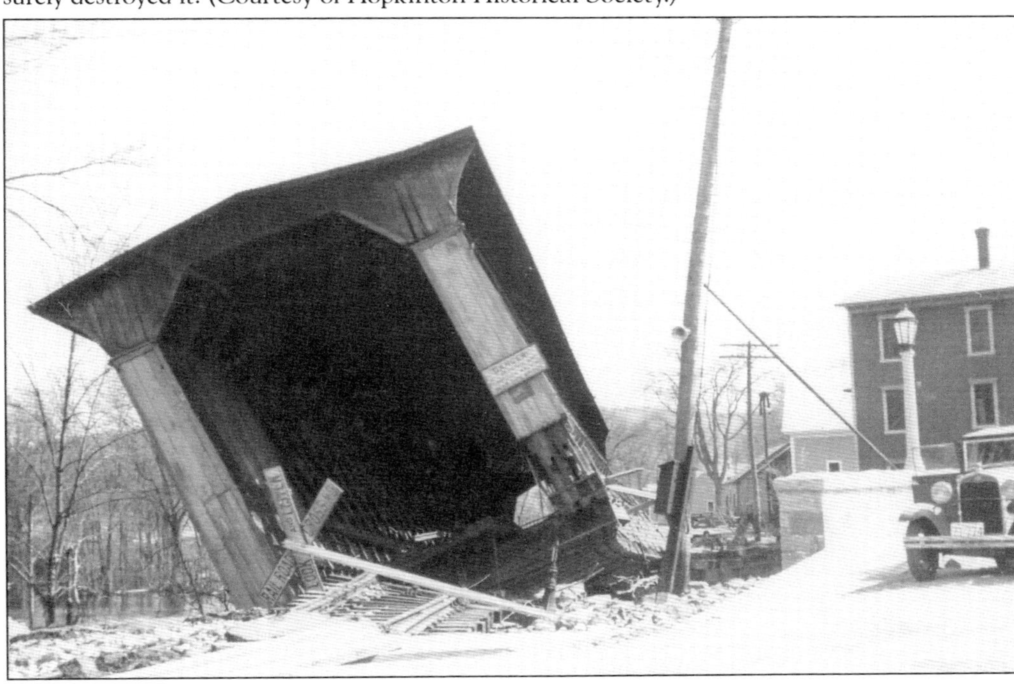

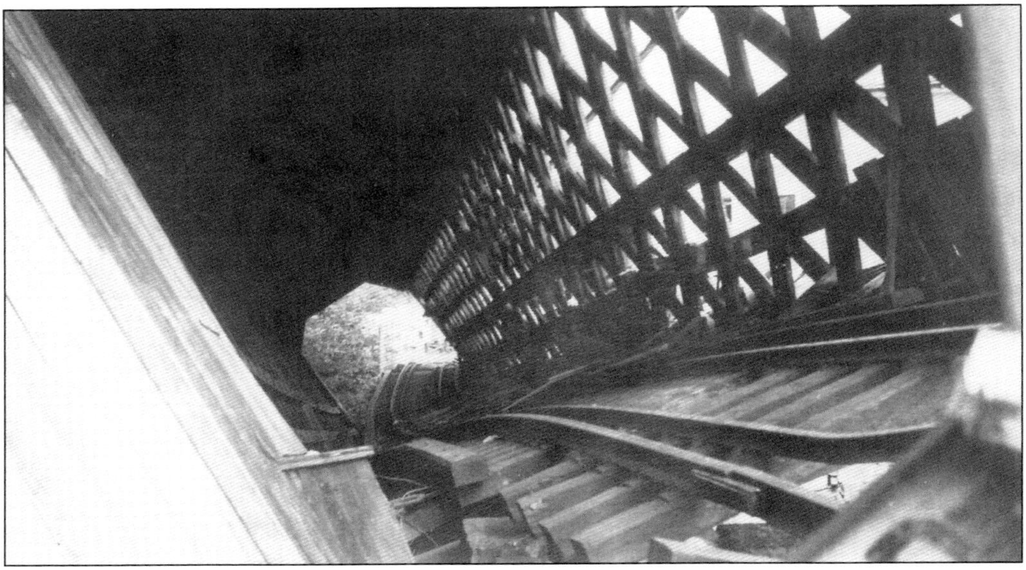

The strength of the steel railroad tracks tethering the covered railroad bridge kept it from being swept downstream by the flood waters in 1936. The flood left the Claremont and Hillsboro Railways, and many other lines as well, heavily damaged. The damage was such that they faced the possibility of being discontinued as people debated whether it was worth repairing the bridges and railroad tracks since the era of rail travel was inevitably coming to its end. However, Claremont had just finished paying the franchise and demanded that the repairs be made, including righting the railroad bridge in Contoocook, so that service could be restored. (Courtesy of Hopkinton Historical Society.)

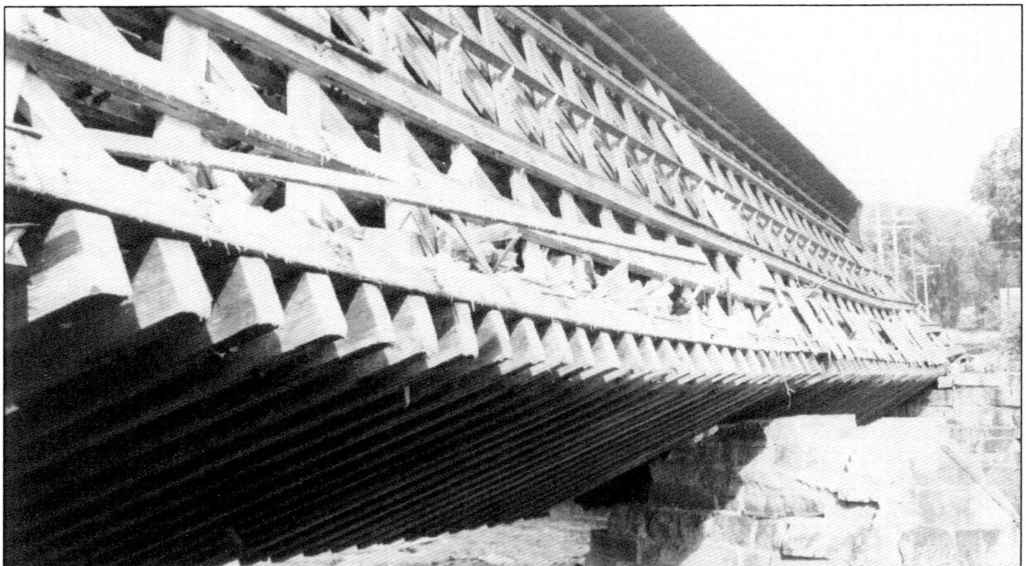

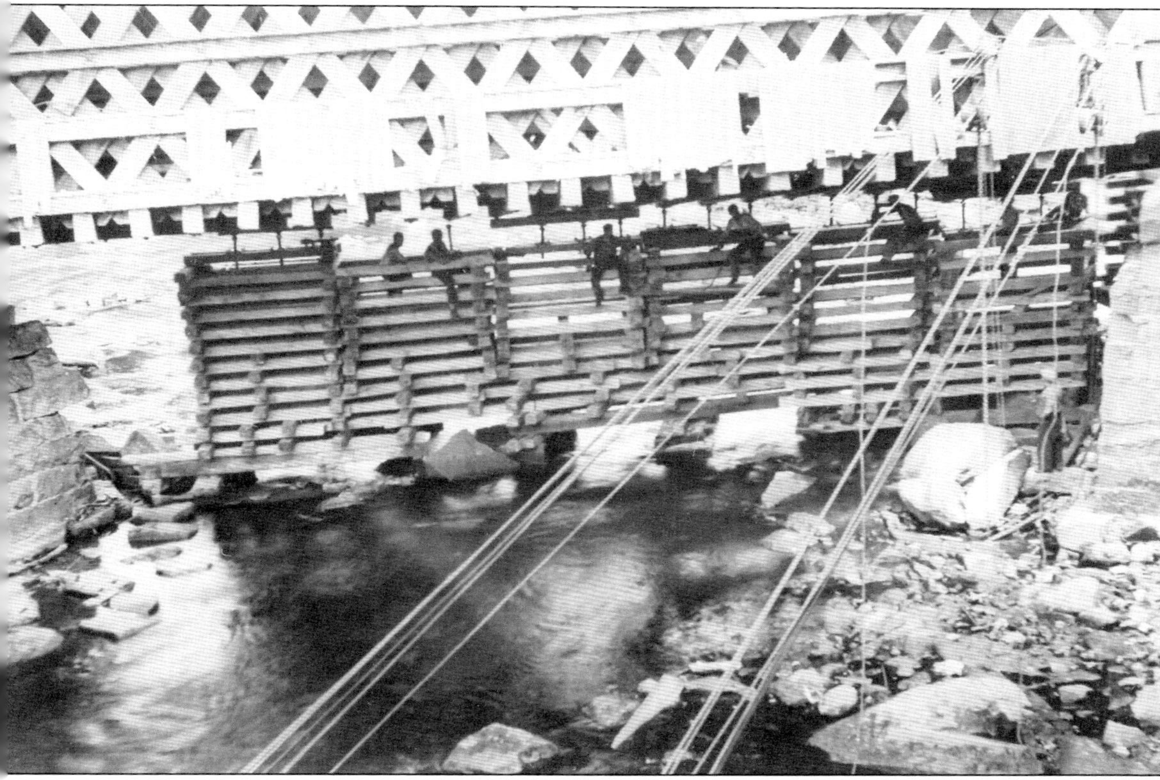

There was an urgency to repair the railroads and restore service as quickly as possible following the flood. In this photograph, workers have secured the bridge with cables as they work to set it upright again. Two years later, in 1938, the bridge would once again be tested by flood waters, and although it tipped again, it remained steadfast. Today this bridge, built in 1889, is the oldest surviving covered railroad bridge in the United States and is listed in the National Register of Historic Places. The bridge is largely unchanged, with only slight modifications being made. In 2006, the bolsters were replaced for the first time since the hurricane of 1938 and the bed timbers were replaced by granite pedestals. In 2010, a sprinkler system, fire alarm system, and LED motion sensor lighting inside the bridge were added at an approximate cost of $123,300. (Courtesy of Hopkinton Historical Society.)

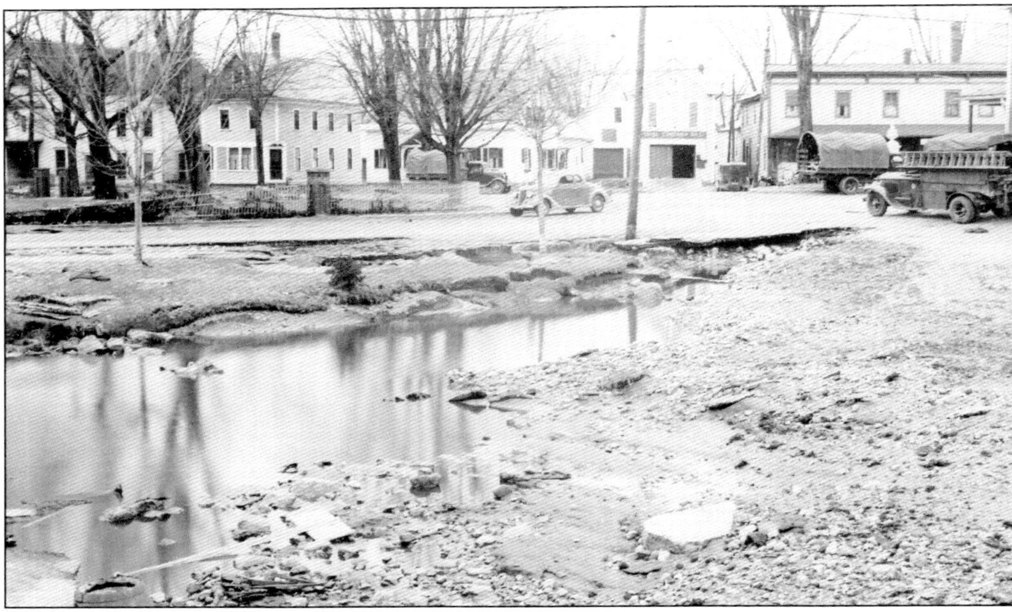

Land, roads, and foundations were eroded by the flood waters in 1936. Above, a photograph taken in the vicinity of the train depot looking toward Fountain Square shows roads and earth washed out by the waters. Street signs, debris, and even the fence of the Walter S. Davis home lay strewn on the ground and chunks of pavement are missing from the roadways. Below, the arduous task of reconstruction begins as men with dump trucks deliver fill to replace the ground that was washed away in front of the train depot. (Courtesy of Hopkinton Historical Society.)

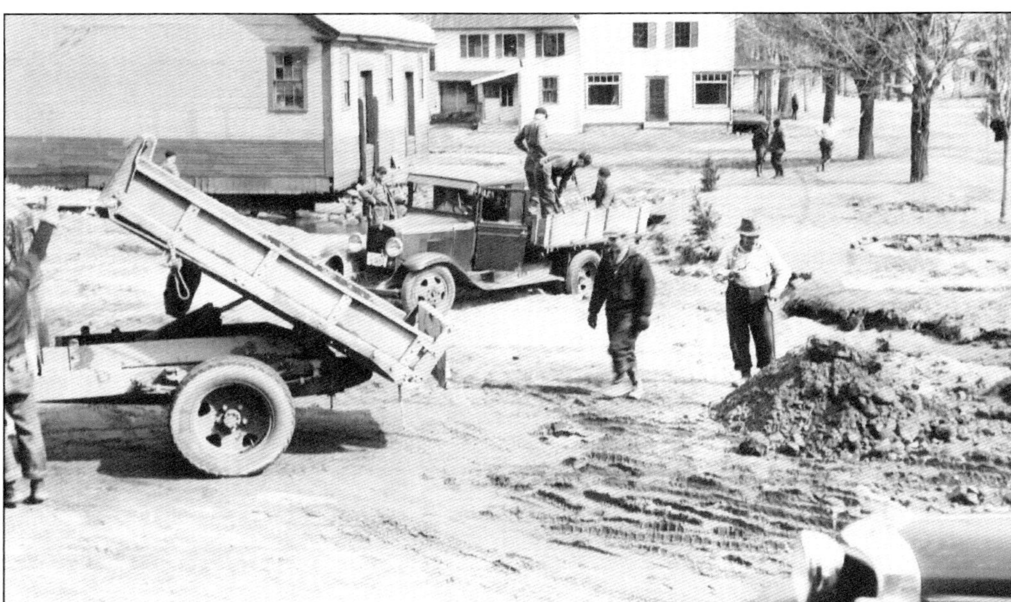

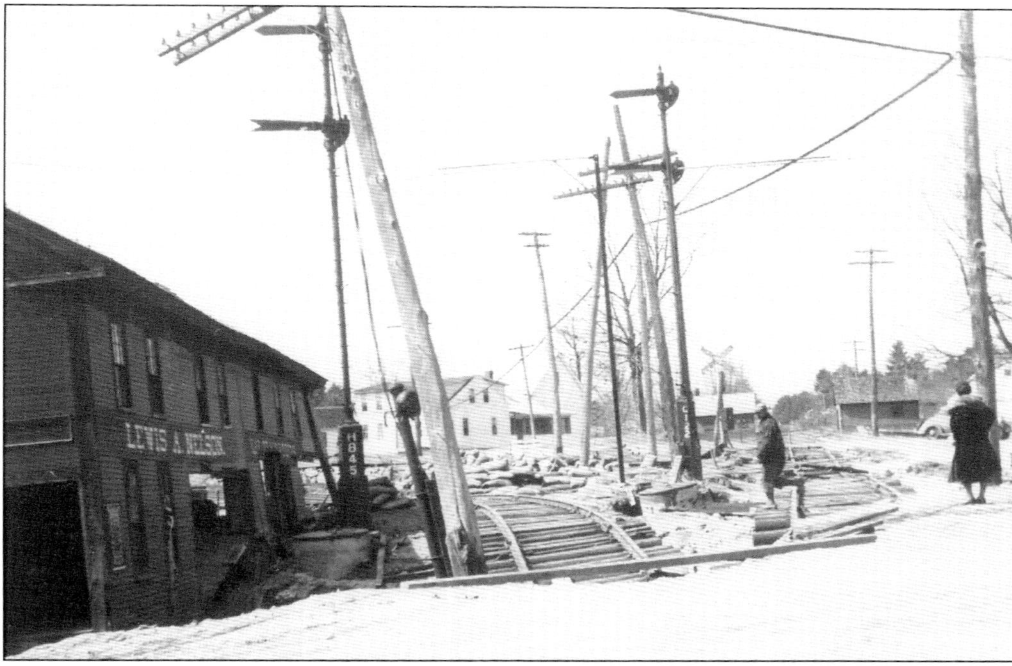

These photographs taken on March 29, 1936, show the massive destruction caused by the flood waters. Bags of grain from Nelson's grain mill were strewn all over the road and as far as the fields behind the house shown below on Park Avenue next to the bridge. The road in the foreground of the photograph above was washed away, as well as the earth beneath the railroad tracks. When dirt was brought to fill in the washed out area and make the road passable, the railroad tracks were buried three to four feet deep. (Courtesy of Hopkinton Historical Society.)

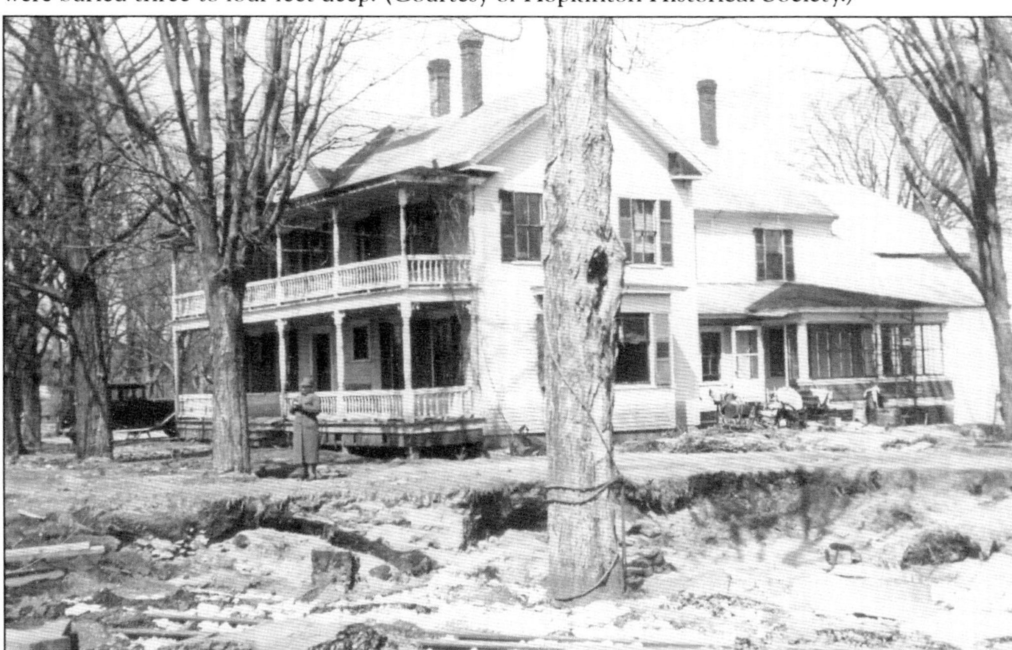

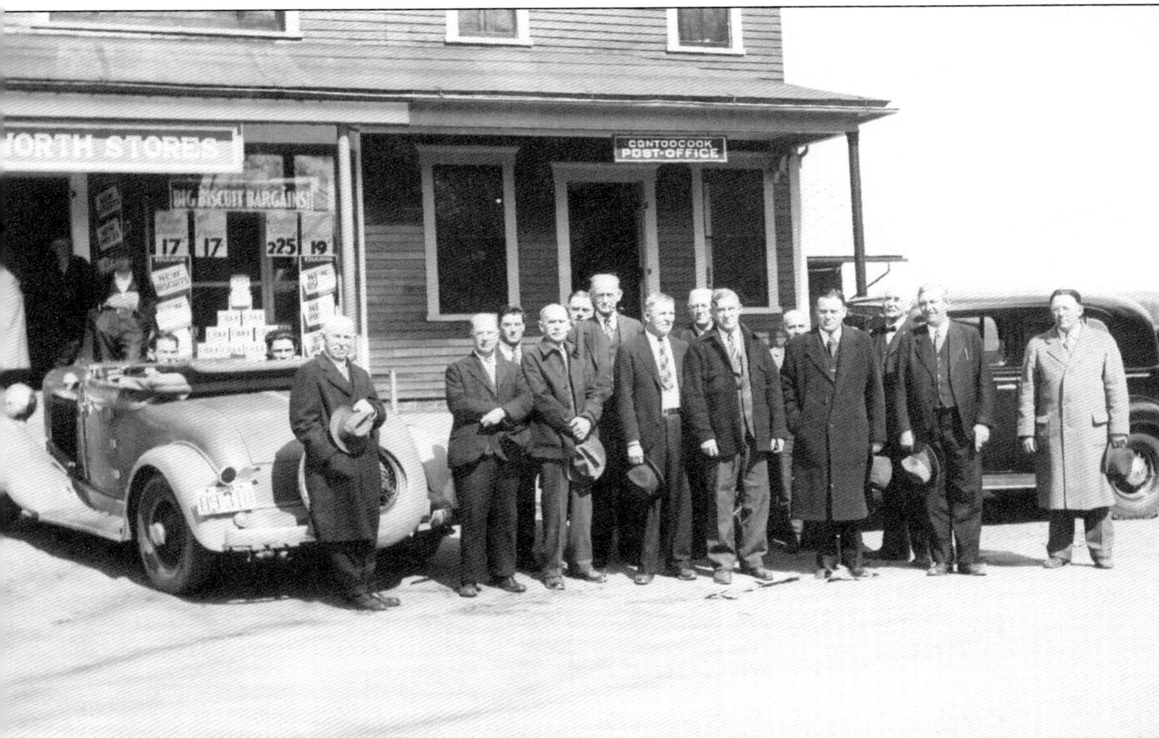

Gov. H. Styles Bridges visited Contoocook to view the damage caused by the flood in 1936. The state as a whole suffered incredible damages and the governor declared it the "worst disaster ever to befall the state of New Hampshire." Local businessmen and leaders posed with the governor in front of the Curtice Block in Fountain Square. Pictured from left to right are (first row) unidentified (leaning against the car), Charles George, unidentified, William Milton (deputy sheriff), unidentified, Lewis A. Nelson (town treasurer), Governor Bridges, John S. Ball (selectman), and Joseph Young (selectman); (second row) Neal Rice, Ralph Crawford, Arthur C. Huntoon (town clerk), Forest Gillingham (railroad agent), and unidentified. (Courtesy of Hopkinton Historical Society.)

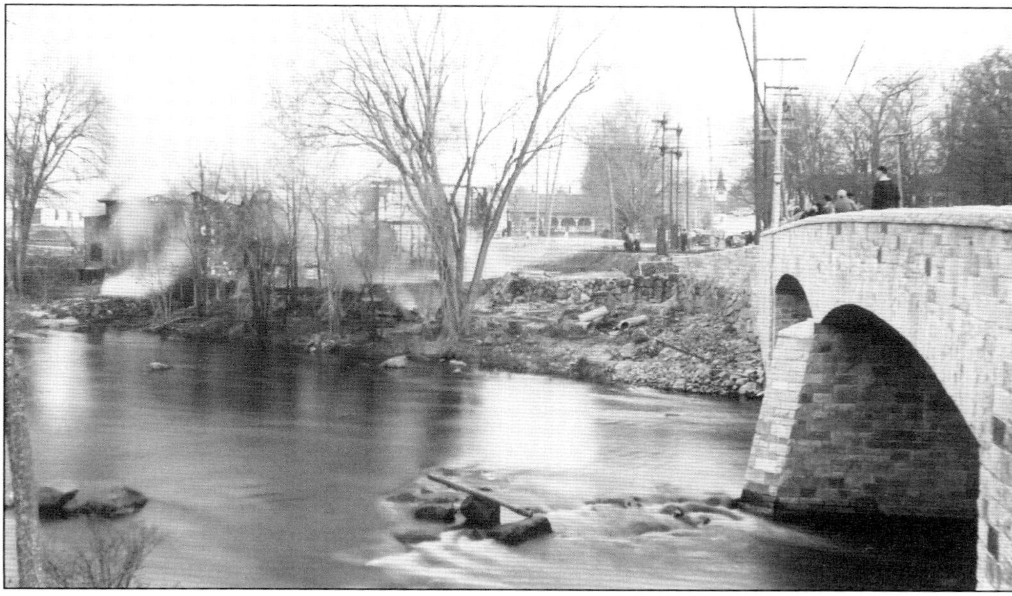

Shortly after the flood of 1936 damaged the grain mill owned by Lewis A. Nelson, the building suffered a final fatal blow when it burned to the ground. The building was originally built around 1835 by Hamilton E. Perkins, father of Comm. George Hamilton Perkins and owner of the manor adjacent to the building. In 1864, the building was owned by the family of Capt. Paul R. George and housed Jonathan M. and George W. Morrill's woolen mill. In these photographs, townspeople line the bridge and Pine Street to watch firefighters extinguish the flames. The grain mill was never rebuilt and the land is now the location of the Contoocook Fire Station. (Courtesy of Hopkinton Historical Society.)

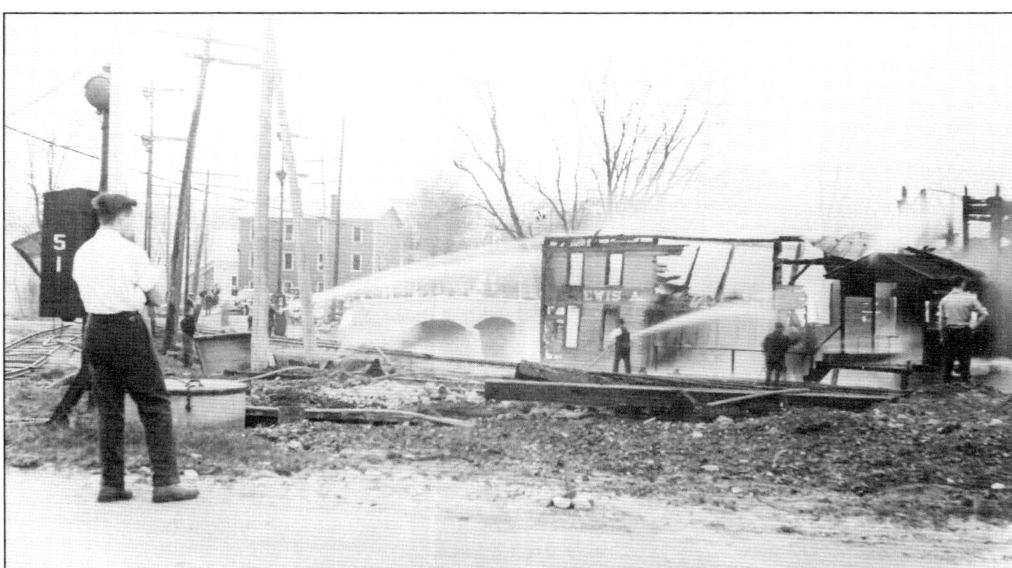

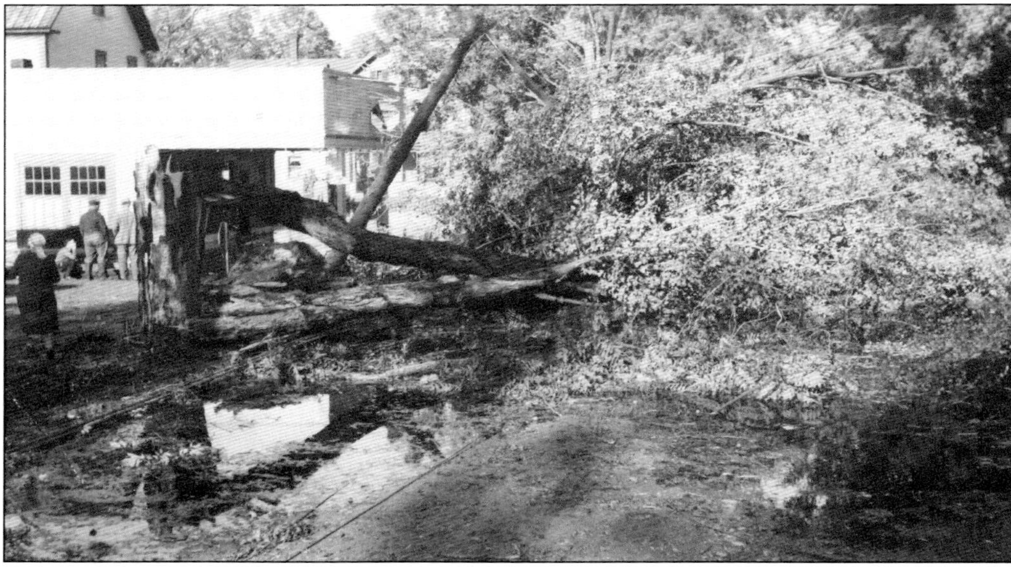

Just over two years after the devastation of the 1936 flood, the town suffered another natural disaster with the 1938 hurricane. Known as the "Long Island Express," the storm hit the night of September 21 and was what would now be identified as a category three hurricane. This was the first major hurricane to hit New England since 1869, with maximum sustained winds of approximately 120 miles per hour. Above, the high winds snapped large trees in front of the Contoocook Garage on Main Street. Below, flooding caused by the hurricane washed out Kearsarge Avenue and utility poles were bent or broken by the wind. (Courtesy of Hopkinton Historical Society.)

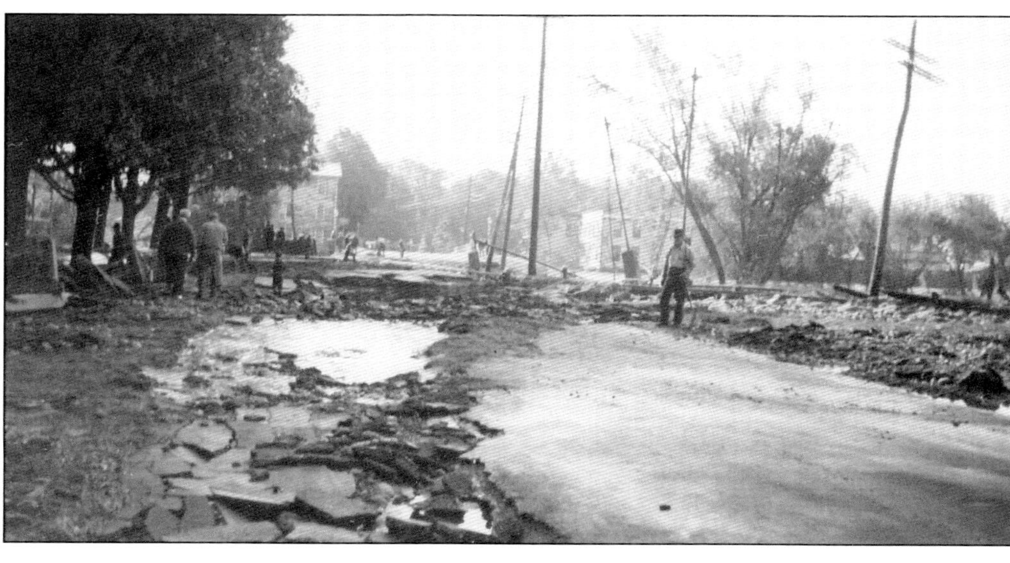

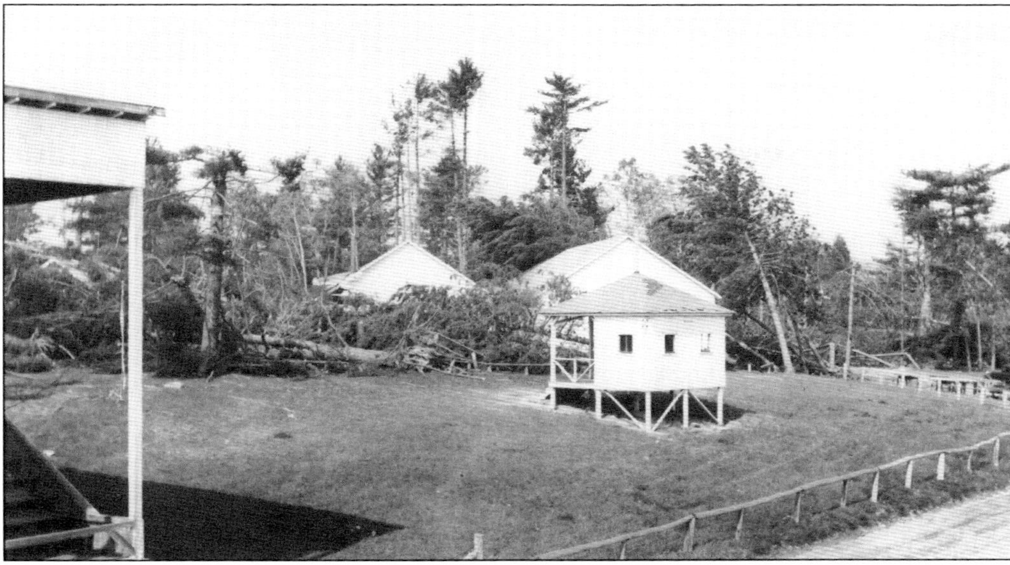

The 1938 hurricane knocked down trees and caused damage at the fair grounds, then located at George's Park. The storm devastated the forests of the Northeast and blew down an estimated two billion trees. With many area residents at risk of losing sizeable sums in ruined timber, resident George M. Putnam, president of the New Hampshire Farm Bureau and a director of the National Farm Bureau, asked Pres. Franklin Roosevelt to assist in a plan to float the fallen timbers in lakes, ponds, and rivers until they could be milled into lumber and sold. (Courtesy of Hopkinton Historical Society.)

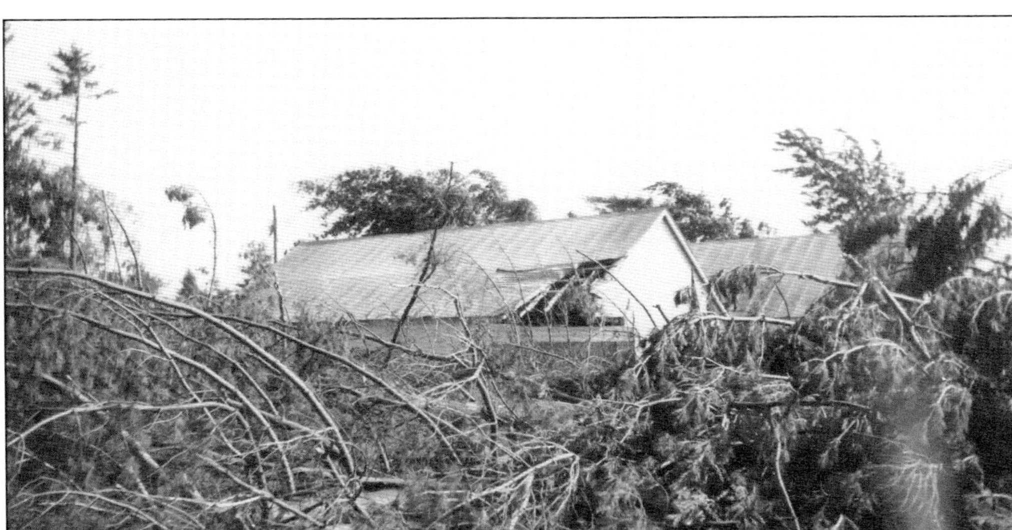

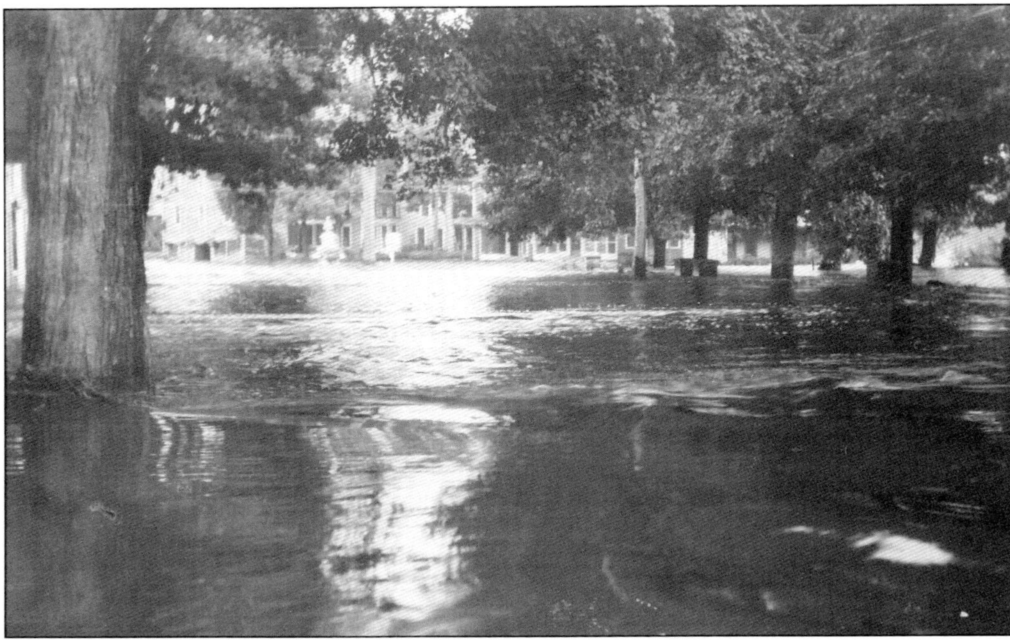

Although the 1938 hurricane tracked farther west through Vermont, the winds and rain caused incredible damage in New Hampshire and killed 13 people. The flooding it caused in Contoocook was reminiscent of the 1936 event, but did not reach the same level. Above, a view down Maple Street shows Fountain Square once again submerged in several feet of water. Below, Cedar Street suffers more flooding from the heavy rainfalls of the hurricane. Plans for creating some sort of flood control had been discussed for years and the hurricane of 1938 provided the necessary momentum for a flood control project. (Courtesy of Hopkinton Historical Society.)

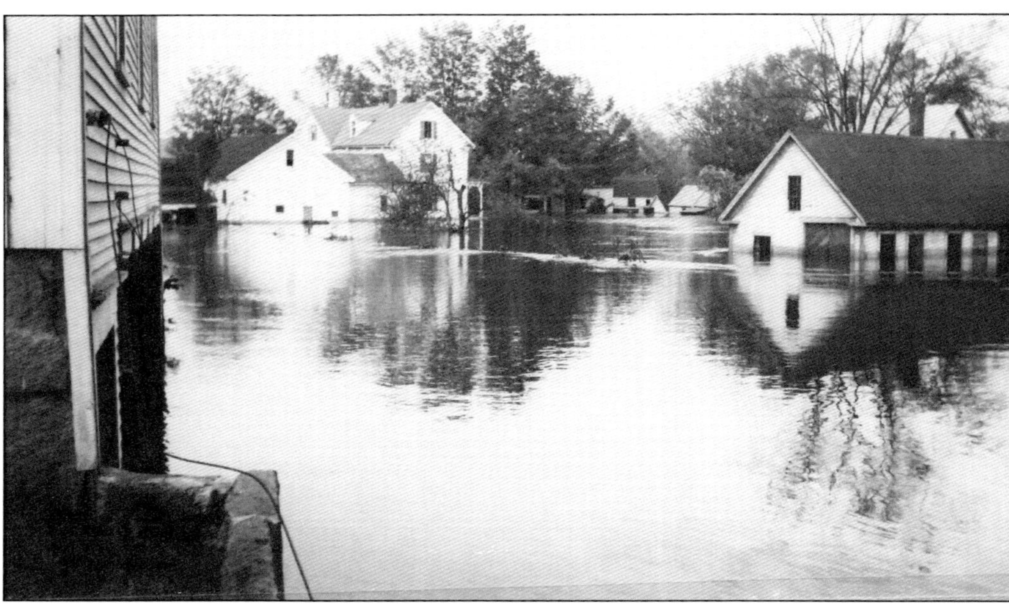

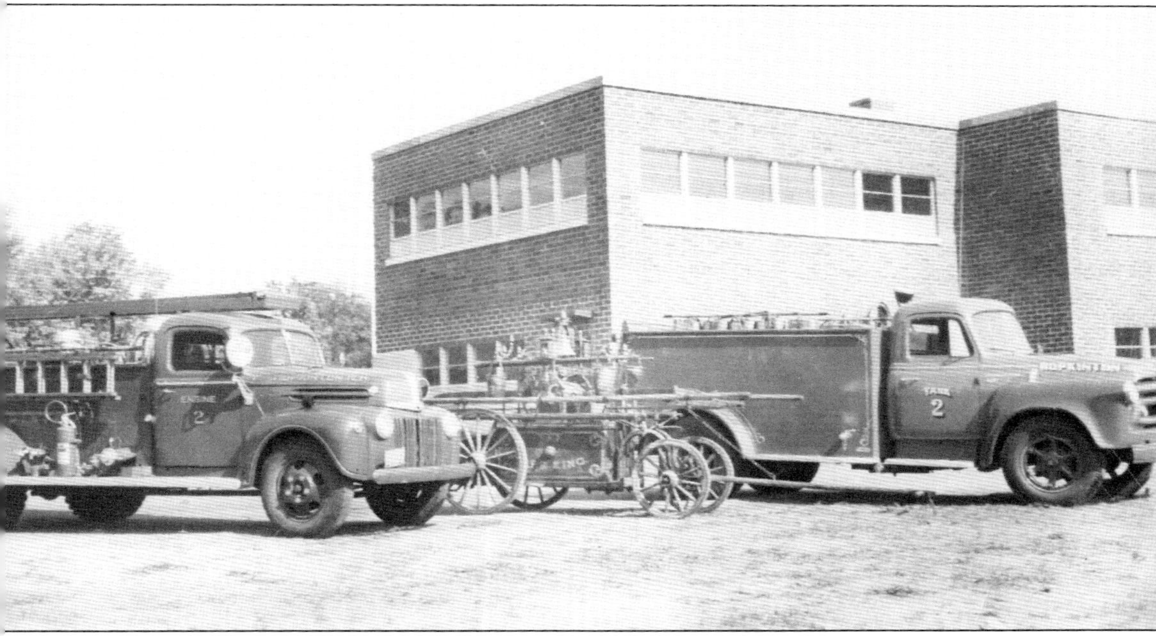

A progression of fire pumpers is displayed in front of the Harold Martin School in this undated photograph. Hopkinton's fire department began when the Hopkinton Aqueduct was created in 1840 with water feeding two large underground tanks installed in the village square. In 1872, a chemical fire engine was purchased by subscription and put into service. A local fire precinct was formed in Hopkinton called the Fire King Engine Company, named after the apparatus seen between the two fire trucks. In 1928, a Maxim fire truck was acquired, the first since the purchase of the *Fire King Two* in 1886. The Contoocook Village Engine Company was incorporated in 1831. The village purchased its first mechanized engine, a Shippet pumper ladder truck, 100 years later. In 1947, Contoocook and Hopkinton fire precincts were merged to create the Hopkinton Fire Department. (Courtesy of Hopkinton Historical Society.)

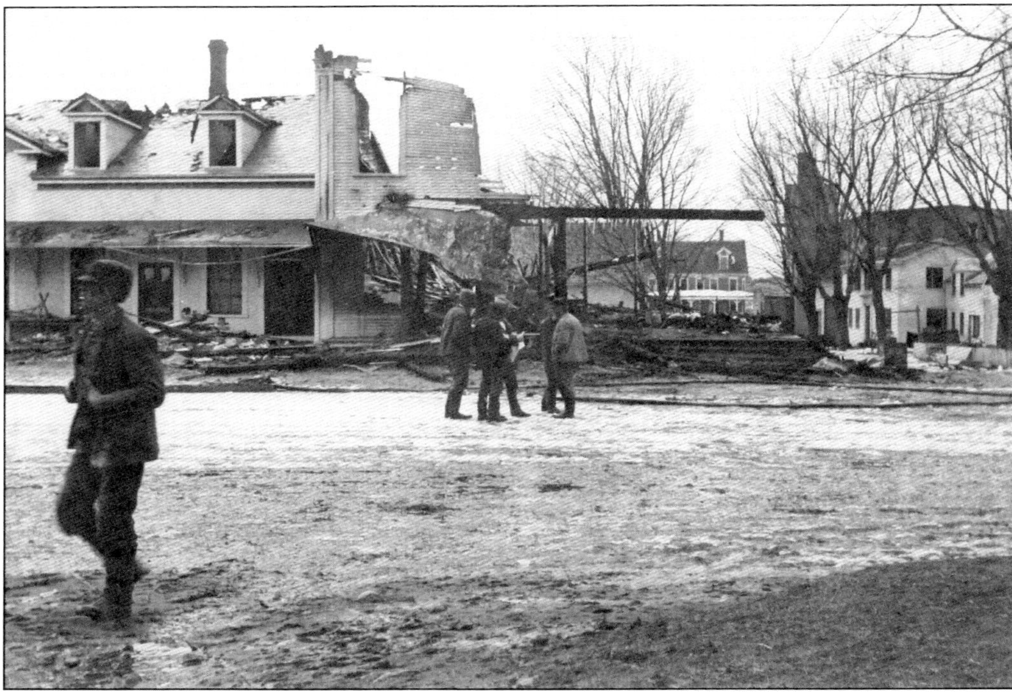

In March 1900, a fire consumed all of the Bailey Block except for the ell on the western corner of Fountain Square in Contoocook. The fire spread to a home across the street on Cedar Street and the store next to it as well as the corner of the covered highway bridge. Above, men stand in front of the burned-out Bailey Block. The ell of the building was saved but badly damaged. The sign for the undertaker can still be seen on the door to the left. Below, townspeople view the damage while debris still smolders. (Photographs by Leown Kelley; courtesy of Hopkinton Historical Society.)

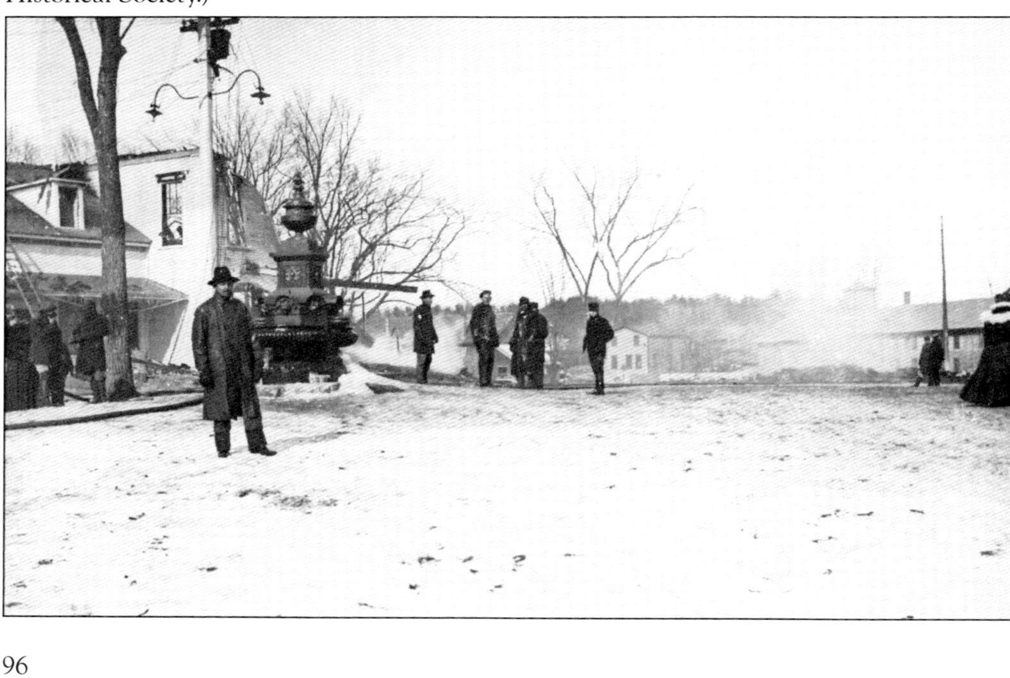

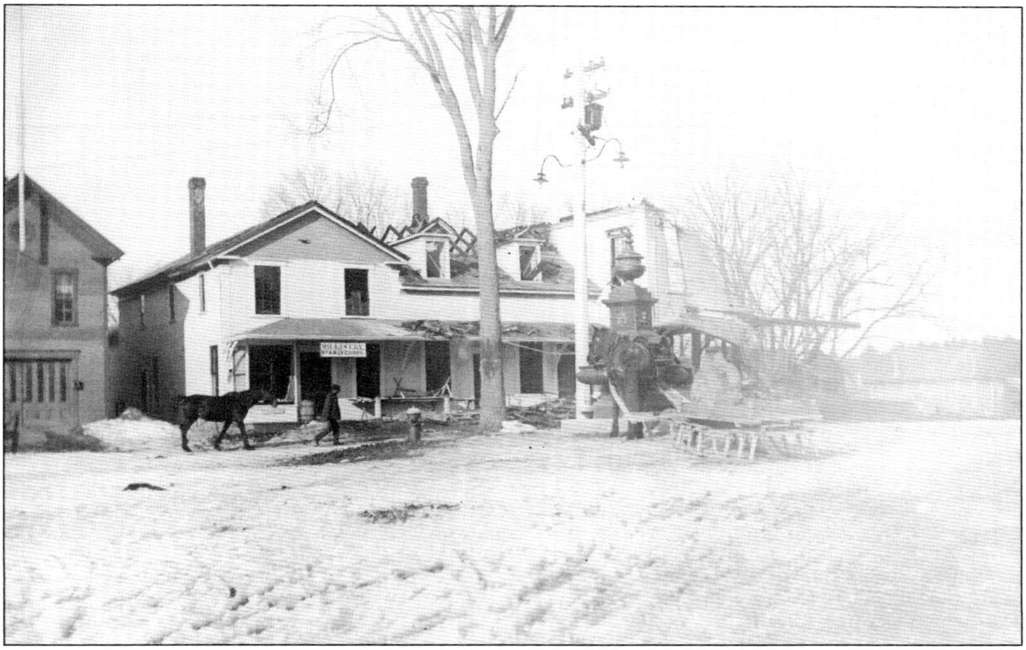

The Contoocook Village Engine Company was incorporated in 1831 and was considered a fire precinct in 1864. Prior to 1889, the means of fire protection consisted of a hand tub and the river. Above, a horse takes a drink at the town fountain in front of the burned-out remains of the Bailey Block in 1900. Below, a view of the damage looking northeast from Cedar Street. The fire destroyed two buildings on the left and the large block on the right. (Photographs by Leown Kelley; courtesy of Hopkinton Historical Society.)

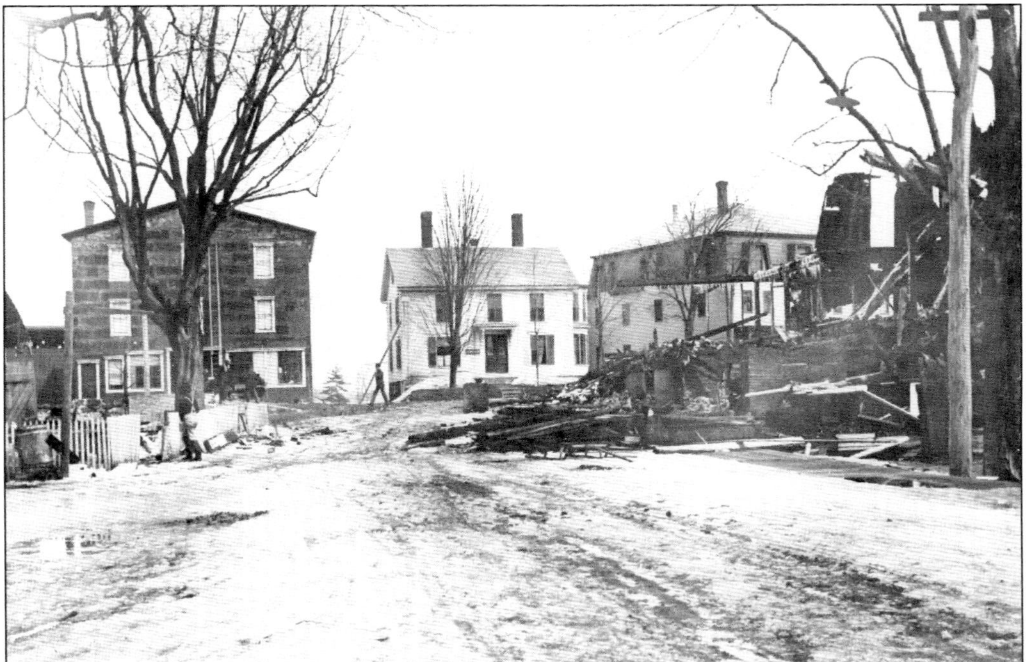

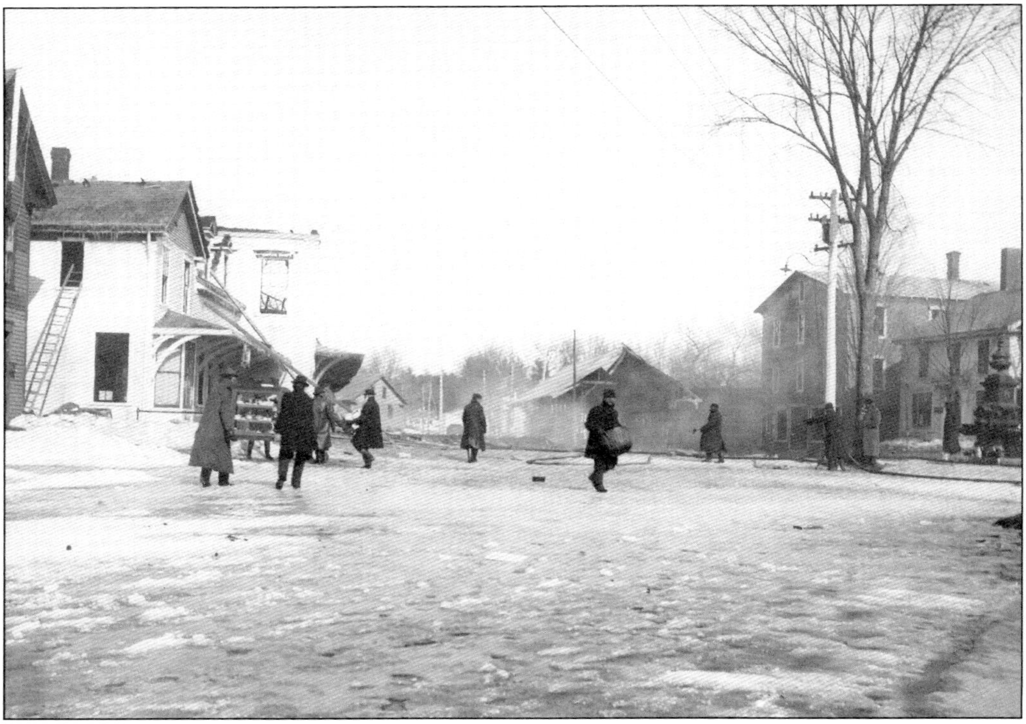

The photograph above shows men salvaging items from the stores that remained standing after the March 1900 fire in Contoocook, including a millinery shop on the southern end of the Bailey Block that was largely spared from the fire. Hoses can be seen on the ground and attached to a hydrant. In 1889, a water line was laid from Bear Pond, five miles west of the village, to supply the hydrant, and hoses were stockpiled around the village. Below is a view of the destruction from across the river. The Jones Block and the house next to it were a total loss. (Photographs by Leown Kelley; courtesy of Hopkinton Historical Society.)

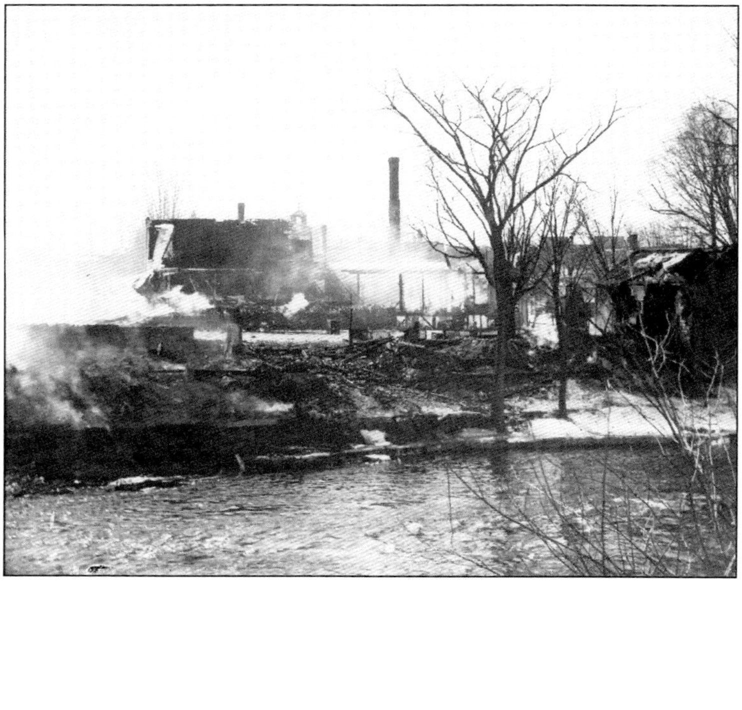

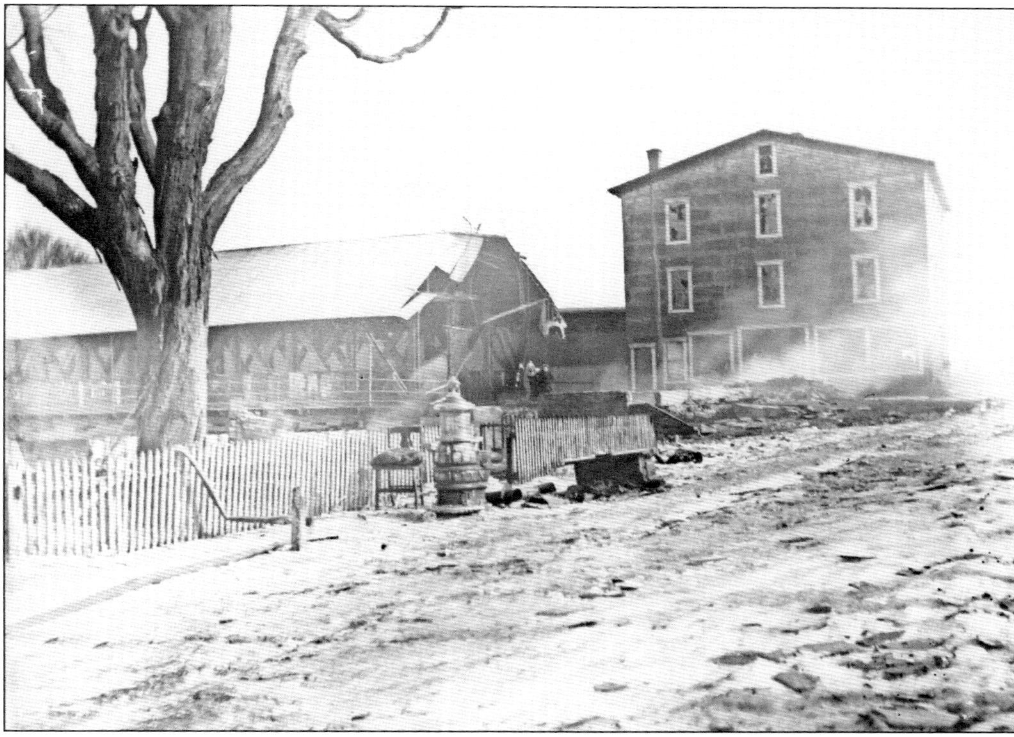

Above on the left, the Jones Building that once housed George Ketchum's stove shop is reduced to smoldering ashes in 1900. His father, Rev. Silas Ketchum, was a founder and president of the New Hampshire Antiquarian Society in 1873. The society's collection of books, specimens, and other historic memorabilia were kept in several rooms of this building. Fortunately, the society (later known as Hopkinton Historical Society) and its collections moved to a new location, the William H. Long Memorial Building in Hopkinton in 1890. Below, a safe salvaged from one of the destroyed buildings sits on Cedar Street. (Photographs by Leown Kelley; courtesy of Hopkinton Historical Society.)

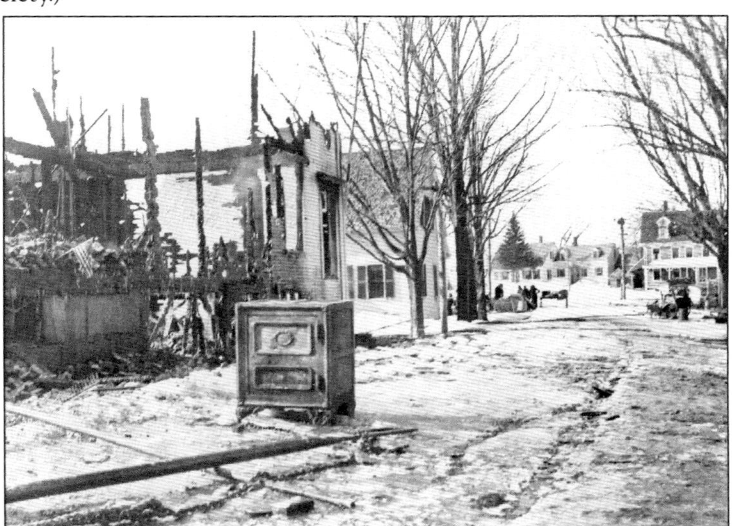

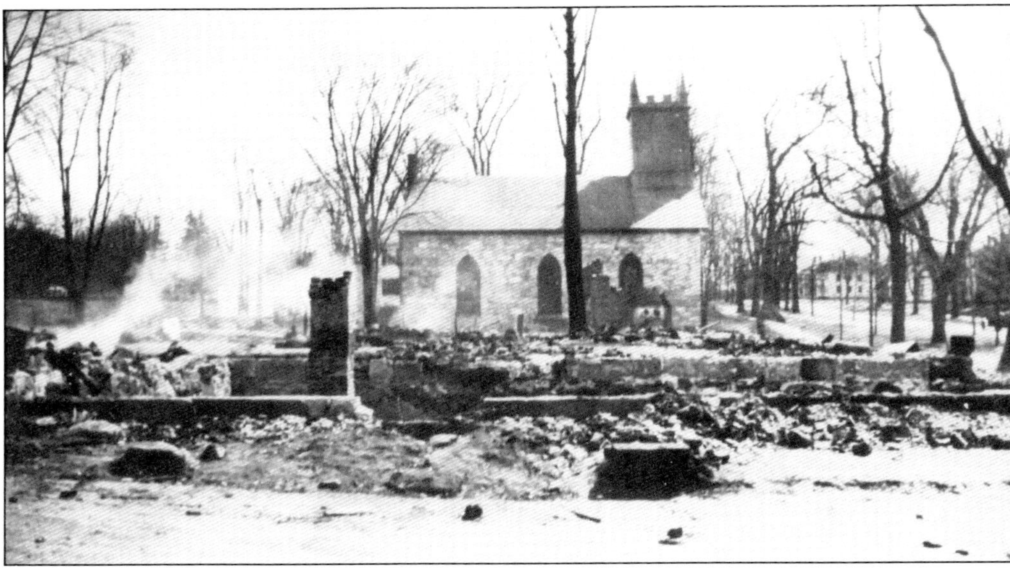

At 4:00 on the morning of April 10, 1927, a fire broke out in the Aiken house, the first house on the right on Briar Hill Road in Hopkinton Village. The fire quickly spread to the village store and down Main Street. It continued and consumed the post office building and a home belonging to Dunbar and Goodspeed, which was located in the historic Wiggins Tavern building, as well as the Lafayette Elm located in front of the house. Fortunately the fire stopped before it damaged St. Andrew's Episcopal Church. Above, the burned remains of the old Wiggins Tavern and post office continue to smolder after the devastating fire. Below, a temporary store is erected near the burned out remains of the four buildings. (Courtesy of Hopkinton Historical Society.)

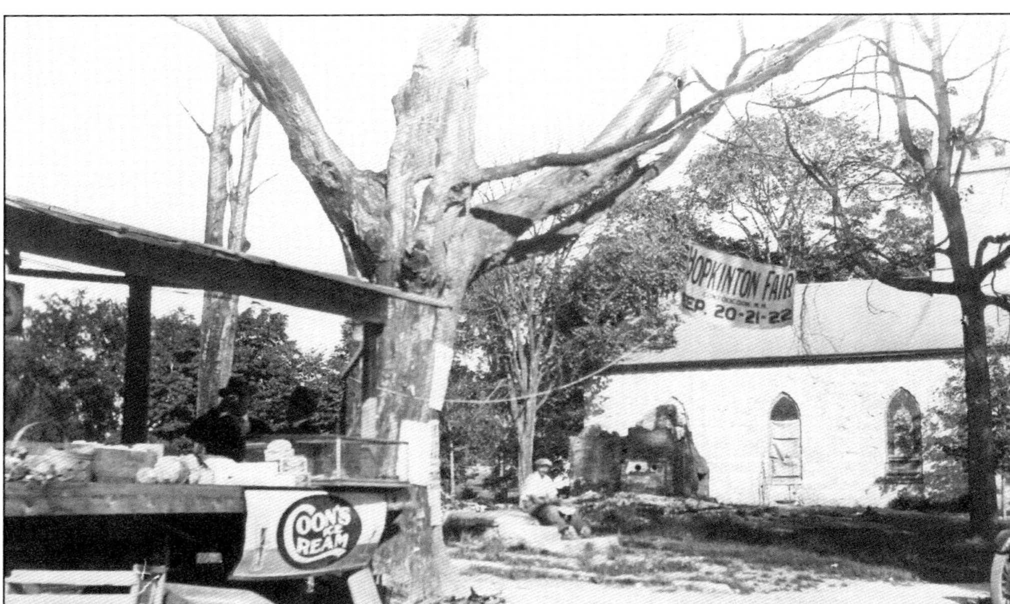

Five

Schools and Churches

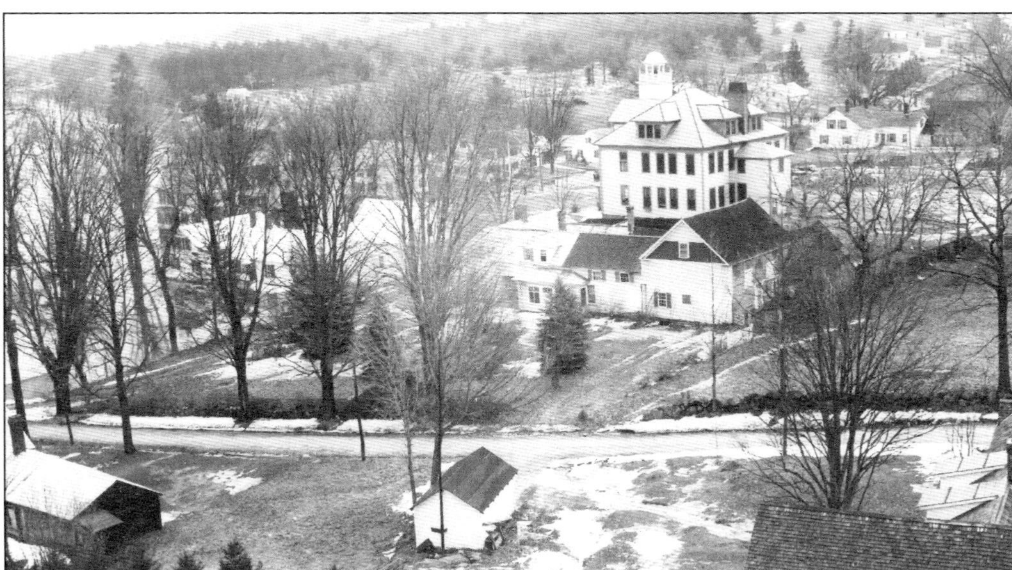

A photograph from March 1936 shows Contoocook Village's school. Prior to 1930, the school accommodated students in grade school through high school. Constructed in 1903 next to the Freewill Baptist Church on Main Street, it housed students until 1953, when a new high school was built and the building was torn down. (Courtesy of Hopkinton Historical Society.)

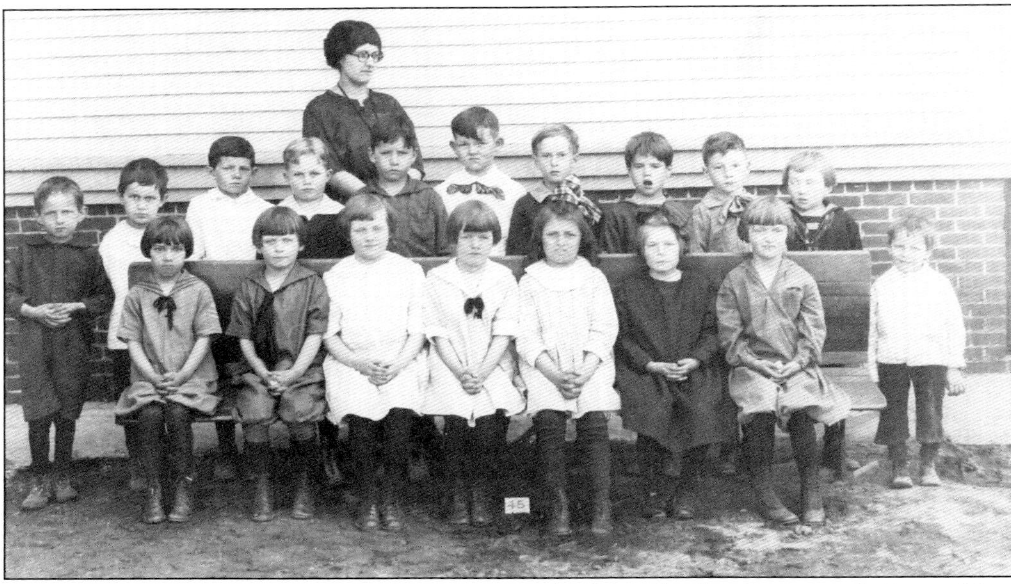

Charlotte Norris's first grade class in 1921 poses outside of the school in Contoocook. Pictured from left to right are (first row) Gertrude Emerson, Ray Pepler, Christine Nelson, Virginia Symonds, Margaret Davis, Helen Krzyzaniak, Helen Harlow, and Albert Kay; (second row) ? Kay, Les Elliott, Eugene Melonson, Ernest Bergstrom, Fred Sawtell, Francis Mitchell, Ben Wescott, Leland Bohanan, George Libby, and Raymond Clough. (Courtesy of Hopkinton Historical Society.)

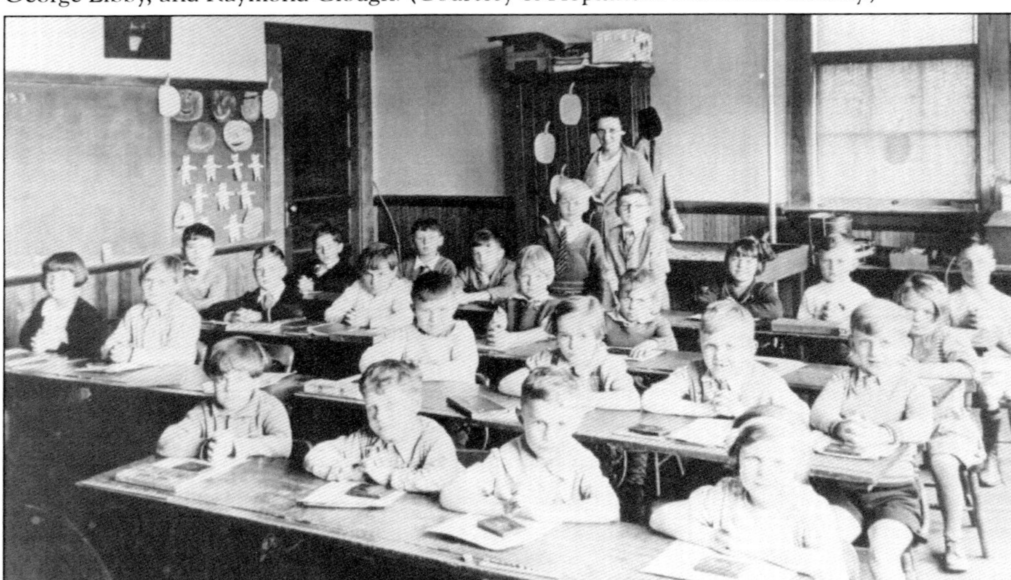

Teacher Dorothy Bangs stands with her first and second grade class at the Contoocook Village school in 1933. The high school students studied on the second and third floor and the younger children took classes on the first floor. Advanced courses included studies in agriculture and home economics. Students who arrived by horse and buggy would stable them in the Baptist church sheds next door while West Hopkinton students could take the train to Contoocook at a special reduced rate. (Courtesy of Barbara Brown Carpenter.)

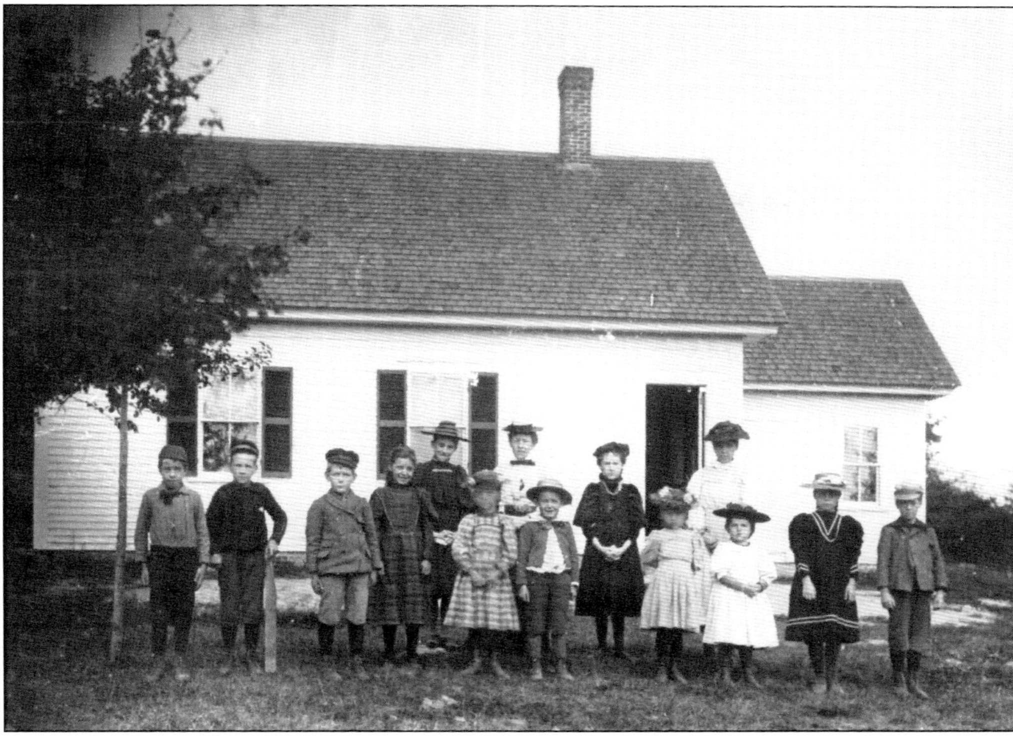

In 1877 there were 22 district schools in Hopkinton. By 1914, only four one-room schools remained, plus the grade schools in Contoocook and Hopkinton. This photograph of the second Putney Hill School shows Flora Clough Putnam's class around 1900. (Courtesy of Hopkinton Historical Society.)

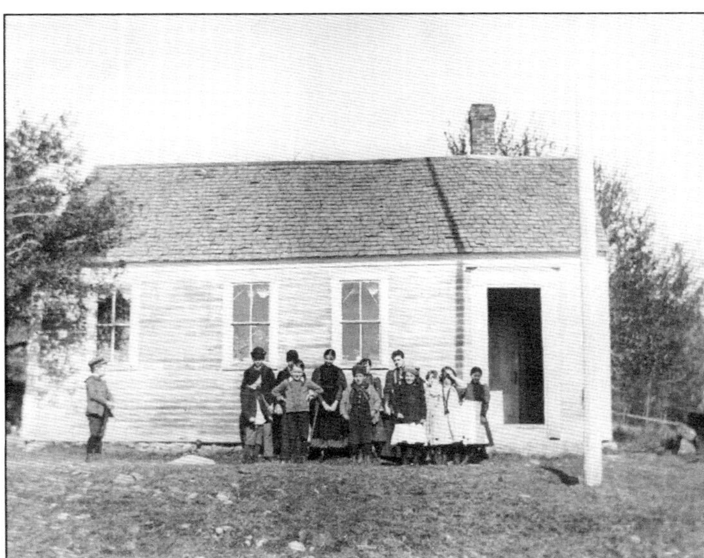

A picture of the students of the Putney Hill School House taken in 1896 shows, from left to right, (first row) Arthur Hunt, Walter Burbank, Francis Clough, Ernest Perry, Edna Perry, Helen Burbank, and Edith Rollins; (second row) Ira Putney, Fred Putney, Alice Rollins, Bertha Perry, Bessie Hoyt (teacher), and Edith Hunt. (Photograph by Leown Kelley; courtesy of Hopkinton Historical Society.)

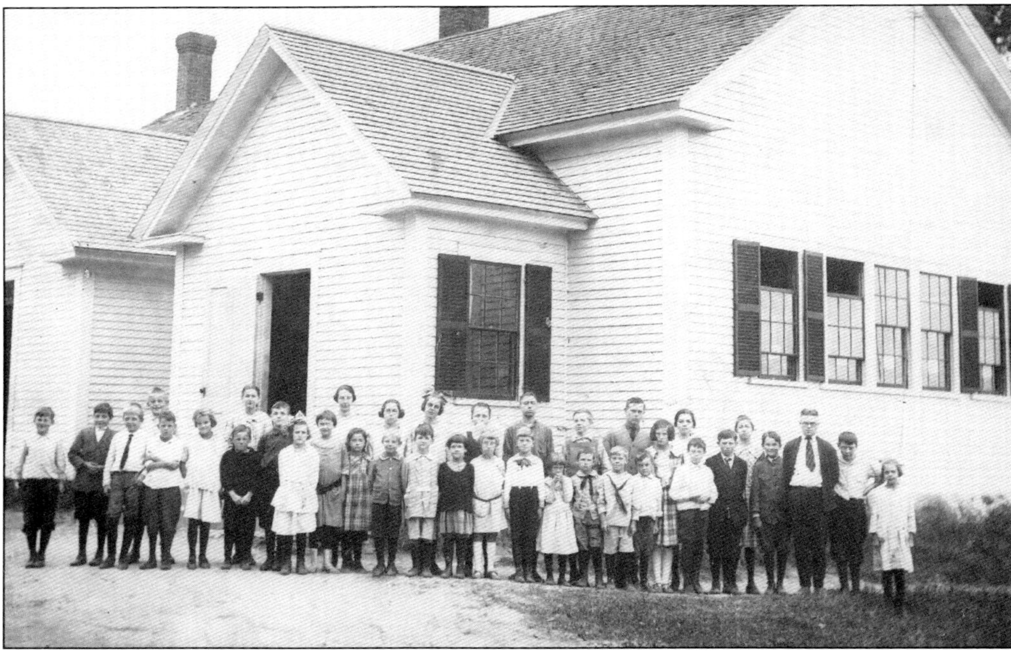

In 1826, Dr. Ebenezer Lerned sparked a movement to establish the Hopkinton Academy in Hopkinton Village. The school opened in the spring of 1827 with 47 male students and 26 female students. It occupied the second floor of the old court house and successfully grew in popularity. By 1835, it had 162 students. On March 29, 1873, the old courthouse was destroyed by a fire, and with it the academy. This photograph is of the Hopkinton Village School located northwest of the square. (Courtesy of Hopkinton Historical Society.)

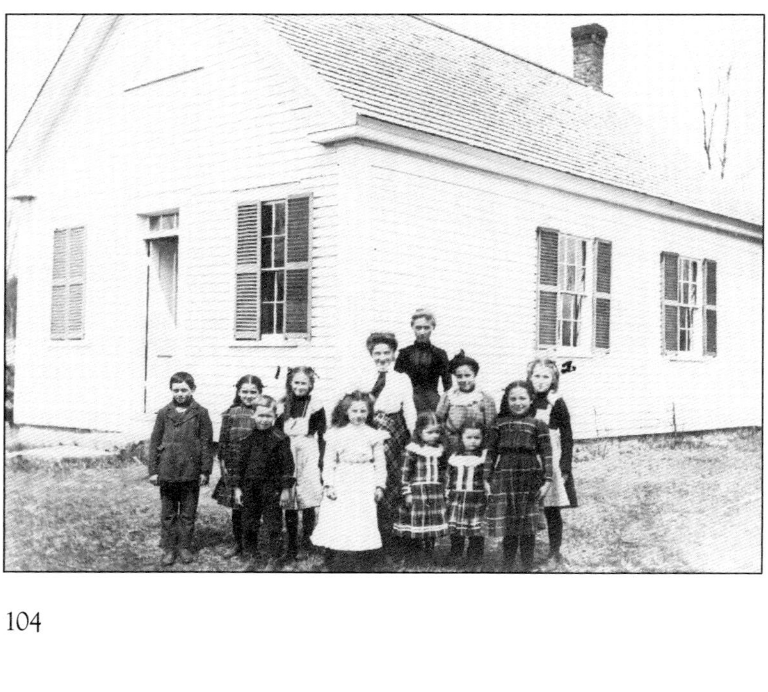

Students pose along with their teacher, Clara Straw, in front of the South Road School in Hopkinton. Schools were placed strategically so the students wouldn't need to walk more than a mile and a half to school. The students were taught together in the same room regardless of age. (Courtesy of Hopkinton Historical Society.)

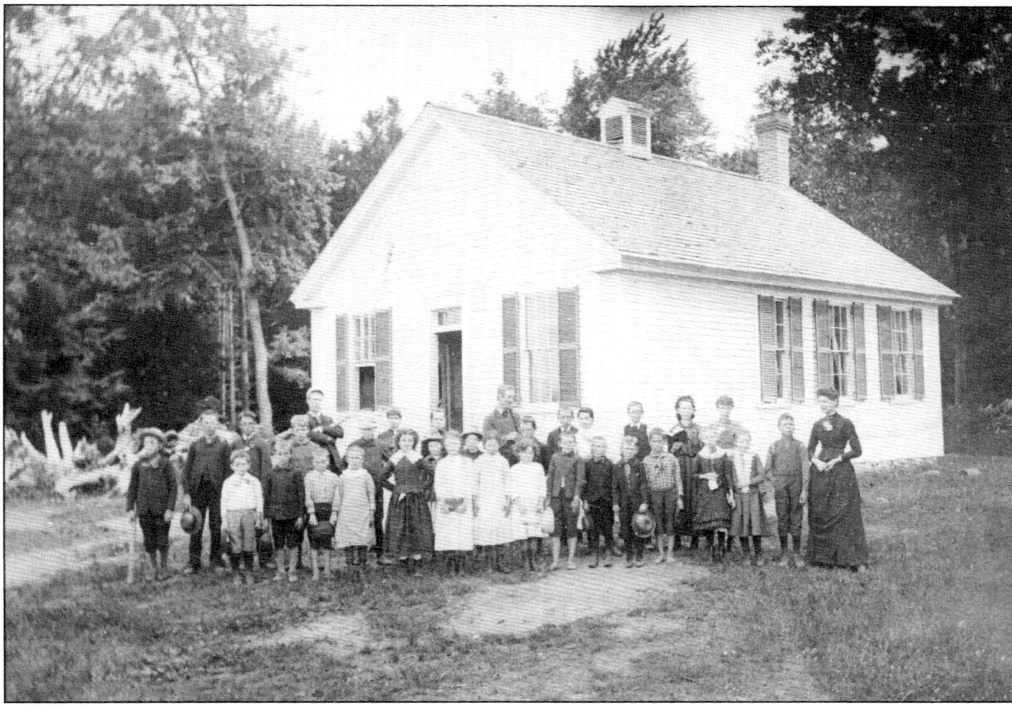

The District No. 20 School, also called the North Contoocook School (seen here in a photograph dated from 1889), was located about a quarter of a mile from Contoocook Village on Kearsarge Avenue next to the former St. Mary's Catholic Church. When it no longer served as a school house, it was used as a cottage. The old school has been enlarged and can still be seen today. (Courtesy of Hopkinton Historical Society.)

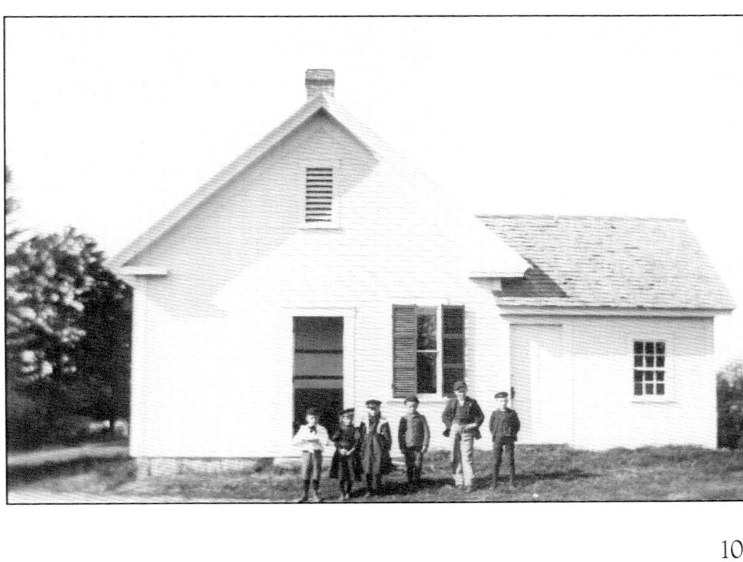

Students pose for this photograph outside of the Jewett Road School in Hopkinton. In 1936, the last two remaining rural schools—West Hopkinton School and the Main Road School—closed, and the era of the one-room schoolhouses came to a close in Hopkinton. (Courtesy of Hopkinton Historical Society.)

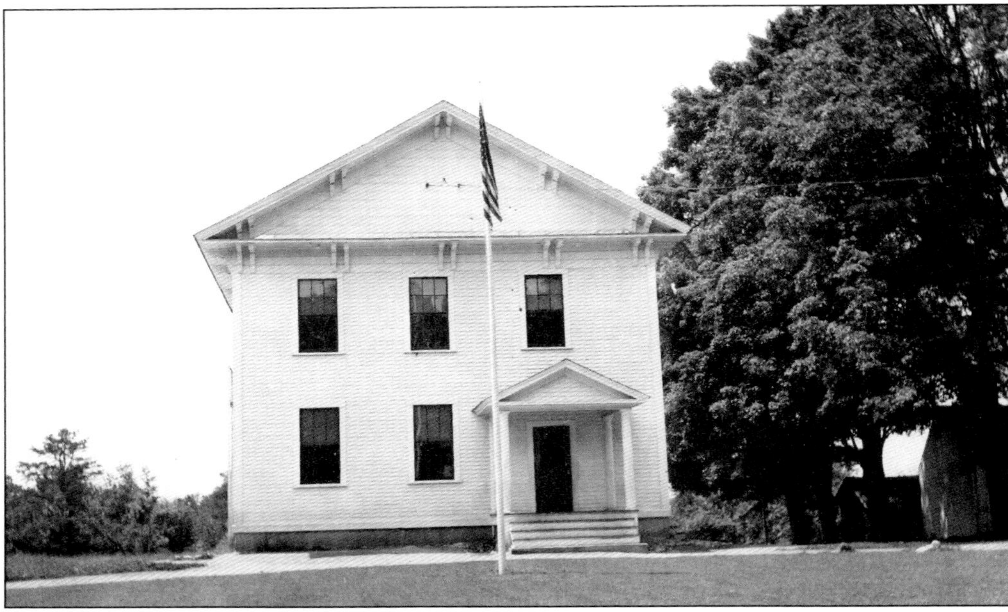

The Contoocook Academy, above, was built in 1856 under the control of the Swedenborgian Church on Maple Street and was funded largely by subscription. When it offered its first term that fall, 80 pupils attended the school. The two-story building contained "Academy Hall" on the second floor, and drawing and recitation rooms on the ground floor. In later years it was used as a rooming house, and in 1930 it was remodeled to serve as a school again when the lower grades from the village school on Main Street were moved to this location. Eventually the school was torn down and Maple Street School was built on the site in 1960, pictured below. (Courtesy of Hopkinton Historical Society.)

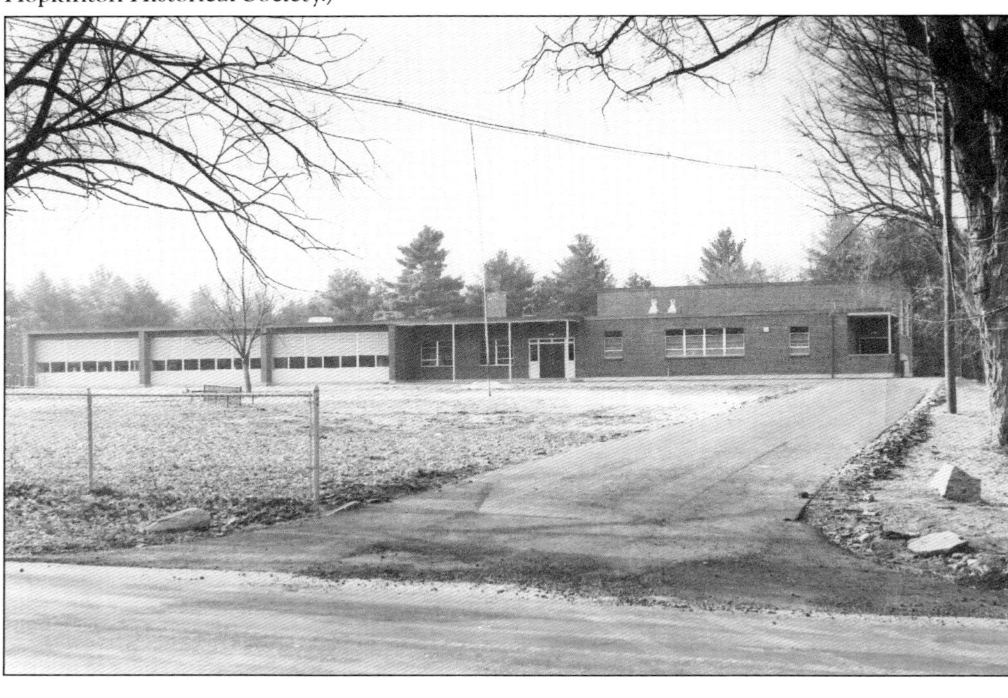

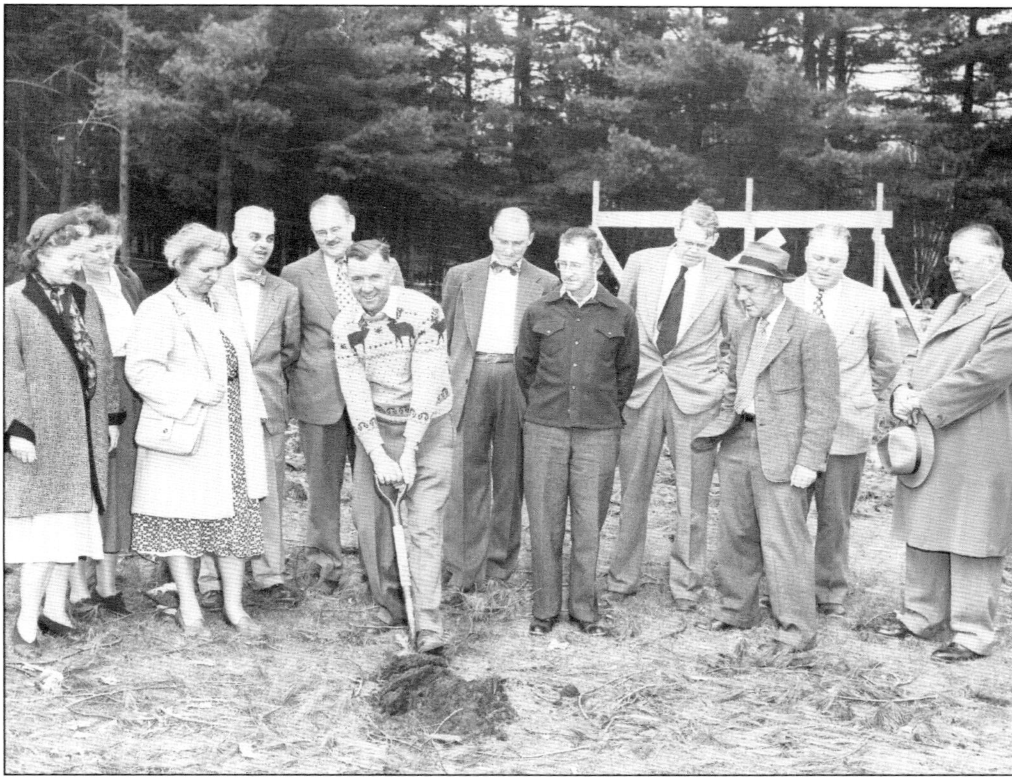

Ground breaking for the Hopkinton High School in 1953 is shown here. From left to right are Mrs. John Wheeler (president of the PTA), Jessie Gould, Gladys Heath, Dr. Pimentel, Dr. J. Howard Lightfoot, Harold Martin, Bert Astles, Earl Rice, William Sterling, Ed Leadbeater, Frank Kimball, and Joe Young. Once the new Hopkinton High School (below) was finished, the old high school was torn down, leaving no school on School Street. (Courtesy of Hopkinton Historical Society.)

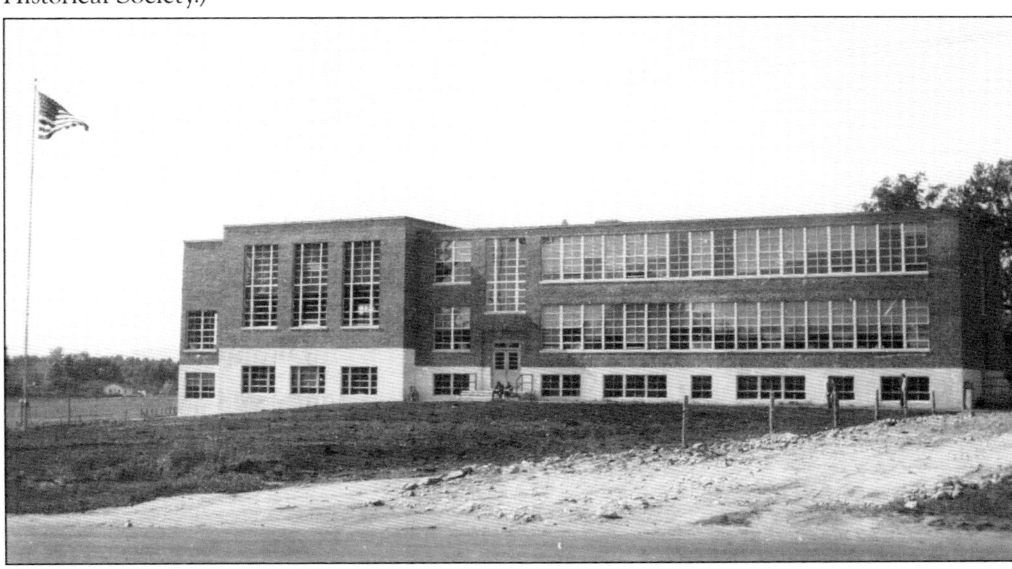

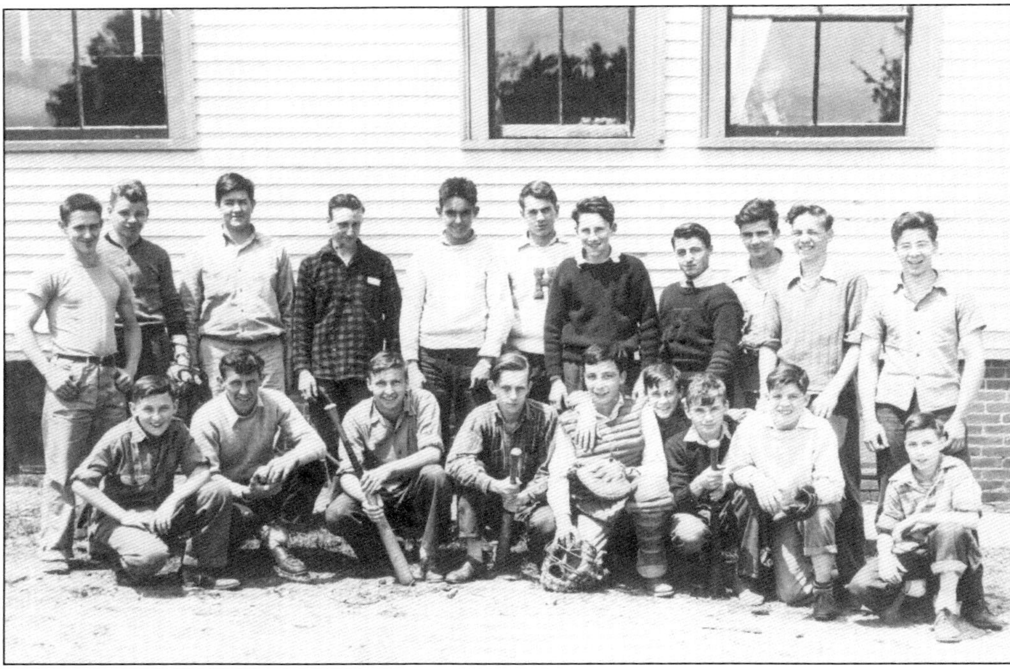

The Hopkinton High School baseball team poses in front of the old high school in the mid-1940s. Pictured from left to right are (first row) Nick Houston, Herrich Geer, James Stoddard, Raymond Aldrich, Bob Houston, Don Symonds, Dick Symonds, Bob Price, and Robin Reed; (second row) Joe Fellows, Gil Ward, Rod Call, Bill Cressy, Spig Holbrook, Jack Babson, Everett Houston, Lyle Holmes, Art Brown, Jack Quigley, and Ron ?. (Courtesy of Barbara Brown Carpenter.)

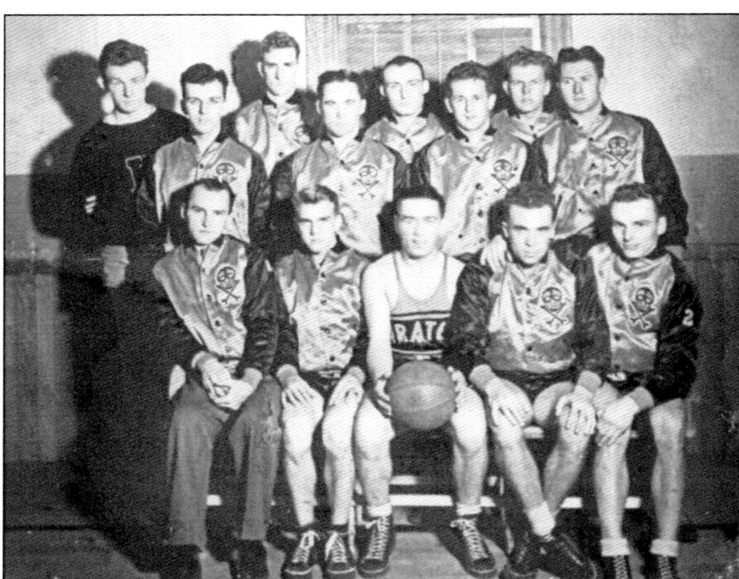

In the 1930s, the Hopkinton High School basketball team was known as the Pirates. Pictured here, from left to right, are (first row) Bert Astles, Raymond Estes, Norman Davis, Kennith Creighton, and Tom Astles; (second row) Bill Billings, Eldon Carruthers, Stan Walters, Win Merrill, Lyle Melcher, Jack Ball, and Bernard Foster. (Courtesy of William Stevens.)

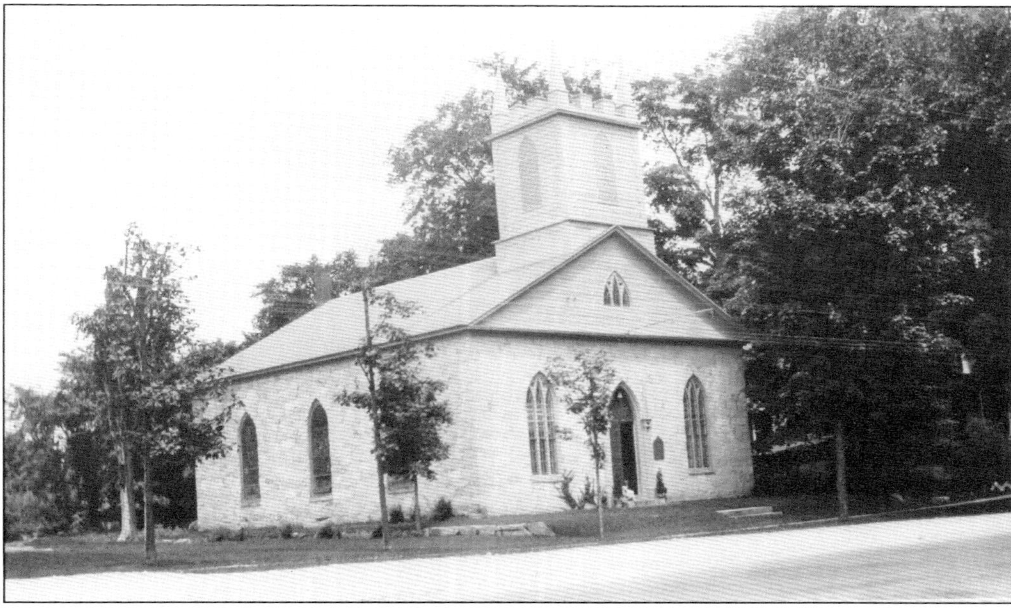

In 1803 an Episcopal society, called Christ Church, was organized and worshipped in the court house (the site of the current town hall). Under Moses B. Chase, a new parish was formed and incorporated in 1827 as St. Andrew's Church. The stone New England "Gothick" style building was built in 1828 from granite quarried in town. The original tower, shown above, was square with no spire. In 1929, a spire with four bells designed by Boston architects Cram and Ferguson was added. The Episcopal Parish House, located between the church and the town hall, was once the home of one of Hopkinton's first lawyers, Baruch Chase, and was built in 1790. (Courtesy of Hopkinton Historical Society.)

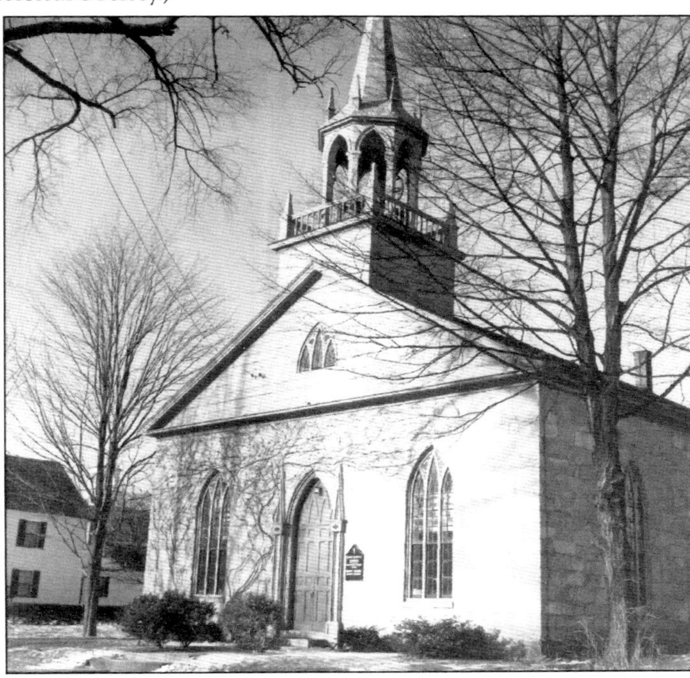

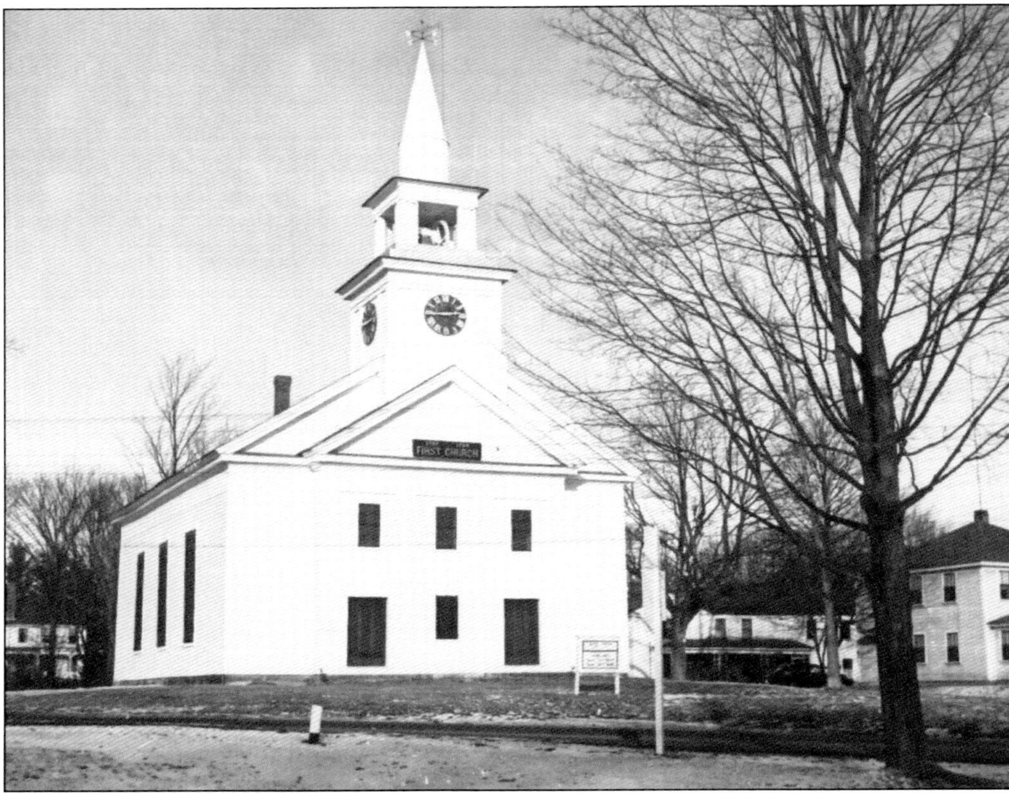

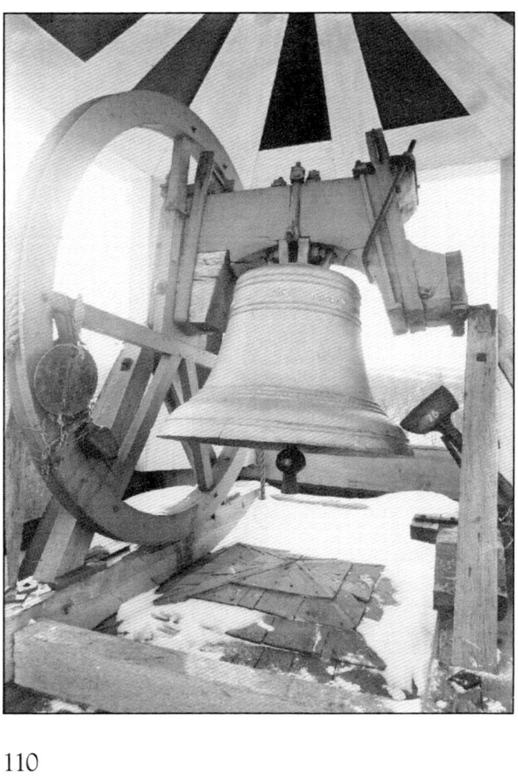

The First Congregational Church of Hopkinton first gathered on November 23, 1757, as the Church of Christ at Hopkinton and the Rev. James Scales was ordained as its first pastor. Services were held at Putney's Fort or the parsonage, both of which were located on Putney Hill. The first meetinghouse, built by the Town of Hopkinton in 1766 on the site of the current building, was destroyed by fire in 1789 and replaced the same year. Despite significant renovations in 1839 and 1963, much of the present building and sanctuary remain the same. Above is an undated exterior photograph of the church. At left is the one-half-ton bell cast by Paul Revere and Son of Boston in 1811, which hangs in the church's tower. (Courtesy of Hopkinton Historical Society.)

The Hopkinton Baptist Church was built in 1831 on Main Street east of the Hopkinton Village square. The church was constructed using timbers from the Old West Hopkinton Congregational Meeting House. In 1869 a parsonage, including a vestry, was erected on the opposite side of the street from the church. The church closed in 1965 and eventually the building was sold and remodeled into apartments. (Courtesy of Hopkinton Historical Society.)

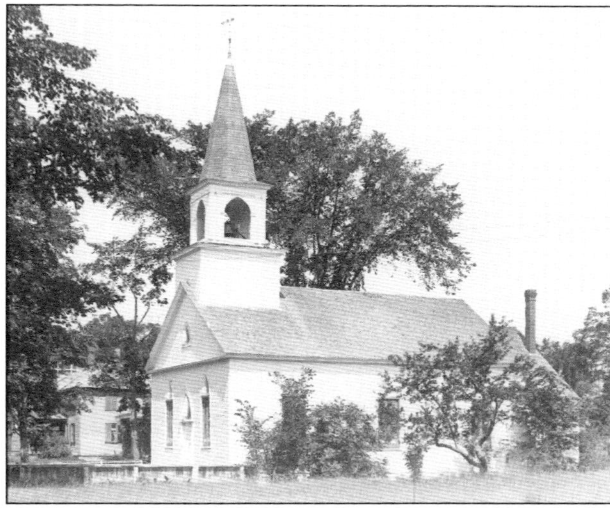

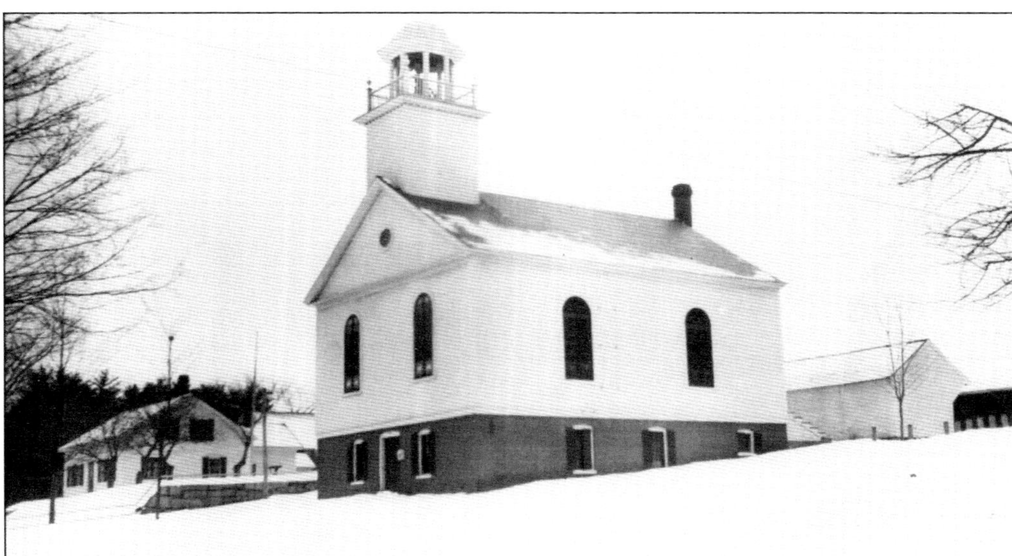

The Union Baptist Society was formed in 1823 under Deacon Jonathan Fowler with 12 members. Four years later, a public meeting house, the Freewill Baptist Church, was constructed and dedicated. The bell was added to the church in 1871, and in 1897 the building was moved forward approximately 10 feet and a brick basement added. The church is now home to Countryside Community Church. (Courtesy of Hopkinton Historical Society.)

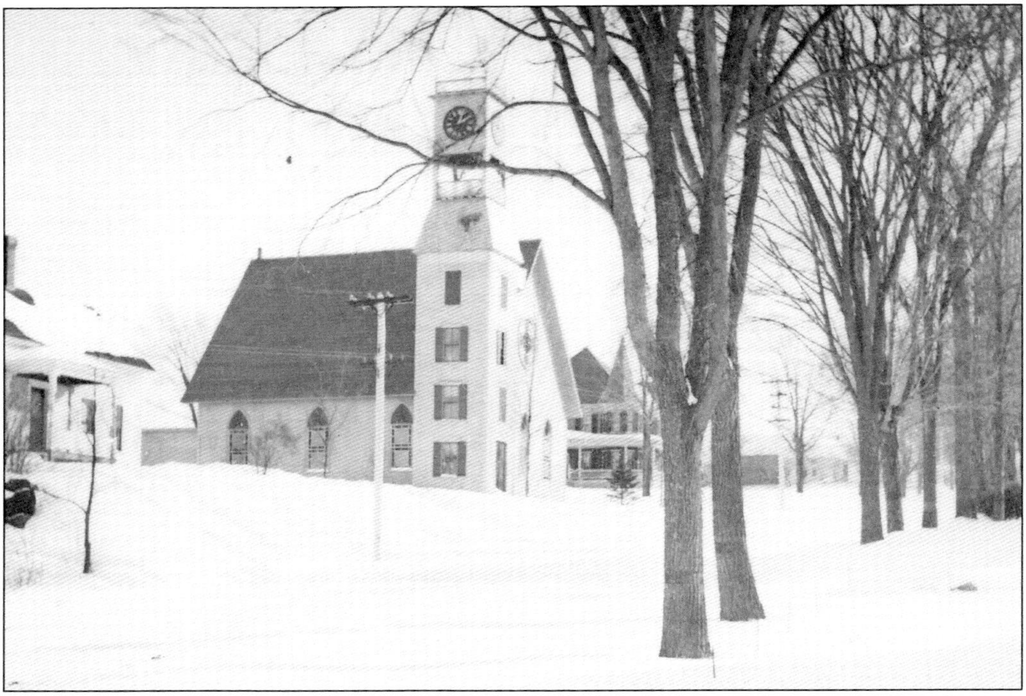

The church (above), located just south of Contoocook Village on Maple Street, was originally built in 1837 by the Universalist Society and known as Union House. In 1851, Rev. Abiel Silver began preaching the works of Emanuel Swedenborg, a Swedish scientist, philosopher, and theologian. Soon interest grew and the New Jerusalem Church, or Swedenborgian Church, was formed. It was under this organization that the Contoocook Academy was formed in 1856. By 1946, the congregation had shrunk in size and the church building was sold to the American Legion. It has since changed hands several times and housed a variety of businesses. Below, young members of the Swedenborgian Church, from left to right, are (first row) Lena Conant Ball, Miriam Chase Emerson, Hiram Conant, and Mary Geer; (second row) Marion Hutchinson, Elfleda Call, Cora Lord, unidentified, Wendall Clough, and Lee Stevens. (Courtesy of Hopkinton Historical Society.)

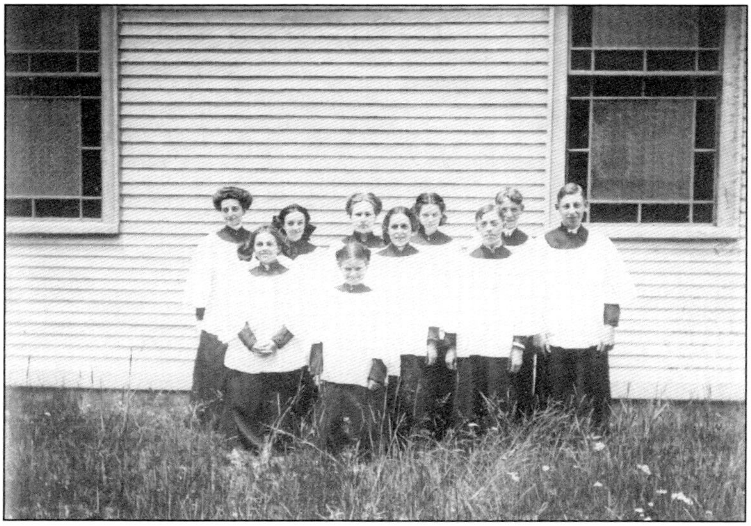

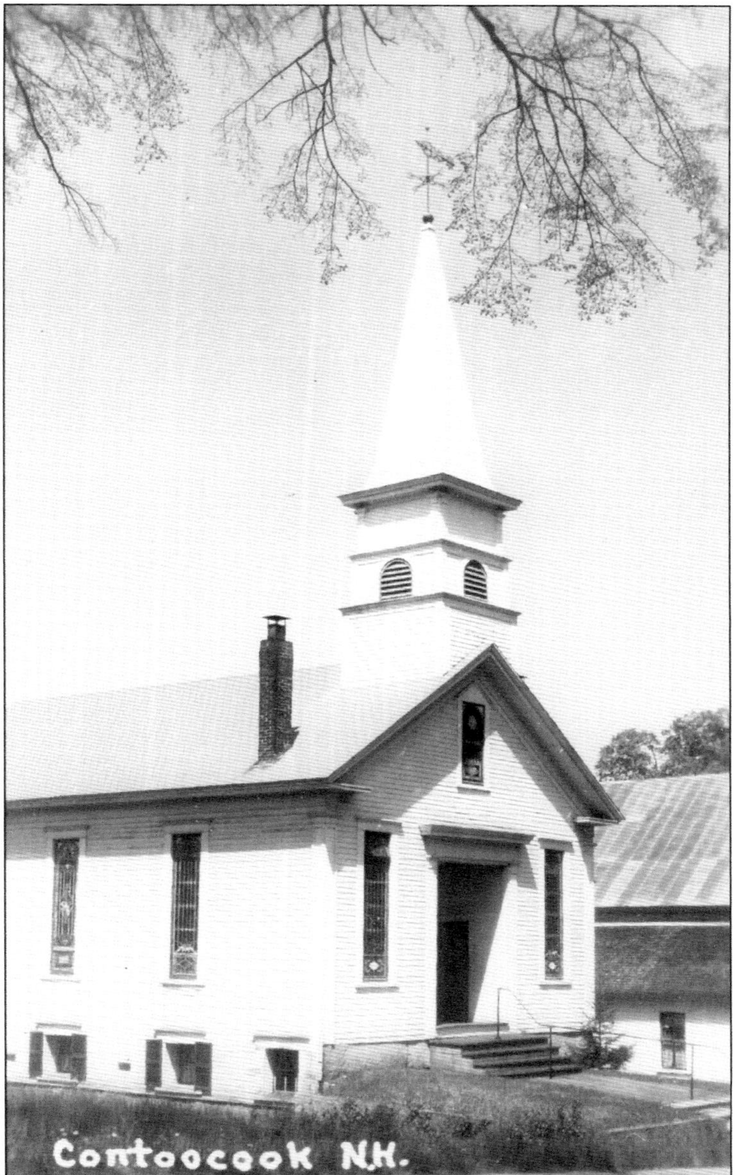

Twenty-one Methodists formed a legal organization on March 20, 1871, at the home of George H. Ketchum in Contoocook. At that time the members met at Charles Taylor's shop in the Curtice Block, and it was proposed that a church be built. Land was purchased on Maple Street from Samuel Curtice, and the Contoocook Methodist Church was erected and dedicated on November 16, 1871. A year later, the church purchased a house and lot, formerly belonging to Ida Kimball, across the street for a parsonage. In 1892, the church was raised and a vestry was built beneath it. Horace J. and Jennie Davis donated the land and building north of the church between the church and Columbia Hall for a parish hall. In 1962, the building adjoining the church was purchased for a parsonage and the old one sold. The following year, an eight-room educational building was added to the south side of the church. In 1968, the church became the Contoocook United Methodist Church. (Courtesy of Hopkinton Historical Society.)

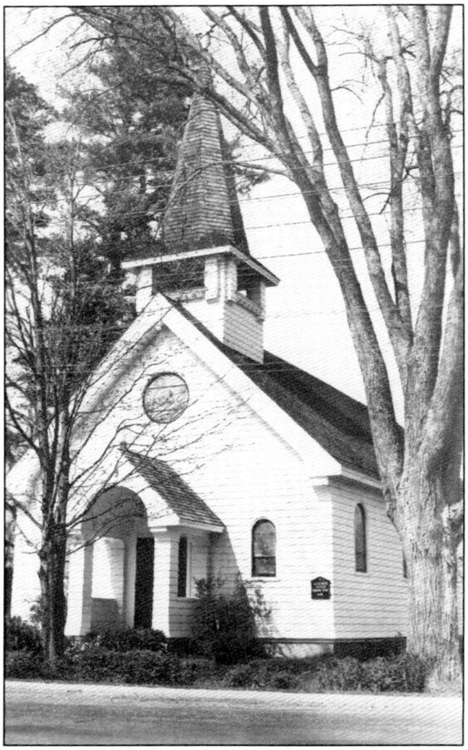

Roman Catholics in town had to travel to St. John's Church in Concord until 1911, when services began to be held in the Hopkinton Town Hall during the winter and in Columbia Hall in Contoocook during the summer. Acknowledging a need for a Catholic church and wishing to honor her Catholic employees, Isabel Weld Perkins Anderson, daughter of Comm. George Hamilton Perkins, donated a plot of land northwest of the Perkins Manor on Kearsarge Avenue for a church to be built. On July 28, 1929, St. Mary of the Assumption in Contoocook was dedicated by Bishop Albert Guertin. In 1945, Rev. Frances E. Butler became pastor of St. Theresa Parish in Henniker and St. Mary became the mission church for St. Theresa's. In 2005, St. Mary's was sold after St. Theresa Parish built a new church in Henniker. (Courtesy of Hopkinton Historical Society.)

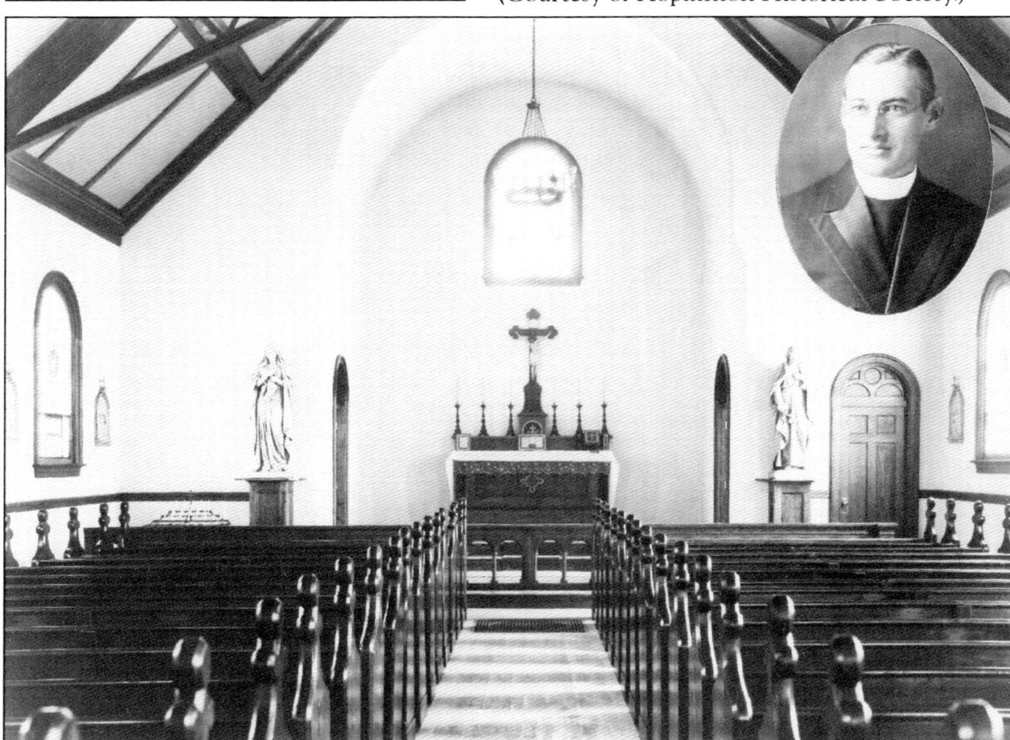

Six

Fairs and Celebrations

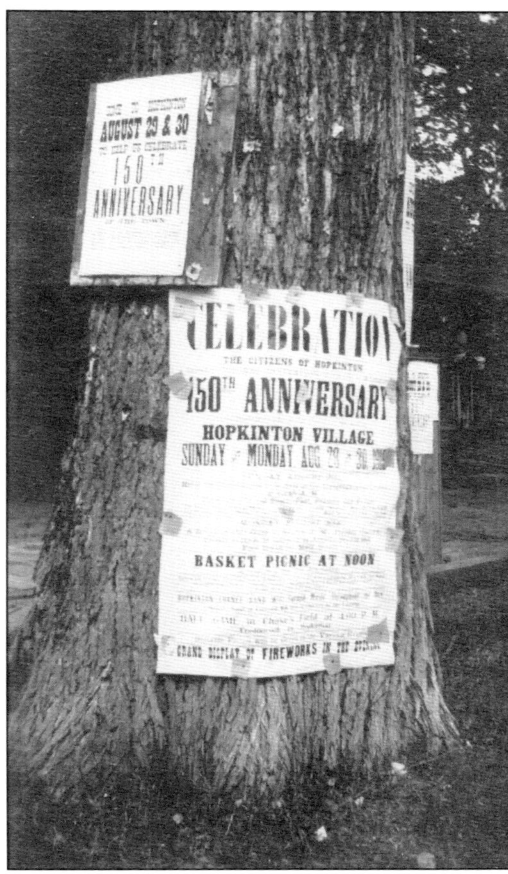

Every Labor Day weekend, people from far and wide descend on the village of Contoocook for the annual festivities of the Hopkinton State Fair. But the fair isn't the only time the town of Hopkinton celebrates. The picturesque town has often had occasion to celebrate its rich history and bright future. These two posters announce the town's sesquicentennial celebration in 1915. (Courtesy of Hopkinton Historical Society.)

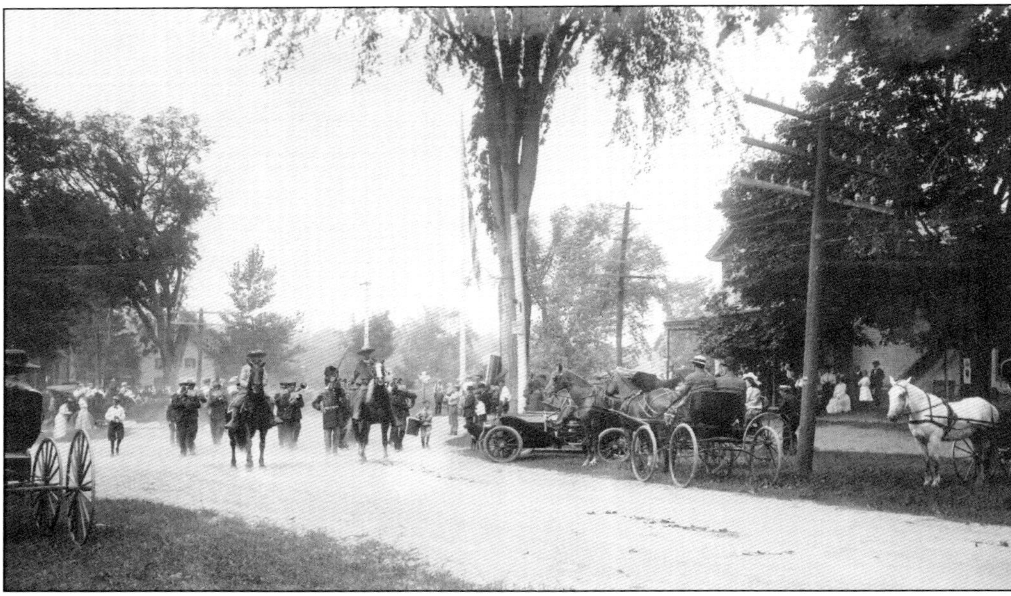

Above is a view of the Old Home Day parade looking west on Main Street towards Hopkinton Village. This photograph is undated, but the absence of Perkins Inn, which would have been visible behind the band, implies that the image was taken after 1907. Below, a wagon full of townspeople pose for a picture by the Kimball and Company Store during the Old Home Day celebration. Horace Gair Chase was a driving force behind the early Old Home Day celebrations in town. Chase was born in Hopkinton in 1827, one of three sons of probate judge Horace Chase. He was a successful businessman—owning a title company, amongst other endeavours— in Chicago and made his fortune after the great Chicago fire of 1872. Chase built a summer home in Hopkinton Village, named "Bergheim," located on the corner of South Road and Main Street. Despite having great success elsewhere, the town of Hopkinton remained close to his heart and Chase was a great supporter of town functions. (Courtesy of Hopkinton Historical Society.)

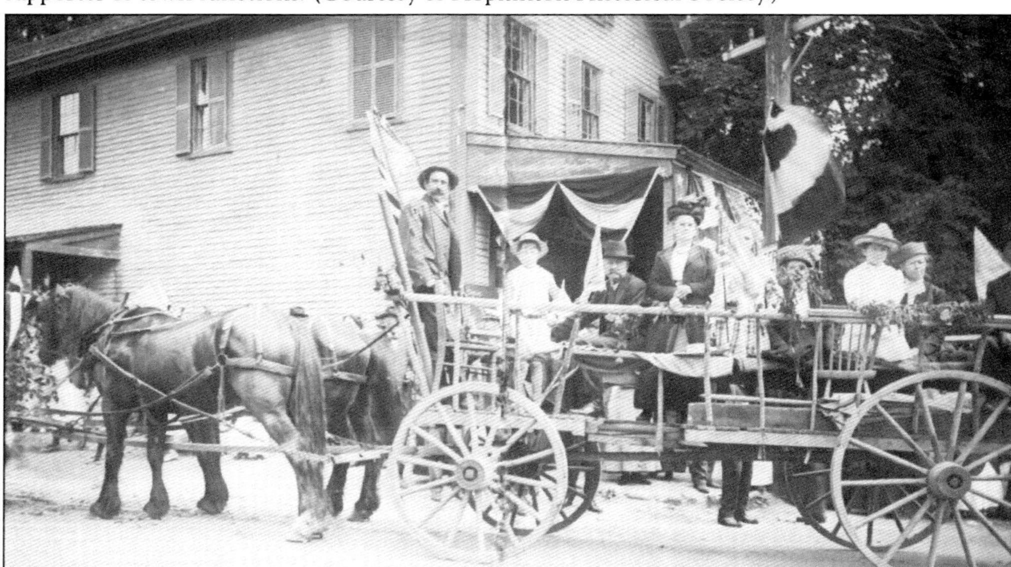

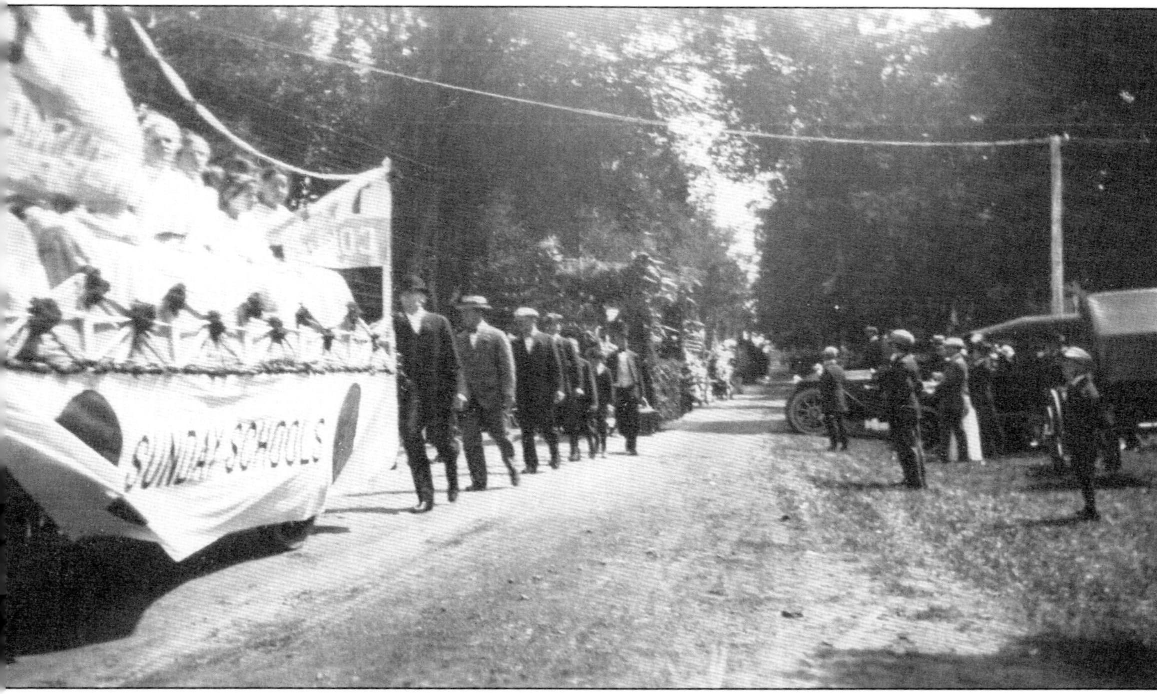

The 150th anniversary of Hopkinton's incorporation was a cause for great celebration in the town. At the March 1915 town meeting, $500 was appropriated for the celebration. A general committee, chaired by Frank I. Morrill, was appointed to determine the time and place and make all the necessary arrangements. Various sub-committees were formed to carry out more specific details. August 29–30 was chosen for the event and the townspeople set to work planning a grand sesquicentennial celebration. The parade pictured here was held on Monday, the second day of the festivities. Dr. Wallace Tarbell, the town physician until he passed away in the fall of 1945, was the parade marshall. (Courtesy of Hopkinton Historical Society.)

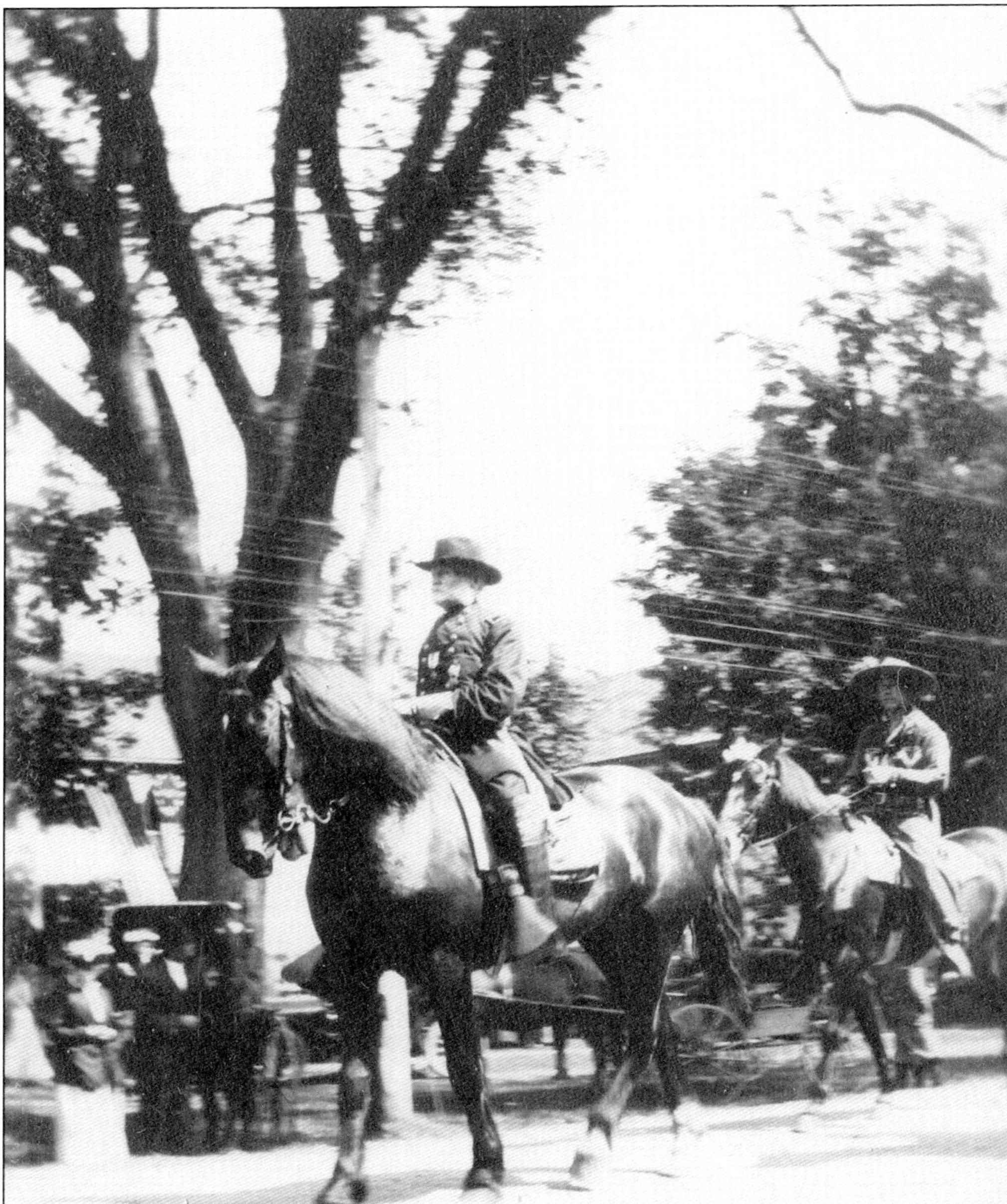

Gen. Joab Nelson Patterson also rode in the parade celebrating the town's 150th anniversary. Patterson, a Hopkinton native, enlisted and soon thereafter set up a recruiting office in Contoocook to form a company of men to fight in the Civil War. By May 1862, he was promoted to captain of Company H, 2nd Regiment of New Hampshire volunteers. On June 3, 1863, he fought and was wounded at the Battle of Gettysburg under Burling's Brigade. By the end of the war, Patterson had risen to the rank of colonel, and at the time he mustered out in December 1865, he had been appointed brevet brigadier general of US volunteers. In 1866, he was elected to the New Hampshire House of Representatives and served as US marshal for the state from 1867 to 1886 and as second auditor of the US Treasury from 1887 to 1893. Patterson continued his service in the Spanish American War. (Courtesy of Hopkinton Historical Society.)

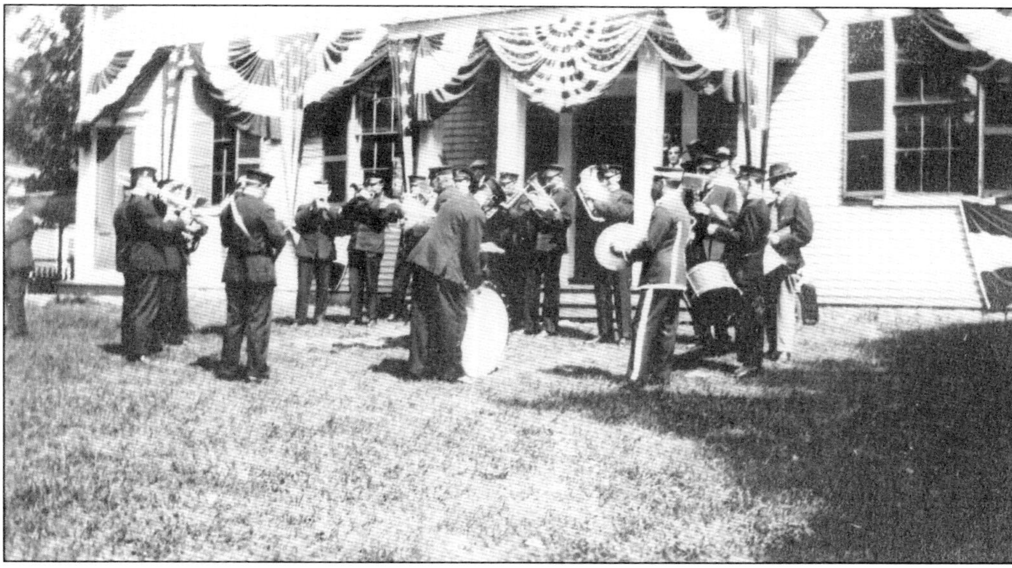

Committees were formed to handle the tasks of putting on such a celebration and well-known figures in town participated in the planning. The decoration committee included carriage painter William A. Baker and photographer Leown Kelley. Religious observances were planned by Rev. Lucian Kimball, amongst others, while the sports activities committee included Contoocook druggist Frank H. Reed and Dr. Wallace H. Tarbell. The grand civil parade was organized by men such as blacksmith Joseph E. Derry, Jack Putney, and store owner Arthur C. Huntoon. The committee to plan the fireworks and 150-gun salute consisted of businessmen Lewis A. Nelson and Charles C. Kimball, to name a few. The Monday schedule of the 150th anniversary celebration included entertainment from the Hopkinton Cornet Band, pictured above. At right, St. Andrew's Church proudly displays its decorations for the celebration. (Courtesy of Hopkinton Historical Society.)

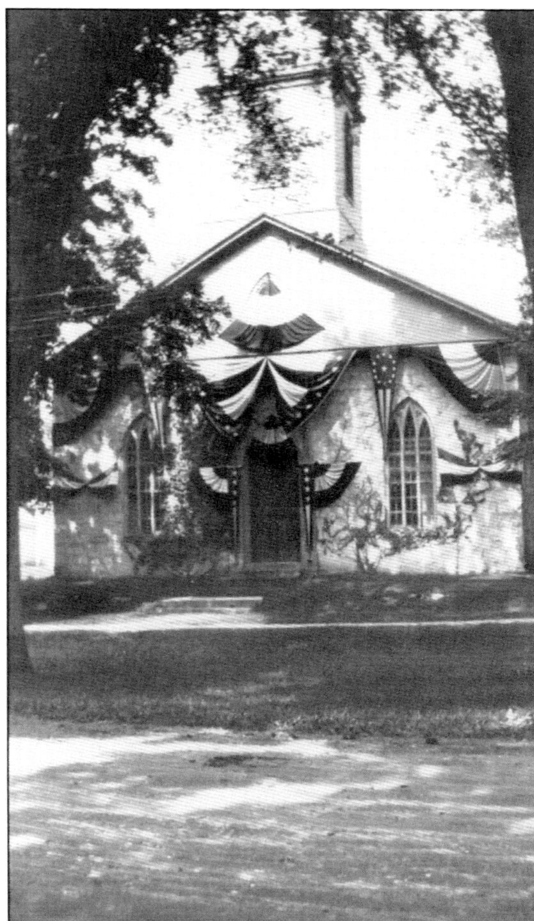

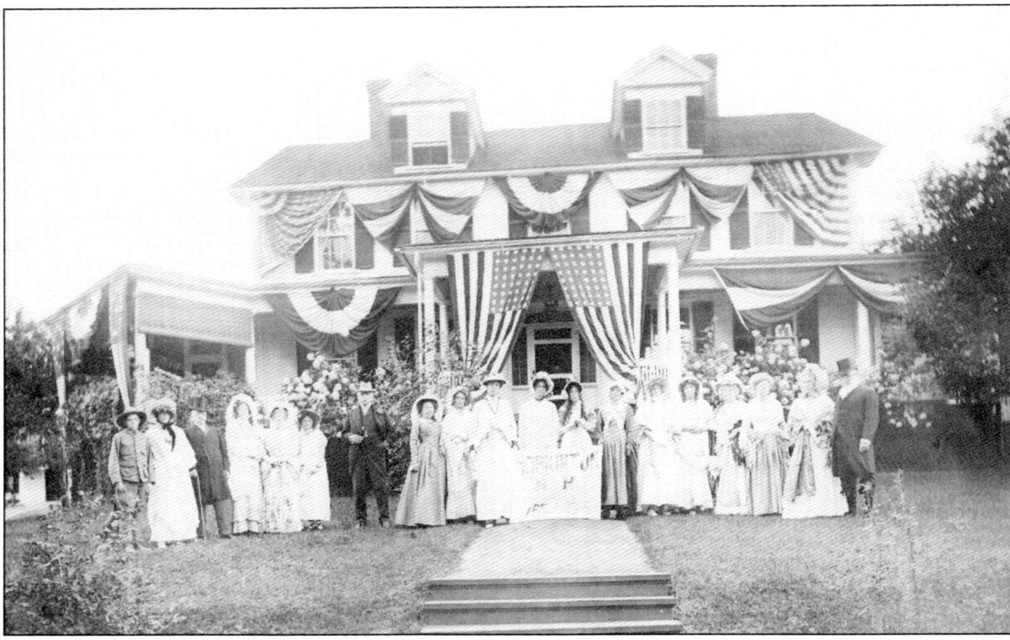

The anniversary program included religious observations on Sunday at the Congregational Church. The following day, townspeople celebrated with a 150-gun salute at sunrise on Mt. Putney near the Mt. Putney Garrison. The parade started at 10:00 a.m., followed by sports and foot races on Main Street. In front of the town hall, historical exercises were performed and the crowd was addressed by chairman Frank I. Morrill. The afternoon activities included historical addresses, a ball game in Chase's field featuring Hopkinton against Contoocook, and the celebration concluded with music and fireworks. Above, even the homes were elaborately decorated for the celebration as a group gathers to commemorate the occasion. Below, a group gathers around a Concord Coach during the town-wide celebration. (Courtesy of Hopkinton Historical Society.)

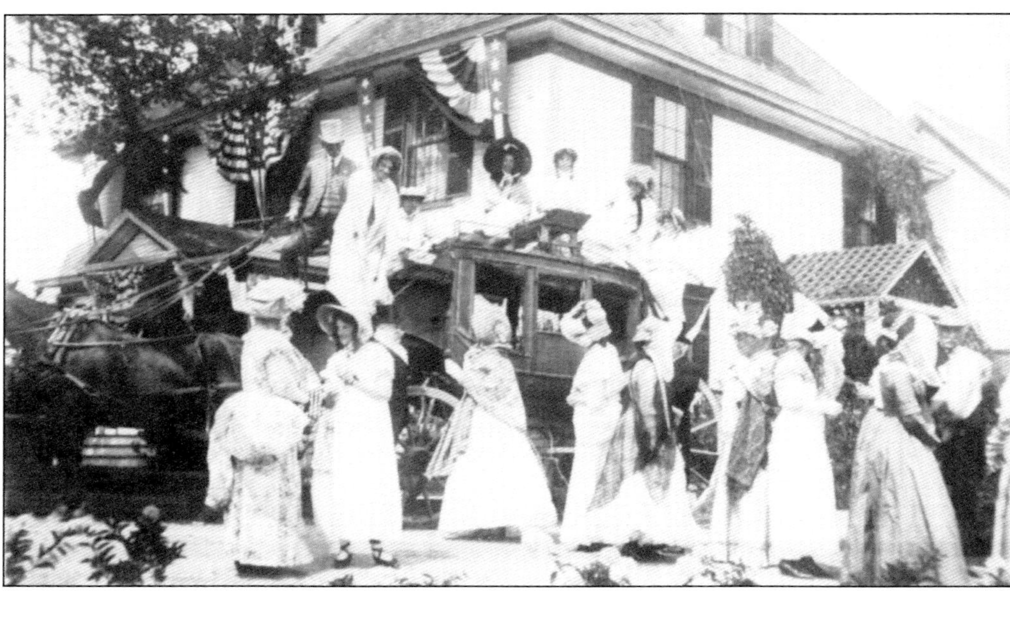

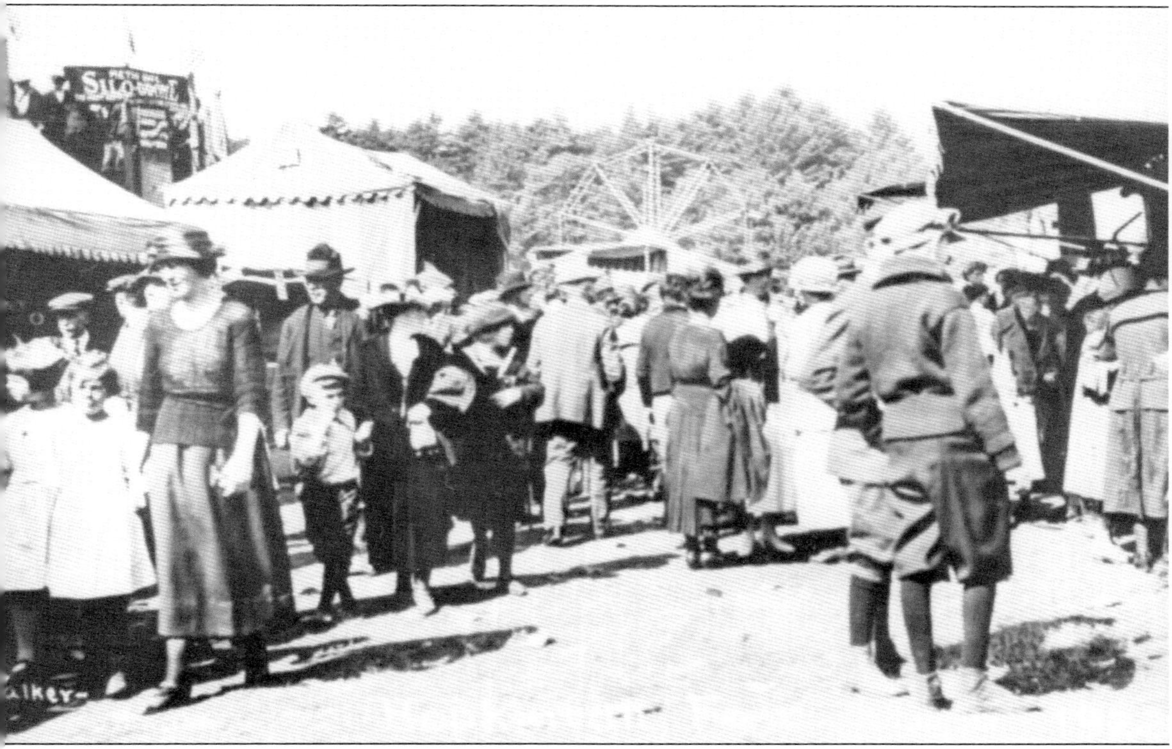

In 1915 the Contoocook Board of Trade decided to hold a two-day event to showcase the local farming industry and the town's rich agricultural history. This event, which would become an annual occasion, was held Tuesday and Wednesday, October 5–6, 1915. The site for the event was George's Park, located about a half mile northwest of Contoocook Village on Park Avenue, where the high school's athletic fields are today. Originally called the Hopkinton Fair, it was also known as the Contoocook Valley Fair, and in the first year the event made a net profit of just under $5. From that first festival the fair has continued to grow and expand from an agricultural event to a fun-filled Labor Day weekend destination for families from all over the region. The photograph above shows fairgoers enjoying the midway in 1922. (Courtesy of Hopkinton Historical Society.)

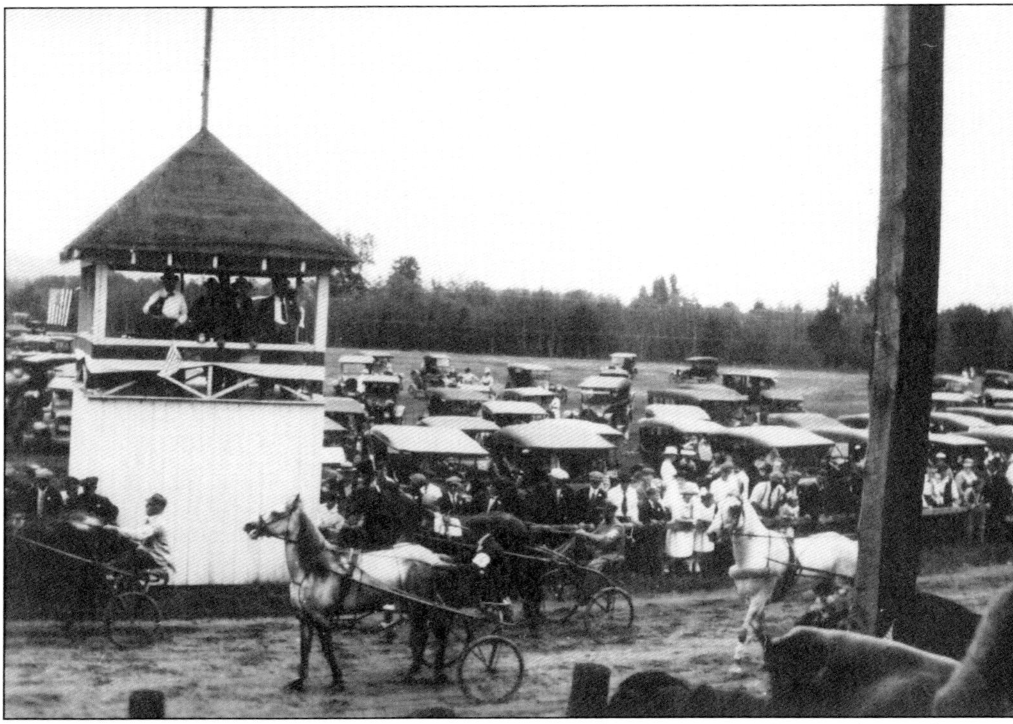

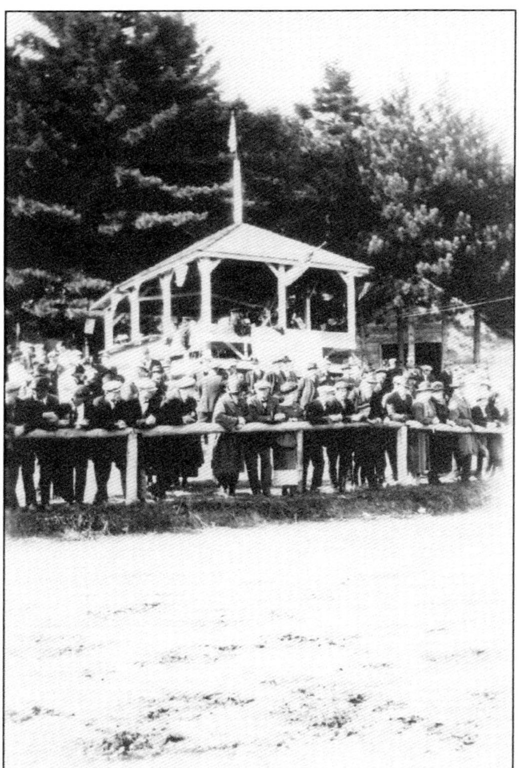

Caroline Livingston George donated George's Park to the people of Contoocook to be used as a public park in 1864 after the death of her husband Captain Paul Rolfe George. The land contained a track where her husband would exercise his horses and enjoy friendly races with other townspeople. The racetrack became a central attraction for the fair and local people would bring their horses to compete in sulky races. When the fair moved to its current location down the road in 1953, a racetrack was constructed and harness races continued for many years. (Courtesy of Hopkinton Historical Society.)

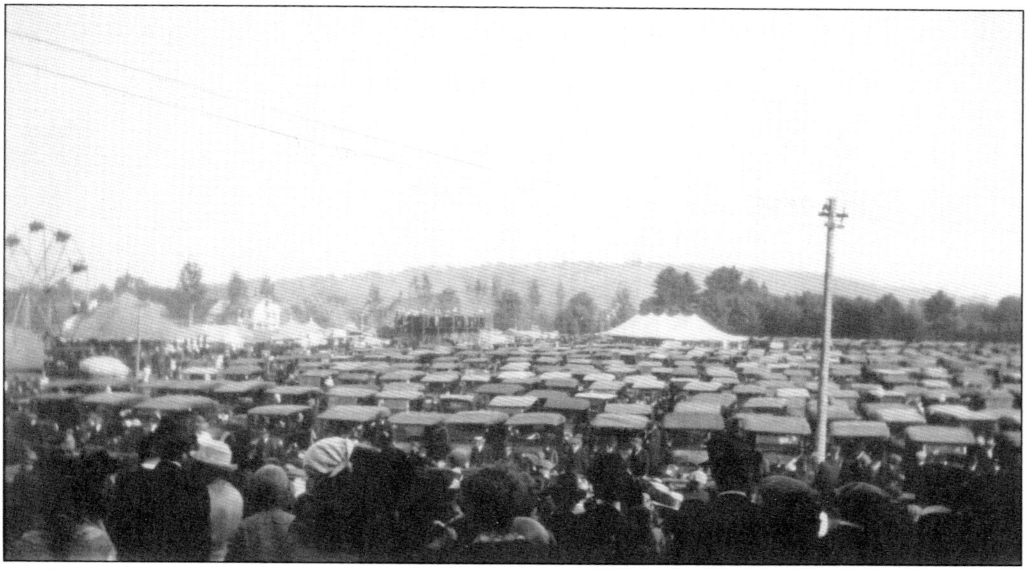

In 1921, the fair became a three-day event, held on Tuesday through Thursday. Stores and businesses often closed early on Wednesday so their employees could enjoy the "big day" at the fair. Around the same time, a large grandstand was constructed at George's Park for spectators to watch the harness racing and other events. The grandstands were torn down in 1958, a few years after the relocation of the fair. Above, the inside of the racetrack was used as a parking lot and contained the midway and a baseball diamond. At right, fairgoers are entertained by a boxing match. (Courtesy of Hopkinton Historical Society.)

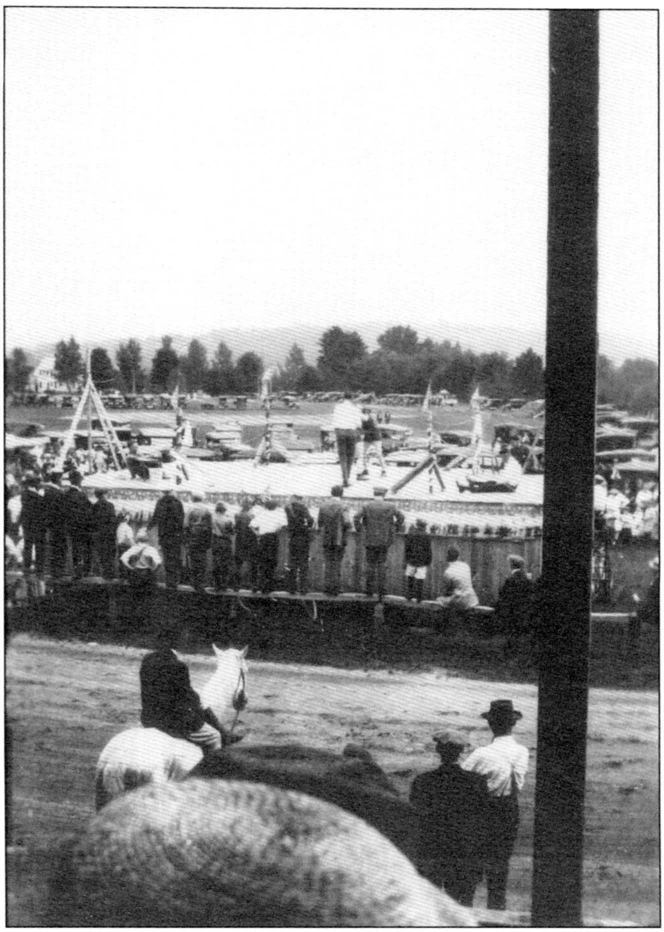

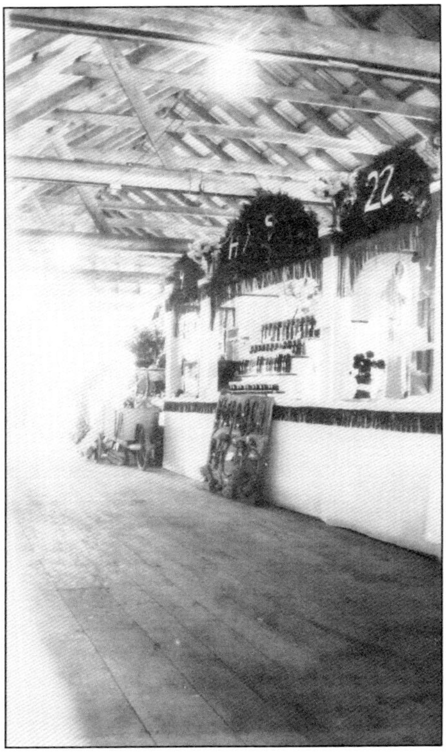

Farmers and exhibitors come from all over Merrimack County to show their livestock, swine, sheep, fowl, and other animals for ribbons and cash prizes. Fruits, vegetables, homemade pastries, canned goods, and home crafts are also exhibited for premiums and bragging rights. In 1921, the fair continued to grow with the building of a new exhibit hall—like the one in the photograph above—and new sheds. In addition to the agricultural events, the midway also drew much attention with amusement rides, games, food stands, and sideshow tents. Pictured below is a tent tempting the crowd to pay to see a mermaid, like that made famous by P.T. Barnum. The "Feejee Mermaid" was later proven to be a hoax consisting of a monkey's head and the tail of a fish. (Courtesy of Hopkinton Historical Society.)

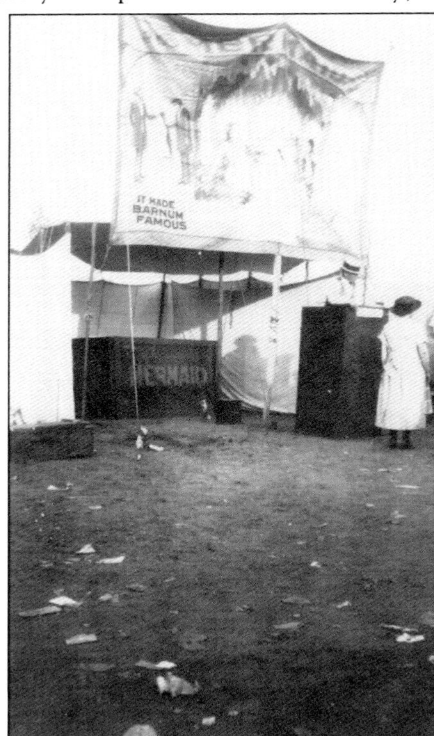

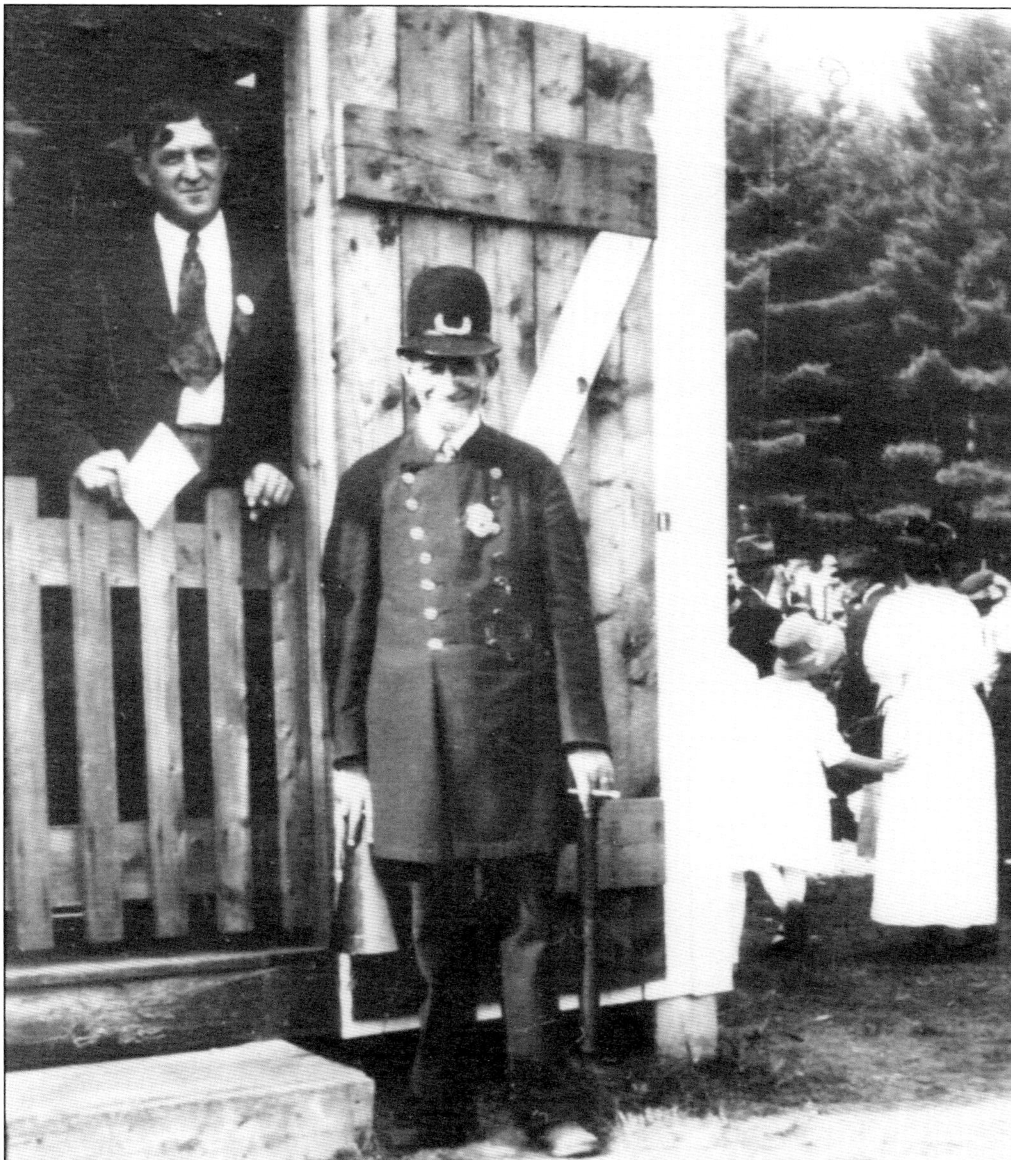

The first officers of the Hopkinton Fair were president C.A. Preston; secretary-treasurer M.F. Davis; directors M.J. Walker, George M. Putnam, George E. Barnard, H.M. Kimball, and J. Arthur Jones; and superintendent of grounds Arthur C. Call. The fair was incorporated under the name of the Contoocook Valley Fair Association in 1934. Year after year the fair continued to grow, and in 1947 it moved from George's Park to the present site of Hopkinton High School. Just a few years later in 1953, the fair needed to move its buildings again as the new high school was to be built where the cow sheds were located. In 1980, it became a full five-day event, opening on Thursday and continuing through Labor Day. On December 2, 1985, the directors of the Hopkinton Fair Association voted to change the name to the Hopkinton State Fair, and it continues to draw thousands of people every year. Pictured is Lewis A. Nelson (left), a fair founder and official for decades. (Courtesy of Hopkinton Historical Society.)

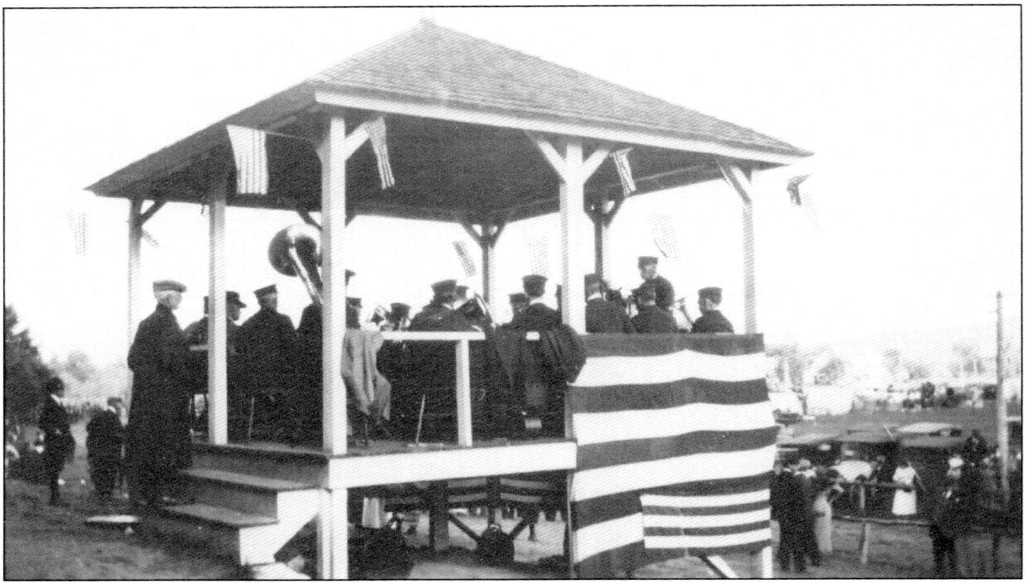

Popular entertainment at the fair included performances of the Hopkinton Cornet Band, pictured above. The original group was organized in 1859 under the leadership of Melvin Colby and continued until 1873 when it disbanded. A new group, using the old name, was created in 1877 by John F. Gage. Contoocook organized its own band in 1861 under the direction of William H. Hardy and reorganized in 1875 under Cyril T. Webber. The two villages' bands were eventually united to form the Hopkinton Cornet Band, and together they alternated between the Contoocook Engine Hall and Hopkinton Town Hall for rehearsals. Pictured below, the Hopkinton Cornet Band marches in the Hopkinton fair parade. (Courtesy of Hopkinton Historical Society.)

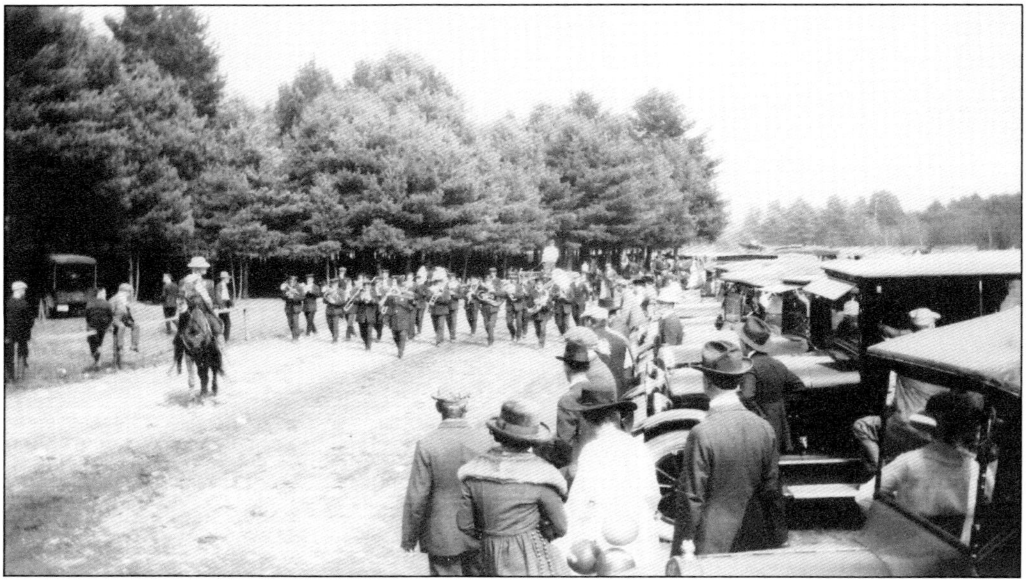

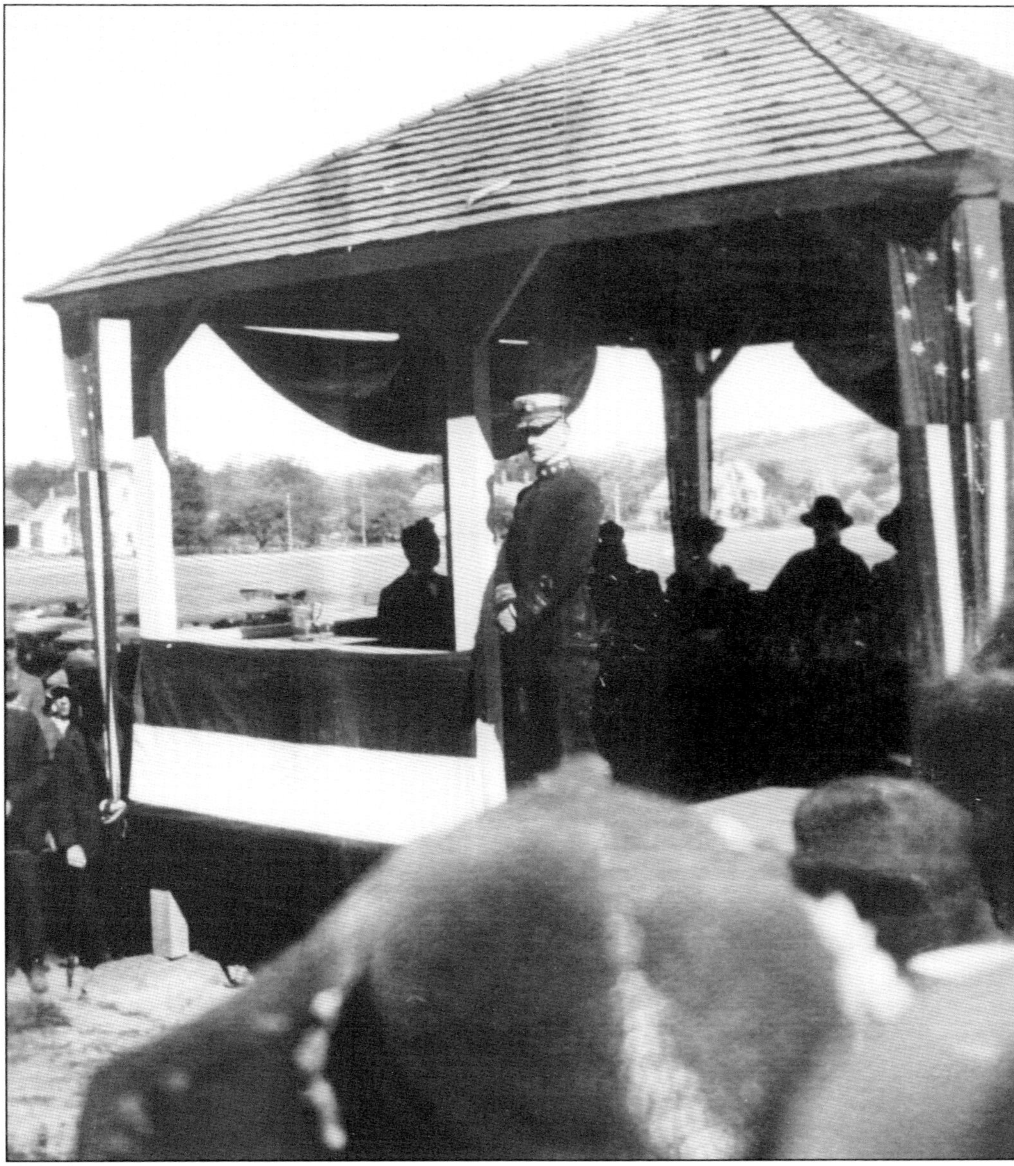

Adm. Guy Hamilton Burrage is pictured here at a celebration of World War I veterans at George's Park. Admiral Burrage was a graduate of the US Naval Academy with a long list of military accomplishments. He served in the Spanish American War, and during World War I was in command of the entire fleet of merchant convoys, which assisted in the transportation of two million men across the Atlantic. During Charles Lindbergh's historic solo transatlantic flight, Admiral Burrage's naval forces were on standby to rescue Lindbergh if his attempt was unsuccessful. Once Lindbergh reached Paris safely, President Roosevelt ordered Admiral Burrage to bring the pilot and the *Spirit of St. Louis* home to the United States. Interestingly, upon seeing the crate that carried the plane, Burrage purchased it from Lindbergh. The 10-by-13-foot wooden box arrived disassembled at the railroad station in Contoocook, and local handymen reconstructed the crate at the admiral's Contoocook home, transforming the box into a summer cottage. Burrage was also a principal player in the negotiations with the supposed Lindbergh baby kidnappers. (Courtesy of Hopkinton Historical Society.)